Epistemology: Internalism and Externalism

D1232203

BLACKWELL READINGS IN PHILOSOPHY
Series Editor: *Steven M. Cahn*

Blackwell Readings in Philosophy are concise, chronologically arranged collections of primary readings from classical and contemporary sources. They represent core positions and important developments with respect to key philosophical concepts. Edited and introduced by leading philosophers, these volumes provide valuable resources for teachers and students of philosophy, and for all those interested in gaining a solid understanding of central topics in philosophy.

EPISTEMOLOGY
Internalism and Externalism

Edited by

Hilary Kornblith

Copyright © Blackwell Publishers Ltd 2001

First published 2001

2 4 6 8 10 9 7 5 3 1

Blackwell Publishers Inc.
350 Main Street
Malden, Massachusetts 02148
USA

Blackwell Publishers Ltd
108 Cowley Road
Oxford OX4 1JF
UK

Library of Congress Cataloging-in-Publication Data

Epistemology : internalism and externalism / edited by Hilary Kornblith.
  p.   cm. – (Blackwell readings in philosophy ; 2)
  Includes bibliographical references and index.
  ISBN 978-0–631-22106-7
paper) 1. Knowledge, Theory of.   I. Kornblith, Hilary.   II. Series.

BD161 .E625   2001
121 – dc21   2001018134

British Library Cataloguing in Publication Data
A CIP catalogue record for this book is available from the British Library.

Typeset in 10½ on 12½ pt Baskerville
by Best-set Typesetter Ltd., Hong Kong

CONTENTS

ACKNOWLEDGMENTS

The authors and publishers gratefully acknowledge the following for permission to reproduce copyright material:

Alston, William P., "Internalism and Externalism in Epistemology," *Philosophical Topics* 14 (1986), courtesy of University of Arkansas Press and the author;

BonJour, Laurence, "Externalist Theories of Empirical Knowledge," *Midwest Studies in Philosophy* 5 (1980);

Conee, Earl and Richard Feldman, "Internalism Defended" (forthcoming), reprinted by permission of North American Philosophical Publications, University of Pittsburgh;

Foley, Richard, "What Am I to Believe?" from S. Wagner and R. Warner (eds.), *Naturalism: A Critical Appraisal* (University of Notre Dame Press, 1993);

Goldman, Alvin, "The Internalist Conception of Justification," *Midwest Studies in Philosophy* 5 (1980);

Goldman, Alvin, "Internalism Exposed," *The Journal of Philosophy* 96 (1999) reprinted by permission of Columbia University;

Kornblith, Hilary, "How Internal Can You Get?" *Synthese* 74 (1988), reprinted by permission of Kluwer Academic Publishers, Dordrecht, The Netherlands;

Schmitt, Frederick, "Epistemic Perspectivism" from J. Heil (ed.), *Rationality, Morality and Self-Interest: Essays Honoring Mark Carl Overvold* (Rowman and Littlefield, Lanham, 1993);

Sosa, Ernest, "Reliabilism and Intellectual Virtue," from E. Sosa, *Knowledge in Perspective: Selected Essays in Epistemology* (Cambridge University Press, 1991);

Stroud, Barry, "Understanding Human Knowledge in General," from M. Clay and K. Lehrer (eds.), *Knowledge and Skepticism* (Westview Press Inc., 1989).

The publishers apologize for any errors or omissions in the above list and would be grateful to be notified of any corrections that should be incorporated in the next edition or reprint of this book.

INTERNALISM AND EXTERNALISM: A BRIEF HISTORICAL INTRODUCTION

Hilary Kornblith

A central focus of work in epistemology for more than the last twenty years has been the debate between internalism and externalism. At issue is the very form of an epistemological theory, and with it, competing conceptions of the epistemological enterprise. This reader brings together ten essays which have played an important role in shaping the debate. In this introduction, I provide some historical background to help orient the reader.

1 The Terms "Internalism" and "Externalism"

The terms "internalism" and "externalism" are used in philosophy in a variety of different senses,[1] but their use in epistemology for anything like the positions which are the focus of this book dates to 1973. More precisely, the word "externalism" was introduced in print by David Armstrong[2] in his book *Belief, Truth and Knowledge*[3] in the following way:

> According to "Externalist" accounts of non-inferential knowledge, what makes a true non-inferential belief a case of *knowledge* is some natural relation which holds between the belief-state, Bap, and the situation which makes the belief true. It is a matter of a certain relation holding between the believer and the world. It is important to notice that, unlike "Cartesian" and "Initial Credibility" theories, Externalist theories are regularly developed as theories of the nature of knowledge *generally* and not simply as theories of non-inferential knowledge. (157)

So in Armstrong's usage, "externalism" is a view about knowledge, and it is the view that when a person knows that a particular claim p is true, there is some sort of "natural relation" which holds between that person's belief that p and the world. One such view, suggested in 1967 by Alvin Goldman, was the Causal Theory of Knowledge.[1] On this view, a person knows that p (for example, that it's raining) when that person's belief that p was caused by the fact that p. A related view, championed by Armstrong and later by Goldman as well, is the Reliability Account of Knowledge, according to which a person knows that p when that person's belief is both true and, in some sense, reliable: on some views, the belief must be a reliable indicator that p; on others, the belief must be produced by a reliable process, that is, one that tends to produce true beliefs. Frank Ramsey[5] was a pioneer in defending a reliability account of knowledge. Particularly influential work in developing such an account was also done by Brian Skyrms,[6] Peter Unger,[7] and Fred Dretske.[8]

Accounts of knowledge which are externalist in Armstrong's sense mark an important break with tradition, according to which knowledge is a kind of justified, true belief. On traditional accounts, in part because justification is an essential ingredient in knowledge, a central task of epistemology is to give an account of what justification consists in. And, according to tradition, what is required for a person to *be* justified in holding a belief is for that person to *have* a certain justification for the belief, where having a justification is typically identified with being in a position, in some relevant sense, to produce an appropriate argument for the belief in question. What is distinctive about externalist accounts of knowledge, as Armstrong saw it, was that they do not require justification, at least in the traditional sense. Knowledge merely requires having a true belief which is appropriately connected with the world.

But while Armstrong's way of viewing reliability accounts of knowledge has them rejecting the view that knowledge requires justified true belief, Alvin Goldman came to offer quite a different way of viewing the import of reliability theories: in 1979, Goldman suggested that instead of seeing reliability accounts as rejecting the claim that knowledge requires justified true belief, we should instead embrace an account which identifies justified belief with reliably produced belief.[9] Reliability theories of knowledge, on this way of understanding them, offer a non-traditional account of what is required for a belief to be justified. This paper of Goldman's, and his subsequent extended development of the idea,[10] have been at the center of epistemological discussion ever since.

The 1980 volume of *Midwest Studies in Philosophy* was devoted to work in epistemology, and two papers in that volume, both reprinted here, inaugurated the current use of the terms "externalism" and "internalism." Laurence BonJour's "Externalist Theories of Empirical Knowledge"[11] presents an argument against accounts which identify knowledge with reliably produced true belief. But while BonJour claims to be following Armstrong's use of the term "externalist," and while his paper is entitled "Externalist Theories of *Knowledge*" [my italics], BonJour's use of the term is, in fact, importantly different from Armstrong's. For BonJour, what is important about the theories he is targeting is that they seem to offer – whether their authors put it in these terms or not – reliability theories of *justification*. The term "externalism," as BonJour uses it, primarily applies to accounts of justified belief, and only derivatively to accounts of knowledge. Thus, BonJour notes:

> When viewed from the general standpoint of the western epistemological tradition, externalism represents a very radical departure. It seems safe to say that until very recent times, no serious philosopher of knowledge would have dreamed of suggesting that a person's beliefs might be epistemically justified simply in virtue of facts or relations that were external to his subjective conception. Descartes, for example, would surely have been quite unimpressed by the suggestion that his problematic beliefs about the external world were justified if only they were in fact reliably related to the world – whether or not he had any reason for thinking this to be so. Clearly his conception, and that of generations of philosophers who followed, was that such a relation could play a justificatory role only if the believer possessed adequate reason for thinking that it obtained.[12]

BonJour argues that reliability theories of justified belief – which he terms "externalist" theories of justification – fly in the face of important intuitions about justification, and worse, fail even to address the most central issues of epistemology. Externalist theories of justification are not merely mistaken in detail, according to BonJour; they are fundamentally misguided in conception.

In the same volume, Alvin Goldman introduces the term "internalism."

> Traditional epistemology . . . has been predominantly *internalist*, or egocentric. On [this] perspective, epistemology's job is to construct a doxastic principle or procedure *from the inside*, from our own individual vantage point. To adopt a Kantian idiom, a [doxastic principle] must not be "heteronomous," or dictated "from without." It must be "autonomous," a law we can give to ourselves and which we have *grounds* for giving to ourselves. The *objective* optimality of a [doxastic principle],

on this view, does not make it right. A [doxastic principle] counts as right only it is "certifiable" *from within.*[13]

Goldman argues that an internalist conception of justification is entirely untenable.

Goldman and BonJour thus independently and simultaneously named this fundamental distinction. Goldman argues that any tenable theory of justification will have to reject internalism; only externalism will do. BonJour argues that any tenable theory of justification will have to reject externalism; only internalism will do.

The debate over the proper form of a theory of justified belief has occupied center stage in epistemological discussions ever since this apt bit of terminology was coined. As the papers in this volume attest, this issue is connected in fundamental ways with questions about the very nature and goals of epistemological theorizing.

2   Descartes' Legacy

Although the terminology of "internalism" and "externalism" is a relatively recent coinage, the question at issue is a longstanding one. Perhaps the best way to understand the debate between internalists and externalists is to see how the issue arose out of the failure of Descartes' epistemology.

Descartes' understanding of the nature of epistemological problems locates them squarely within the first-person perspective. *The Meditations*, written in a confessional style, presents the reader with Descartes' concerns: Descartes recognizes that he, like all of us, has had mistaken beliefs in the past, and thus it is inevitable that his current body of beliefs should contain mistakes as well. Descartes wishes to have an accurate understanding of the world around him, and simply building on the beliefs he already has, taking them at face-value, would surely involve building on those very mistaken beliefs. Thus, in order to improve his understanding of the world, he resolves to suspend belief in any claim which might be wrong; this idea leads very quickly, by way of the Dream Argument, to total suspension of belief. Descartes must begin again; he must form his beliefs anew, "from the very foundation," as he puts it.

Now one of the interesting things about the Cartesian epistemological project is that Descartes holds that he can figure out, from this internal perspective, precisely how it is that he should go on. Moreover, Descartes holds that the principles of belief acquisition which he comes to endorse are guaranteed to result in accurate beliefs about the world around him. This is far more optimistic than any philosopher has been ever since, but it is precisely Descartes' optimism about the powers of human reason that lays the foundation for the debate between internalism and externalism.

On the one hand, Descartes proceeds from the first-person, thinking about epistemological problems as any internalist would. He is concerned to figure out which principles of reasoning appear to be best; he then wishes to take those principles and apply them so as to form beliefs which conform to the principles he has endorsed. In so doing, Descartes forms his beliefs in a thoroughly responsible way: he is not merely acquiring beliefs will-nilly, but in a careful, self-conscious, and calculated manner, designed to get him at the truth.

But this is not all which Descartes claims to achieve. Descartes does not believe that he has merely discovered a set of principles which *seem* to assist him in his goal of coming to understand the world as it actually is. Rather, Descartes believes that he has shown, from within his own subjective perspective, that these principles must in fact succeed in getting him at the truth.

If Descartes could have done this, he would have achieved something quite remarkable. First, he would have discovered a set of principles for forming beliefs which, from his own subjective perspective, appear to be optimal in getting at the truth. He would not form a single belief which did not meet his own subjective standards. Second, he would have discovered a set of principles which, in fact, are optimal in getting at the truth. Thus, all of the beliefs formed would in fact meet these objective standards. Third, he would have devised a proof, from within his own subjective perspective, which would assure that those principles meeting his subjective standards are in fact objectively successful. The fact that his subjective standards are objectively correct would thus in no way depend on lucky accidents; all of the necessary conditions for objective validity would be fully available and certifiable from within Descartes' subjective perspective. This combination of features would allow him to effectively respond to the skeptic on the skeptic's own terms: Descartes could conclusively prove that his beliefs are true.

Now the problems which arise for this project do not depend upon Descartes' optimism in thinking that he had discovered principles which would guarantee that his beliefs be true. For if Descartes had only thought that he had discovered principles which guaranteed the likelihood, in some objective sense, that his beliefs be true, his position would still have been problematic. For consider an individual who reasons very badly. Imagine that this individual is not someone who is unconcerned about getting at the truth. Rather, he cares deeply about having true beliefs, and before forming any belief, he very carefully scrutinizes his evidence for and against it. Or rather, he scrutinizes the evidence for and against it to the extent to which he is capable; and he is not very capable at all. From the inside, he is aware of trying very hard to form true beliefs, and indeed, he is trying very hard. He is thinking about epistemological issues as hard as he can. But his reasoning ability simply does not meet any reasonable objective standard. Unfortunately, he lives in a fool's paradise: he believes that he is reasoning well; he believes that he is reasoning perfectly, but in actual fact, he is reasoning very poorly indeed. Although this individual has fully met his own subjective standards for good reasoning, and although he has shown to his own satisfaction that his own subjective standards cannot fail to have a real purchase on the truth, he is reasoning so poorly that a very large percentage of his beliefs are throughly mistaken.

Now it surely seems that there could be such an individual, and, if this is correct, then we need to know how it is that Descartes could possibly show that he is not in the very position which our fool finds himself in. And it seems quite clear that he cannot. For to show that he satisfies his own subjective standards does not distinguish him from our fool, and to show that, by his own subjective standards, he genuinely does have a real purchase on the truth does not distinguish him from our fool either.

Now if one grants that this is correct, one will have to grant that the project Descartes attempted to carry out could not possibly have succeeded. On the one hand, there is the laudable goal in Descartes to form beliefs in a way which manifests a kind of intellectual integrity: he wishes to form beliefs which fully satisfy his own subjective standards. On the other hand, he has another laudable goal: he wishes to form beliefs in ways which have some objective purchase on the truth. The internalist is someone who identifies justified belief with beliefs satisfying something like the first of these goals. The externalist, on the other hand, is someone who identifies justified belief with something like satisfying the second. Descartes thought he had a proof that whatever satisfies the first goal automatically satisfies the second as well. But it now seems that that is not so. And if it is not so, then the idea that we might have a conception of justified belief which answers to both of these goals simultaneously must be rejected as well. But where then should we locate the concept of justified belief? The debate between internalists and externalists attempts to answer this question.

I have been intentionally vague in saying just what internalism and externalism are committed to. While the broad outlines of these two views are clear enough, precisely what each position comes to is itself a subject of current controversy. It would thus be a mistake to provide precise accounts of these two views in this introduction; the state of the art will not allow it.

3   The Essays

The essays contained here show the evolution of this debate over the past twenty years. Reading through them will bring the reader up to date. The volume begins with the essays by BonJour and Goldman which placed this issue at the center of epistemological discussion. Chapter 3, by William P. Alston, "Internalism and Externalism in Epistemology," distinguishes two different kinds of internalism: perspectival internalism and access internalism. According to the first of these, only features which are, in some appropriate sense, within an agent's perspective may serve to determine the justificatory status of that agent's beliefs; according to the second, only states to which an agent has appropriate access may determine a belief's justificatory status. Alston examines the motivations for each of these kinds of internalism and argues that, in the end, "existing forms of internalism are in serious trouble." In chapter 4, "How Internal Can You Get?," I further explore the motivation behind internalism and argue that the very coherence of the position depends on an implausibly strong Cartesian premise. Barry Stroud examines the nature of the philosophical enterprise in chapter 5, "Understanding Human Knowledge in General." A philosophical understanding of the nature of knowledge differs in important ways from the scientific enterprise of understanding human knowledge, and Stroud develops a view about what a successful philosophical understanding of human knowledge would entail. Stroud argues that neither traditional Cartesian views about knowledge nor their externalist rivals can provide a satisfying account of knowledge in general. In chapter 6, "Reliabilism and Intellectual Virtue," Ernest Sosa makes the case for a kind of virtue epistemology which blends both internalist and externalist elements. On Sosa's view, no successful epistemology can ignore either of these two dimensions of epistemic appraisal. Richard Foley develops an internalist perspective on epistemology in chapter 7, "What Am I to Believe?" Foley argues that the most fundamental questions in epistemology must inevitably be addressed from the first-person, or egocentric, perspective. In chapter 8, "Epistemic Perspectivism," Frederick Schmitt presents a thorough account of the many different views which identify justified belief with belief somehow sanctioned by the agent's perspective. Schmitt argues that none of these views is defensible. Alvin Goldman presents a case against internalism in chapter 9, "Internalism Exposed." Goldman argues that internalism faces insurmountable problems, not only of detail, but of fundamental conception. The case in favor of internalism is taken up by Earl Conee and Richard Feldman in chapter 10, "Internalism Defended." Internalism, they argue, survives the many assaults mounted against it.

There is an extensive literature on this subject, and anyone interested in pursuing this issue in more detail should consult the Further Reading section at the end of the volume.

Notes

1 Aside from their use in epistemology, these terms are used as labels for quite different pairs of positions in moral philosophy and in philosophy of language and mind. The issue which divides internalist from externalist theories of mental content, now very widely discussed, is not entirely unrelated to the subject of this reader – both hinge on questions about the extent to which the first-person perspective is epistemically privileged – but neither is it identical with it.

2 Armstrong gives credit to Gregory O'Hair for introducing the term in unpublished work.

3 David M. Armstrong, *Belief, Truth and Knowledge* (Cambridge University Press, 1973).

4 Alvin Goldman, "A Causal Theory of Knowing," *Journal of Philosophy*, 64 (1967), 357–72.

5 Frank Ramsey, *The Foundations of Mathematics, and Other Logical Essays* (Routledge, 1931).

6 Brian Skyrms, "The Explication of 'X knows that p'," *Journal of Philosophy*, 64 (1967), 373–89.

7 Peter Unger, "An Analysis of Factual Knowledge," *Journal of Philosophy*, 65 (1968), 157–70.

8 Fred Dretske, "Conclusive Reasons," *Australasian Journal of Philosophy*, 49 (1971), 1–22.

9 Alvin Goldman, "What Is Justified Belief?," in G. Pappas, ed., *Justification and Knowledge: New Studies in Epistemology* (Reidel, 1979), 1–23.

10 See especially Alvin Goldman, *Epistemology and Cognition* (Harvard University Press, 1986).

11 Laurence BonJour, "Externalist Theories of Empirical Knowledge," *Midwest Studies in Philosophy*, 5 (1980), 53–73.

12 Ibid., 56.

13 Alvin Goldman, "The Internalist Conception of Justification," *Midwest Studies in Philosophy*, 5 (1980), 32.

1

EXTERNALIST THEORIES OF EMPIRICAL KNOWLEDGE

Laurence BonJour

Of the many problems that would have to be solved by a satisfactory theory of empirical knowledge, perhaps the most central is a general structural problem which I shall call *the epistemic regress problem*: the problem of how to avoid an infinite and presumably vicious regress of justification in one's account of the justification of empirical beliefs. *Foundationalist* theories of empirical knowledge, as we shall see further below, attempt to avoid the regress by locating a class of empirical beliefs whose justification does not depend on that of other empirical beliefs. *Externalist* theories, the topic of the present paper, represent one species of foundationalism.

I

I begin with a brief look at the epistemic regress problem. The source of the problem is the requirement that beliefs that are to constitute knowledge must be *epistemically justified*. Such a requirement is of course an essential part of the "traditional" conception of knowledge as justified true belief, but it also figures in at least most of the revisions of that conception which have been inspired by the Gettier problem. Indeed, if this requirement is understood in a sufficiently generic way, as meaning roughly that the acceptance of the belief must be epistemically rational, that it must not be epistemically irresponsible, then it becomes hard to see how any adequate conception of knowledge can fail to include it.

How then are empirical beliefs epistemically justified? Certainly the most obvious way to *show* that such a belief is justified is by producing a justificatory argument in which the belief to be justified is shown to follow inferentially from some other (perhaps conjunctive) belief, which is thus offered as a reason for accepting it. Beliefs whose justification would, if made explicit, take this form may be said to be *inferentially justified*. (Of course, such a justificatory argument would usually be explicitly rehearsed only in the face of some specific problem or challenge. Notice also that an inferentially justified belief need not have been *arrived at* through inference, though it often will have been.)

The important point about inferential justification, however, is that if the justificandum belief is to be genuinely justified by the proffered argument, then the belief that provides the premise of the argument must itself be justified in some fashion. This premise belief might of course itself be inferentially justified, but this would only raise a new issue of justification with respect to the premise(s) of this new justificatory argument, and so on, so that empirical knowledge is threatened by an infinite and seemingly vicious regress of epistemic justification, with a thoroughgoing skepticism as the eventual outcome. So long as each new step of justification is inferential, it appears that justification can never be completed, indeed can never really even get started, and hence that there is no justification and no knowledge. Thus the epistemic regress problem.

What is the eventual outcome of this regress? There are a variety of possibilities, but the majority of philosophers who have considered the problem have believed that the only outcome that does not lead more or less directly to skepticism is *foundationalism*: the view that the regress terminates by reaching empirical beliefs (a) that are genuinely justified, but (b) whose justification is not inferentially dependent on that of any further empirical belief(s), so that no further issue of empirical justification is thereby raised. These non-inferentially justified beliefs, or *basic beliefs* as I shall call them, are claimed to provide the foundation upon which the edifice of empirical knowledge rests. And the central argument for foundationalism is simply that all other possible outcomes of the regress lead inexorably to skepticism.[1]

This argument has undeniable force. Nonetheless, the central concept of foundationalism, the concept of a basic belief, is itself by no means unproblematic. The fundamental question that must be answered by any acceptable version of foundationalism is: *how are basic beliefs possible?* How, that is, is it possible for there to be an empirical belief that is epistemically justified in a way completely independent of any believed premises that might provide reasons for accepting it? As Chisholm suggests, a basic belief seems to be in effect an epistemologically unmoved (or perhaps self-moved) mover.

But such a status is surely no less paradoxical in epistemology than it is in theology.

This intuitive difficulty with the idea of a basic empirical belief may be elaborated by considering briefly the fundamental concept of epistemic justification. There are two points to be made. First, the idea of justification is generic, admitting in principle of many different species. Thus, for example, the acceptance of an empirical belief might be morally justified, or pragmatically justified, or justified in some still different sense. But a belief's being justified in one of these other senses will not satisfy the justification condition for knowledge. What knowledge requires is *epistemic* justification. And the distinguishing characteristic of this particular species of justification is, I submit, its internal relationship to the cognitive goal of *truth*. A cognitive act is epistemically justified, on this conception, only if and to the extent that is aimed at this goal – which means at a minimum that one accepts only beliefs that there is adequate reason to think are true.

Second, the concept of epistemic justification is fundamentally a normative concept. It has to do with what one has a duty or obligation to do, from an epistemic or intellectual standpoint. As Chisholm suggests, one's purely intellectual duty is to accept beliefs that are true, or likely to be true, and reject beliefs that are false, or likely to be false. To accept beliefs on some other basis is to violate one's epistemic duty – to be, one might say, *epistemically irresponsible* – even though such acceptance might be desirable or even mandatory from some other, non-epistemic standpoint.

Thus if basic beliefs are to provide a suitable foundation for empirical knowledge, if inference from them is to be the sole basis for the justification of other empirical beliefs, then that feature, whatever it may be, in virtue of which an empirical belief qualifies as basic, must also constitute an adequate reason for thinking that the belief is true. And now if we assume, plausibly enough, that the person for whom a belief is basic must *himself* possess the justification for that belief if *his* acceptance of it is to be epistemically rational or responsible, and thus apparently that he must believe *with justification* both (a) that the belief has the feature in question and (b) that beliefs having that feature are likely to be true, then we get the result that this belief is not basic after all, since its justification depends on that of these other beliefs. If this result is correct, then foundationalism is untenable as a solution to the regress problem.[2]

What strategies are available to the foundationalist for avoiding this objection? One possibility would be to grant that the believer must be in possession of the reason for thinking that his basic belief is true but hold that the believer's cognitive grasp of that reason does not involve further *beliefs*, which would then require justification, but instead cognitive states of a different and more rudimentary kind: *intuitions* or *immediate apprehensions*, which are somehow capable of conferring justification upon beliefs without themselves requiring justification. Some such view as this seems implicit in most traditional versions of foundationalism.[3]

My concern in the present paper, however, is with an alternative foundationalist strategy, one of comparatively recent innovation. One way, perhaps somewhat tendentious, to put this alternative approach is to say that according to it, though there must in a sense be a reason why a basic belief is likely to be true, the person for whom such a belief is basic need not have any cognitive grasp of this reason. On this view, the epistemic justification or reasonableness of a basic belief depends on the obtaining of an appropriate relation, generally causal or nomological in character, between the believer and the world. This relation, which is differently characterized by different versions of the view, is such as to make it either nomologically certain or else highly probable that the belief is true. It would thus provide, *for anyone who knew about it*, an undeniably excellent reason for accepting such a belief. But according to proponents of the view under discussion, the person for whom the belief is basic need not (and in general will not) have any cognitive grasp of any kind of this reason or of the relation that is the basis for it in order for this basic belief to be justified; all these matters may be entirely *external* to the person's subjective conception of the situation. Thus the justification of a basic belief need not involve any further beliefs (or other cognitive states) so that no further regress of justification is generated. D. M. Armstrong calls this an "externalist" solution to the regress problem, and I shall adopt this label.

My purpose in this paper is to examine such externalist views. I am not concerned with problems of detail in formulating a view of this kind, though some of these will be mentioned in passing, but rather with the overall acceptability of an externalist solution to the regress problem and thus of an externalist version of foundationalism. I shall attempt to argue that externalism is not acceptable. But there is a methodological problem with respect to such an argument which must be faced at the outset, since it determines the basic approach of the paper.

When viewed from the general standpoint of the western epistemological tradition, externalism represents a very radical departure. It seems safe to say that until very recent times, no serious philosopher of knowledge would have dreamed of suggesting that a person's beliefs might be epistemically justified simply in virtue of facts or relations that were external to his subjective conception. Descartes, for example, would surely have been quite unimpressed by the suggestion that his problematic beliefs about the external world were justified if only they were in fact reliably related to the world – whether or not he had any reason for thinking this to be so. Clearly his conception, and that of generations of philosophers who followed, was that such a relation could play a justificatory role only if the believer possessed adequate reason for thinking that it obtained. Thus the suggestion embodied in externalism would have been regarded by most epistemologists as simply irrelevant to the main epistemological issue, so much so that the philosopher who suggested it would have been taken either to be hopelessly confused or to be simply changing the subject (as I note below, this may be what some externalists in fact intend to be doing). The problem, however, is that this very radicalism has the effect of insulating the externalist from any very direct refutation: any attempt at such a refutation is almost certain to appeal to premises that a thoroughgoing externalist would not accept. My solution to this threatened impasse will be to proceed on an intuitive level as far as possible. By considering a series of examples, I shall attempt to exhibit as clearly as possible the fundamental intuition about epistemic rationality that externalism seems to violate. Although this intuition may not constitute a conclusive objection to the view, it is enough, I believe, to shift the burden of proof decisively to the externalist. In the final section of the paper, I shall consider briefly whether he can discharge this burden.

II

Our first task will be the formulation of a clear and relatively adequate version of externalism. The recent epistemological literature contains a reasonably large number of externalist and quasi-externalist views. Some of these, however, are not clearly relevant to our present concerns, either because they are aimed primarily at the Gettier problem, so that their implications for a foundationalist solution of the regress problem are not made clear, or because they *seem*, on the surface at least, to involve a repudiation of the very conception of epistemic justification or reasonableness as a requirement for knowledge. Views of the latter sort seem to me to be very difficult to take seriously; but if they are seriously intended, they would have the consequence that the regress problem, at least in the form discussed here, would simply not arise, so that there would be no need for any solution, foundationalist or otherwise. My immediate concern here is with versions of externalism that claim to *solve* the regress problem and thus that also claim that the acceptance of beliefs satisfying the externalist conditions is epistemically justified or rational or warranted. Only such an externalist position genuinely constitutes a version of foundationalism, and hence the more radical views, if any such are in fact seriously intended, may safely be left aside for the time being.

The most completely developed externalist view of the sort we are interested in is that of Armstrong, as presented in his book, *Belief, Truth and Knowledge*.[1] Armstrong is explicitly concerned with the regress problem, though he
formulates it in terms of knowledge rather than justification. And it seems
reasonably clear that he wants to say that beliefs satisfying his externalist criterion are epistemically justified or rational, though he is not as explicit as one
might like on this point.[5] In what follows, I shall in any case assume such an
interpretation of Armstrong and formulate his position accordingly.

Another version of externalism, which fairly closely resembles Armstrong's
except for being limited to knowledge derived from visual perception, is
offered by Dretske in *Seeing and Knowing*.[6] Goldman, in several papers, also
suggests views of an externalist sort,[7] and the view that Alston calls "Simple
Foundationalism" and claims to be the most defensible version of foundationalism seems to be essentially externalist in character.[8] The most extreme
version of externalism would be one that held that the external condition
required for justification is simply the *truth* of the belief in question. Such a
view could not be held in general, of course, without obliterating the distinction between knowledge and mere true belief, thereby turning every lucky
guess into knowledge. But it might be held with respect to some more limited
class of beliefs. Such a view is mentioned by Alston as one possible account
of privileged access,[9] and seems, surprisingly enough, to be advocated by
Chisholm (though it is very hard to be sure that this is what Chisholm really
means).[10]

Here I shall concentrate mainly on Armstrong's view. Like all externalists,
Armstrong makes the acceptability of a basic belief depend on an external
relation between the believer and his belief, on the one hand, and the world,
on the other, specifically a law-like connection: "there must be a *law-like connection* between the state of affairs *Bap* [i.e., *a*'s believing that *p*] and the state
of affairs which makes '*p*' true, such that, given *Bap*, it must be the case that
p" (166). This is what Armstrong calls the "thermometer-model" of non-
inferential knowledge: just as the readings of a reliable thermometer lawfully
reflect the temperature, so one's basic beliefs lawfully reflect the states of
affairs that make them true. A person whose beliefs satisfy this condition is in
effect a reliable cognitive instrument; and it is, according to Armstrong, precisely in virtue of this reliability that these basic beliefs are justified.

Of course, not all thermometers are reliable, and even a reliable one may
be accurate only under certain conditions. Similarly, it is not a requirement
for the justification of a basic belief on Armstrong's view that all beliefs of
that general kind or even all beliefs of that kind held by that particular believer
be reliable. Thus the law linking the having of the belief with the state of
affairs that makes it true will have to mention properties, including relational

properties, of the believer beyond his merely having that belief. Incorporating this modification yields the following schematic formulation of the conditions under which a non-inferential belief is justified and therefore basic: a non-inferential belief is justified if and only if there is some property H of the believer, such that it is a law of nature that whenever a person satisfies H and has that belief, then the belief is true (197).[11] Here H may be as complicated as one likes and may include facts about the believer's mental processes, sensory apparatus, environment, and so on. But presumably, though Armstrong does not mention this point, H is not to include anything that would entail the truth of the belief; such a logical connection would not count as a law of nature.

Armstrong adds several qualifications to this account, aimed at warding off various objections, of which I shall mention only two. First, the nomological connection between the belief and the state of affairs that makes it true is to be restricted to "that of *completely reliable sign* to thing signified" (182). What this is intended to exclude is the case where the belief itself *causes* the state of affairs that makes it true. In such a case, it seems intuitively that the belief is not a case of knowledge even though it satisfies the condition of complete reliability formulated above. Second, the property H of the believer which is involved in the law of nature must not be "too specific"; there must be a "real possibility" of a recurrence of the situation described by the law. What Armstrong is worried about here is the possibility of a "veridical hallucination," i.e., a case in which a hallucinatory belief happens to be correct. In such a case, if the state of affairs that makes the belief true happens to be part of the cause of the hallucination and if the believer and his environment are described in enough detail, it might turn out to be nomologically necessary that such a state of affairs obtain, simply because all alternative possible causes for the hallucinatory belief have been ruled out by the specificity of the description. Again, such a case intuitively should not count as a case of knowledge, but it would satisfy Armstrong's criterion in the absence of this additional stipulation. (Obviously this requirement of nonspecificity or repeatability is extremely vague and seems in fact to be no more than an *ad hoc* solution to this problem; but I shall not pursue this issue here.)

There are various problems of detail, similar to those just discussed, which could be raised about Armstrong's view, but these have little relevance to the main theme of the present paper. Here I am concerned with the more fundamental issue of whether Armstrong's view, or any other externalist view of this general sort, is acceptable as a solution to the regress problem and the basis for a foundationalist account of empirical knowledge. When considered from this perspective, Armstrong's view seems at the very least to

be in need of considerable refinement in the face of fairly obvious counterexamples. Thus our first task will be to develop some of these counterexamples and suggest modifications in the view accordingly. This discussion
will also lead, however, to a fundamental intuitive objection to all forms of
externalism.

III

Although it is formulated in more general terms, the main concern of an
externalist view like Armstrong's is obviously those non-inferential beliefs
which arise from ordinary sources like sense-perception and introspection. For
it is, of course, these beliefs which will on any plausible foundationalist view
provide the actual foundations of empirical knowledge. Nevertheless, cases
involving sense-perception and introspection are not very suitable for an
intuitive assessment of externalism, since one central issue between externalism and other foundationalist and non-foundationalist views is precisely
whether in such cases a further basis for justification beyond the externalist
one is typically present. Thus it will be useful to begin by considering the
application of externalism to other possible cases of non-inferential knowledge, cases of a less familiar sort where it will be easier to stipulate in a way
that will be effective on an intuitive level that only the externalist sort of justification is present. Specifically, in this section and the next, our focus will be
on possible cases of clairvoyant knowledge. Clairvoyance, the alleged psychic
power of perceiving or intuiting the existence and character of distant states
of affairs without the aid of any sensory input, remains the subject of considerable scientific controversy. Although many would like to dismiss out of
hand the very idea of such a cognitive power, there remains a certain amount
of evidence in favor of its existence which it is difficult to entirely discount.
But in any case, the actual existence of clairvoyance does not matter at all for
present purposes, so long as it is conceded to represent a coherent possibility.
For externalism, as a general philosophical account of the foundations of
empirical knowledge, must of course apply to all possible modes of non-
inferential empirical knowledge, and not just to those that in fact happen to
be realized.

The intuitive difficulty with externalism that the following discussion is
intended to delineate and develop is this: on the externalist view, a person
may be ever so irrational and irresponsible in accepting a belief, when judged
in light of his own subjective conception of the situation, and may still turn
out to be epistemically justified, i.e., may still turn out to satisfy Armstrong's
general criterion of reliability. This belief may in fact be reliable, even though

the person has no reason for thinking that it is reliable – or even though he has good reason to think that it is not reliable. But such a person seems nonetheless to be thoroughly irresponsible from an epistemic standpoint in accepting such a belief, and hence not justified, contrary to externalism. The following cases may help bring out this problem more clearly.

Consider first the following case:

> Case I. Samantha believes herself to have the power of clairvoyance, though she has no reasons for or against this belief. One day she comes to believe, for no apparent reason, that the President is in New York City. She maintains this belief, appealing to her alleged clairvoyant power, even though she is at the same time aware of a massive amount of apparently cogent evidence, consisting of news reports, press releases, allegedly live television pictures, etc., indicating that the President is at that time in Washington, D.C. Now the President is in fact in New York City, the evidence to the contrary being part of a massive official hoax mounted in the face of an assassination threat. Moreover, Samantha does in fact have completely reliable clairvoyant power, under the conditions that were then satisfied, and her belief about the President did result from the operation of that power.

In this case, it is clear that Armstrong's criterion of reliability is satisfied. There will be some complicated description of Samantha, including the conditions then operative, from which it will follow, by the law describing her clairvoyant power, that her belief is true.[12] But it seems intuitively clear nevertheless that this is not a case of justified belief or of knowledge: Samantha is being thoroughly irrational and irresponsible in disregarding cogent evidence that the President is not in New York City on the basis of a clairvoyant power which she has no reason at all to think that she possesses; and this irrationality is not somehow canceled by the fact that she happens to be right. Thus, I submit, Samantha's irrationality and irresponsibility prevent her belief from being epistemically justified.

This case and others like it suggest the need for a further condition to supplement Armstrong's original one: not only must it be true that there is a law-like connection between a person's belief and the state of affairs that makes it true, such that given the belief, the state of affairs cannot fail to obtain, but it must also be true that the person in question does not possess cogent reasons for thinking that the belief in question is false. For, as this case seems to show, the possession of such reasons renders the acceptance of the belief irrational in a way that cannot be overridden by a purely externalist justification.

Nor is this the end of the difficulty for Armstrong. Suppose that the clair-voyant believer, instead of having evidence against the particular belief in question, has evidence against his possession of such a cognitive power, as in the following case:

Case II. Casper believes himself to have the power of clairvoyance, though he has no reasons for this belief. He maintains his belief despite the fact that on the numerous occasions on which he has attempted to confirm one of his allegedly clairvoyant beliefs, it has always turned out apparently to be false. One day Casper comes to believe, for no appar-ent reason, that the President is in New York City, and he maintains this belief, appealing to his alleged clairvoyant power. Now in fact the President is in New York City; and Casper does, under the conditions that were then satisfied, have completely reliable clairvoyant power, from which this belief in fact resulted. The apparent falsity of his other clair-voyant beliefs was due in some cases to his being in the wrong condi-tions for the operation of his power and in other cases to deception and misinformation.

Is Casper justified in believing that the President is in New York City, so that he then knows that this is the case? According to Armstrong's account, even with the modification just suggested, we must apparently say that the belief is justified and hence a case of knowledge: the reliability condition is satisfied, and Casper possesses no reason for thinking that the President is not in New York City. But this result still seems mistaken. Casper is being quite irrational and irresponsible from an epistemic standpoint in disregarding evidence that his beliefs of this sort are not reliable and should not be trusted. And for this reason, the belief in question is not justified.

In the foregoing case, Casper possessed good reasons for thinking that he did not possess the sort of cognitive ability that he believed himself to possess. But the result would be the same, I believe, if someone instead possessed good reasons for thinking that *in general* there could be no such cognitive ability, as in the following case:

Case III. Maud believes herself to have the power of clairvoyance, though she has no reasons for this belief. She maintains her belief despite being inundated by her embarrassed friends and relatives with massive quantities of apparently cogent scientific evidence that no such power is possible. One day Maud comes to believe, for no apparent reason, that the President is in New York City, and she maintains this belief, despite the lack of any independent evidence, appealing to her alleged clairvoyant power. Now in fact the President is in New York City, and Maud does, under the conditions then satisfied, have completely reliable clairvoyant power. Moreover, her belief about the President did result from the operation of that power.

Again, Armstrong's criterion of reliability seems to be satisfied. But it also seems to me that Maud, like Casper, is not justified in her belief about the President and does not have knowledge. Maud has excellent reasons for thinking that no cognitive power such as she believes herself to possess is possible, and it is irrational and irresponsible of her to maintain her belief in that power in the face of that evidence and to continue to accept and maintain beliefs on this dubious basis.

Cases like these two suggest the need for a further modification of Armstrong's account: in addition to the law-like connection between belief and truth and the absence of any reasons against the particular belief in question, it must also be the case that the believer in question has no cogent reasons, either relative to his own case or in general, for thinking that such a law-like connection does *not* exist, i.e., that beliefs of that kind are not reliable.

IV

So far the modifications suggested for Armstrong's criterion are consistent with the basic thrust of externalism as a response to the regress problem. What emerges is in fact a significantly more plausible externalist position. But these cases and the modifications made in response to them also suggest an important moral which leads to a basic intuitive objection to externalism: external or objective reliability is not enough to offset subjective irrationality. If the acceptance of a belief is seriously unreasonable or unwarranted from the believer's own standpoint, then the mere fact that unbeknownst to the believer its existence in those circumstances lawfully guarantees its truth will not suffice to render the belief epistemically justified and thereby an instance of knowledge. So far we have been concerned only with situations in which the believer's subjective irrationality took the form of ignoring positive grounds in his possession for questioning either that specific belief or beliefs arrived at in that way. But now we must ask whether even in a case where these positive reasons for a charge of irrationality are not present, the acceptance of a belief where only an externalist justification is available cannot still be said to be subjectively irrational in a sense that rules out its being epistemically justified.

We may begin by considering one further case of clairvoyance, in which Armstrong's criterion with all the suggested modifications is satisfied:

Case IV. Norman, under certain conditions that usually obtain, is a completely reliable clairvoyant with respect to certain kinds of subject matter. He possesses no evidence or reasons of any kind for or against the general possibility of such a cognitive power, or for or against the thesis that he possesses it. One day Norman comes to believe that the President is in New York City, though he has no evidence either for or against this belief. In fact the belief is true and results from his clairvoyant power, under circumstances in which it is completely reliable.

Is Norman epistemically justified in believing that the President is in New York City, so that his belief is an instance of knowledge? According to the modified externalist position, we must apparently say that he is. But is this the right result? Are there not still sufficient grounds for a charge of subjective irrationality to prevent Norman's being epistemically justified?

One thing that might seem relevant to this issue, which I have deliberately omitted from the specification of the case, is whether Norman *believes* himself to have clairvoyant power, even though he has no justification for such a belief. Let us consider both possibilities. Suppose, first, that Norman does have such a belief and that it contributes to his acceptance of his original belief about the President's whereabouts in the sense that were Norman to become convinced that he did not have this power, he would also cease to accept the belief about the President.[13] But is it not obviously irrational, from an epistemic standpoint, for Norman to hold such a belief when he has no reasons at all for thinking that it is true or even for thinking that such a power is possible? This belief about his clairvoyance fails after all to possess even an externalist justification. And if we say that the belief about his clairvoyance is epistemically irrational and unjustified, must we not say the same thing about the belief about the President which *ex hypothesi* depends upon it?[14]

A possible response to this challenge would be to add one further condition to our modified externalist position, *viz.*, that the believer not even *believe* that the law-like connection in question obtains, since such a belief will not in general be justified (or at least that his continued acceptance of the particular belief that is at issue not depend on his acceptance of such a general belief). In our present case, this would mean that Norman must not believe that he has the power of clairvoyance (or at least that his acceptance of the belief about the President's whereabouts not depend on his having such a general belief). But if this specification is added to the case, it now becomes more than a little puzzling to understand what Norman thinks is going on. From his standpoint, there is apparently no way in which he *could* know the President's whereabouts. Why then does he continue to maintain the belief that the President is in New York City? Why is not the mere fact that there is no way, as far as he knows or believes, for him to have obtained this information a sufficient reason for classifying this belief as an unfounded hunch and ceasing to accept it? And if Norman does not do this, is he not thereby being epistemically irrational and irresponsible?

For these reasons, I submit, Norman's acceptance of the belief about the President's whereabouts is epistemically irrational and irresponsible, and thereby unjustified, whether or not he believes himself to have clairvoyant power, so long as he has no justification for such a belief. Part of one's epistemic duty is to reflect critically upon one's beliefs, and such critical reflection precludes believing things to which one has, to one's knowledge, no reliable means of epistemic access.[15]

We are now face-to-face with the fundamental – and seemingly obvious – intuitive problem with externalism: *why* should the mere fact that such an external relation obtains mean that Norman's belief is epistemically justified, when the relation in question is entirely outside his ken? As remarked earlier, it is clear that one who knew that Armstrong's criterion was satisfied would be in a position to construct a simple and quite cogent justifying argument for the belief in question: if Norman has property H (being a completely reliable clairvoyant under the existing conditions and arriving at the belief on that basis), then he holds the belief in question only if it is true; Norman does have property H and does hold the belief in question; therefore, the belief is true. But Norman himself is by stipulation not in a position to employ this argument, and it is unclear why the mere fact that it is, so to speak, potentially available in the situation should justify *his* acceptance of the belief. Precisely what generates the regress problem in the first place, after all, is the requirement that for a belief to be justified for a particular person, not only is it necessary that there be true premises somehow available in the situation which could in principle provide a basis for a justification, but also that the believer in question know or at least justifiably believe some such set of premises and thus be in a position to employ the corresponding argument. The externalist position seems to amount merely to waiving this general requirement in a certain class of cases, and the question is why this should be acceptable in these cases when it is not acceptable generally. (If it were acceptable generally, then it seems likely that *any* true belief would be justified, unless some severe requirement is imposed as to how immediately available such premises must be. But any such requirement seems utterly arbitrary, once the natural one of actual access by the believer is abandoned.)

Thus externalism looks like a purely *ad hoc* solution to the epistemic regress problem.

One reason why externalism may seem initially plausible is that if the external relation in question genuinely obtains, then Norman will in fact not go wrong in accepting the belief, and it is, *in a sense*, not an accident that this is so. But how is this supposed to justify Norman's belief? From his subjective perspective, it *is* an accident that the belief is true. Of course, it would not be an accident from the standpoint of our hypothetical external observer who knows all the relevant facts and laws. Such an observer, having constructed the justifying argument sketched above, would be thereby in a position to justify *his own* acceptance of the belief. Thus Norman, as Armstrong's thermometer image suggests, could serve as a useful epistemic instrument for such an observer, a kind of cognitive thermometer; and it is to this fact, as we have seen, that Armstrong appeals in arguing that a belief like Norman's can be correctly said to be reasonable or justifiable (183). But none of this seems in fact to justify Norman's *own* acceptance of the belief, for Norman, unlike the hypothetical external observer, has no reason at all for thinking that the belief is true. And the suggestion here is that the rationality or justifiability of Norman's belief should be judged from Norman's own perspective, rather than from one that is unavailable to him.[16]

This basic objection to externalism seems to me to be intuitively compelling. But it is sufficiently close to being simply a statement of what the externalist wants to deny to make it helpful to buttress it a bit by appealing to some related intuitions.

First, we may consider an analogy with moral philosophy. The same conflict between perspectives which we have seen to arise in the process of epistemic assessment can also arise with regard to the moral assessment of a person's action: the agent's subjective conception of what he is doing may differ dramatically from that which would in principle be available to an external observer who had access to facts about the situation that are beyond the agent's ken. And now we can imagine an approximate moral analogue of externalism which would hold that the moral justifiability of an agent's action was, in certain cases at least, properly to be determined from the external perspective, entirely irrespective of the agent's own conception of the situation.

Consider first the moral analogue of Armstrong's original, unmodified version of externalism. If we assume, purely for the sake of simplicity, a utilitarian moral theory, such a view would say that an action might on occasion be morally justified simply in virtue of the fact that in the situation then obtaining, it would as a matter of objective fact lead to the best overall consequences – even if the agent planned and anticipated that it would lead to a very different, perhaps extremely undesirable, consequences. But such a view seems plainly mistaken. There is no doubt a point to the objective, external assessment: we can say correctly that it turns out to be objectively a good thing that the agent performed the action. But this is not at all inconsistent with saying that his action was morally unjustified and reprehensible, given his subjective conception of the likely consequences.

Thus our envisaged moral externalism must at least be modified in a way that parallels the modifications earlier suggested for epistemological externalism. Without attempting to make the analogy exact, it will suffice for our present purposes to add to the original requirement for moral justification, *viz.*, that the action will in fact lead to the best overall consequences, the further condition that the agent not believe or intend that it lead to undesirable consequences. Since it is also, of course, not required by moral externalism that the agent believe that the action will lead to good consequences, the sort of case we are now considering is one in which an agent acts in a way that will in fact produce the best overall consequences, but has *no belief at all* about the likely consequences of his action. Although such an agent is no doubt preferable to one who acts in the belief that his action will lead to undesirable consequences, surely he is not morally justified in what he does. On the contrary, he is being highly irresponsible, from a moral standpoint, in performing the action in the absence of any evaluation of what will result from it. His moral duty, from our assumed utilitarian standpoint, is to do what will lead to the best consequences, but this duty is not satisfied by the fact that he produces this result willy-nilly, without any idea that he is doing so.[17] And similarly, the fact that a given sort of belief is objectively reliable, and thus that accepting it is in fact conducive to arriving at the truth, need not prevent our judging that the epistemic agent who accepts it without any inkling that this is the case violates his epistemic duty and is epistemically irresponsible and unjustified in doing so.

Second, we may appeal to the connection between knowledge and rational action. Suppose that Norman, in addition to the clairvoyant belief described earlier, also believes that the Attorney-General is in Chicago. This latter belief, however, is not a clairvoyant belief but is based upon ordinary empirical evidence in Norman's possession, evidence strong enough to give the belief some fairly high degree of reasonableness, but *not* strong enough to satisfy the requirement for knowledge.[18] Suppose further that Norman finds himself in a situation where he is forced to bet a very large amount, perhaps even his life or the life of someone else, on the whereabouts of either the President or the Attorney-General. Given his epistemic situation as described, which bet is it more reasonable for him to make? It seems relatively clear that it is more reasonable for him to bet the Attorney-General is in Chicago than to bet that the President is in New York City. But then we have the paradoxical result that from the externalist standpoint it is more rational to act on a merely reasonable belief than to act on one that is adequately justified to qualify as knowledge (and which in fact *is* knowledge). It is very hard to see how this could be so. If greater epistemic reasonableness does not carry with it greater reasonableness of action, then it becomes most difficult to see why it should be sought in the first place. (Of course, the externalist could simply bite the bullet and insist that it is in fact more reasonable for Norman to bet on the President's whereabouts than the Attorney-General's, but such a view seems very implausible.)

I have been attempting in this section to articulate the fundamental intuition about epistemic rationality, and rationality generally, that externalism seems to violate. This intuition the externalist would of course reject, and thus my discussion does not constitute a refutation of the externalist position on its own ground. Nevertheless it seems to me to have sufficient intuitive force at least to place the burden of proof squarely on the externalist. In the final section of the paper, I shall consider briefly some of the responses that seem to be available to him.

V

One possible defense for the externalist in the face of the foregoing intuitive objection would be to narrow his position by restricting it to those commonsensical varieties of non-inferential knowledge which are his primary concern, *viz.*, sense-perception and introspection, thereby rendering the cases set forth above strictly irrelevant. Such a move seems, however, utterly *ad hoc*. Admittedly it is more difficult to construct intuitively compelling counterexamples involving sense-perception and introspection, mainly because our intuitions that beliefs of those kinds are in fact warranted in *some* way or other are very strong. But this does nothing to establish that the externalist account of their warrant is the correct one. Thus unless the externalist can give some positive account of why the same conclusion that seems to hold for non-standard cases like clairvoyance does not also hold for sense-perception and introspection, this narrowing of his position seems to do him no good.

If the externalist cannot escape the force of the objection in this way, can he perhaps balance it with positive arguments in favor of his position? Many attempts to argue for externalism are in effect arguments by elimination and depend on the claim that alternative accounts of empirical knowledge are unacceptable, either because they cannot solve the regress problem or for some other reason. Most such arguments, depending as they do on a detailed consideration of the alternatives, are beyond the scope of the present paper. But one such argument depends only on very general features of the competing positions and thus can usefully be considered here.

The basic factual premise of this argument is that in very many cases that are commonsensically instances of justified belief and of knowledge, there seem to be no justifying factors explicitly present beyond those appealed to by the externalist. An ordinary person in such a case may have no idea at all of the character of his immediate experience, of the coherence of his system of beliefs, etc., and yet may still have knowledge. Alternative theories, so the argument goes, may describe correctly cases of knowledge involving a knower who is extremely reflective and sophisticated, but they are obviously too demanding and too grandiose when applied to these more ordinary cases. In these cases, *only* the externalist condition is satisfied, and this shows that no more than that is necessary for justification and for knowledge, though more might still be epistemically desirable.

Although the precise extent to which it holds could be disputed, in the main this factual premise must be simply conceded. Any non-externalist account of empirical knowledge that has any plausibility will impose standards for justification which very many beliefs that seem commonsensically to be cases of knowledge fail to meet in any full and explicit fashion. And thus on such a view, such beliefs will not *strictly speaking* be instances of adequate justification and of knowledge. But it does not follow that externalism must be correct. This would follow only with the addition of the premise that the judgments of common sense in this area are sacrosanct, that any departure from them is enough to demonstrate that a theory of knowledge is inadequate. But such a premise seems entirely too strong. There seems in fact to be no basis for more than a reasonably strong presumption in favor of the correctness of common sense, but one which is still quite defeasible. And what it would take to defeat this presumption depends in part on how great a departure from common sense is being advocated. Thus, although it would take very strong grounds to justify a very strong form of skepticism, not nearly so much would be required to make acceptable the view that what common sense regards as cases of justification and of knowledge are in fact only rough approximations to an epistemic ideal which *strictly speaking* they do not satisfy.

Of course, a really adequate reply to the externalist would have to spell out in some detail the precise way in which such beliefs really do approximately satisfy some acceptable alternative standard, a task which obviously cannot be attempted here. But even without such elaboration, it seems reasonable to conclude that this argument in favor of externalism fails to carry very much weight as it stands and would require serious buttressing in order to give it any chance of offsetting the intuitive objection to externalism: either the advocacy and defense of a quite strong presumption in favor of common sense, or a detailed showing that alternative theories cannot in fact grant to the cases favored by common sense even the status of approximations to justification and to knowledge.

The other pro-externalist argument I want to consider does not depend in any important way on consideration of alternative positions. This argument is hinted at by Armstrong (185–8), among others, but I know of no place where it is developed very explicitly. Its basic claim is that only an externalist theory can handle a certain version of the lottery paradox.

The lottery paradox is standardly formulated as a problem confronting accounts of inductive logic that contain a rule of acceptance or detachment, but we shall be concerned here with a somewhat modified version. This version arises when we ask how much or what degree of epistemic justification is required for a belief to qualify as knowledge, given that the other necessary conditions for knowledge are satisfied. Given the intimate connection, discussed earlier, between epistemic justification and likelihood of truth, it seems initially reasonable to take likelihood or probability of truth as a measure of the degree of epistemic justification, and thus to interpret the foregoing question as asking how likely or probable it must be, relative to the justification of one's belief, that the belief be true, in order for that belief to satisfy the justification requirement for knowledge. Most historical theories of knowledge tended to answer that knowledge requires *certainty* of truth, relative to one's justification. But more recent epistemological views have tended to reject this answer, for familiar reasons, and to hold instead that knowledge requires only a reasonably high likelihood of truth. And now, if this high likelihood of truth is interpreted in the obvious way as meaning that, relative to one's justification, the numerical probability that one's belief is true must equal or exceed some fixed value, the lottery paradox at once rears its head.

Suppose, for example, that we decide that a belief is adequately justified to satisfy the requirement for knowledge if the probability of its truth, relative to its justification, is 0.99 or greater. Imagine now that a lottery is to be held, about which we know the following facts: exactly 100 tickets have been sold, the drawing will indeed be held, it will be a fair drawing, and there will be only one winning ticket. Consider now each of the 100 propositions of the form:

Ticket number n will lose

where n is replaced by the numbers of one of the tickets. Since there are 100 tickets and only one winner, the probability of each such proposition is 0.99;

and hence if we believe each of them, our individual beliefs will be adequately justified to satisfy the requirement for knowledge. And then, given only the seemingly reasonable assumptions, first, that if one has adequate justification for believing each of a set of propositions, one also has adequate justification for believing the conjunction of the members of the set, and, second, that if one has adequate justification for believing a proposition, one also has adequate justification for believing any further proposition entailed by the first proposition, it follows that we are adequately justified in believing that no ticket will win, contradicting our other information.

Clearly this is a mistaken result, but how is it to be avoided? In the first place, it will plainly do no good to simply increase the level of numerical probability required for adequate justification. For no matter how high it is raised, short of certainty, it will obviously be possible to duplicate the paradoxical result by simply choosing a large enough lottery. Nor do the standard responses to the lottery paradox, whatever their merits may be in dealing with other versions of the paradox, seem to be of much help here. Most of them are ruled out simply by insisting that we do know that empirical propositions are true, not merely that they are probable, and that such knowledge is not in general relative to particular contexts of inquiry. This leaves only the possibility of avoiding the paradoxical result by rejecting the two assumptions stated in the preceding paragraph. But this would be extremely implausible – involving in effect a denial that one may always justifiably deduce conclusions from one's putative knowledge – and in any case would still leave the intuitively unacceptable result that one could on this basis come to know separately the 99 true propositions about various tickets losing (though not of course the false one). In fact, it seems intuitively clear that I do not *know* any of these propositions to be true: if I own one of the tickets, I do not know that it will lose, even if in fact it will, and would not know no matter how large the total number of tickets might be.

At this stage, it may seem that the only way to avoid the paradox is to return to the traditional idea that any degree of probability or likelihood of truth less than certainty is insufficient for knowledge, that only certainty, relative to one's justification, will suffice. The standard objection to such a view is that it seems to lead at once to the skeptical conclusion that we have little or no empirical knowledge. For it seems quite clear that there are no empirical beliefs, with the possible and extremely problematic exception of beliefs about one's own mental states, for which we have justification adequate to exclude all possibility of error. Such a solution seems as bad as the original problem.

It is at this point that externalism may seem to offer a way out. For an externalist position allows one to hold that the justification of an empirical belief must make it certain that the belief is true, while still escaping the clutches of skepticism. This is so precisely because the externalist justification need not be within the cognitive grasp of the believer or indeed of anyone. It need only be true that there is *some* description of the believer, however complex and practically unknowable it may be, which, together with *some* true law of nature, ensures the truth of the belief. Thus, e.g., my perceptual belief that there is a cup on my desk is not certain, on any view, relative to the evidence or justification that is in my possession; I might be hallucinating or there might be an evil demon who is deceiving me. But it seems reasonable to suppose that if the belief is indeed true, then there is *some* external description of me and my situation and *some* true law of nature, relative to which the truth of the belief is guaranteed, and if so it would satisfy the requirement for knowledge.

In some ways, this is a neat and appealing solution to the paradox. Nonetheless, it seems doubtful that it is ultimately satisfactory. In the first place, there is surely something intuitively fishy about solving the problem by appealing to an in-principle guarantee of truth which will almost certainly in practice be available to no one. A second problem, which cannot be elaborated here, is that insisting on this sort of solution seems likely to create insuperable difficulties for knowledge of general and theoretical propositions. But in any case, the externalist solution seems to yield intuitively incorrect results in certain kinds of cases. A look at one of these may also suggest the beginnings of a more satisfactory solution.

Consider then the following case:

> Case V. Agatha, seated at her desk, believes herself to be perceiving a cup on the desk. She also knows, however, that she is one of a group of 100 people who have been selected for a philosophical experiment by a Cartesian evil demon. The conditions have been so arranged that all 100 will at this particular time seem to themselves to be perceiving a cup upon their respective desks, with no significant differences in the subjective character of their respective experiences. But in fact, though 99 of the people will be perceiving a cup in the normal way, the last one will be caused by the demon to have a complete hallucination (including perceptual conditions, etc.) of a non-existent cup. Agatha knows all this, but she does not have any further information as to whether she is the one who is hallucinating, though as it happens she is not.

Is Agatha epistemically justified in her belief that there is a cup on the desk and does she know this to be so? According to the externalist view, we must say that she is justified and does know. For there is, we may assume, an external description of Agatha and her situation relative to which it is nomologically certain that her belief is true. (Indeed, according to Armstrong's original, unmodified view, she would be justified and would know even if she also knew instead that 99 of 100 persons were being deceived by the demon, so long as she was in fact the odd one who was perceiving normally.) But this result is, I submit, intuitively mistaken. If Agatha knows that she is perceiving a cup, then she also knows that she is not the one who is being deceived. But she does not know this, for reasons that parallel those operative in the lottery case.

Is there then no way out of the paradox? The foregoing case and others like it seem to me to suggest the following approach to at least the present version of the paradox, though I can offer only an exceedingly brief sketch here. Intuitively, what the lottery case and the case of Agatha have in common is the presence of a large number of relevantly similar, alternative possibilities, all individually very unlikely, but such that the person in question *knows* that at least one of them will in fact be realized. In such a case, since there is no relevant way of distinguishing among these possibilities, the person cannot believe with adequate justification and *a fortiori* cannot know that any particular possibility will not be realized, even though the probability that it will not be realized may be made as high as one likes by simply increasing the total number of possibilities. Such cases do show that high probability is not by itself enough to satisfy the justification condition for knowledge. They do not show, however, that certainty is required instead. For what rules out knowledge in such a case is not merely the fact that the probability of truth is less than certainty but also the fact that the person *knows* that at least one of these highly probable propositions is false. It is a necessary condition for justification and for knowledge that this not be so. But there are many cases in which a person's justification for a belief fails to make it certain that the belief is true, but in which the person also does not know that some possible situation in which the belief would be false is one of a set of relevantly similar, alternative possibilities, at least one of which will definitely be realized. And in such a case, the lottery paradox provides no reason to think that the person does not know.[19]

An example may help to make this point clear. Consider again my apparent perception of the cup on my desk. I think that I do in fact know that there is a cup there. But the justification that is in my possession surely does not make it certain that my belief is true. Thus, for example, it seems to be possible, relative to my subjective justification, that I am being deceived by an evil demon, who is causing me to have a hallucinatory experience of the cup, together with accompanying conditions of perception. But it does not follow from this that I do not know that there is a cup on the desk, because it does not follow and I do not know that there is some class of relevantly similar cases in at least one of which a person is in fact deceived by such a demon. Although it is only probable and not certain that there is no demon, it is still possible for all I *know* that never in the history of the universe, past, present, or future, is there a case in which someone in a relevantly similar perceptual situation is actually deceived by such a demon. And, as far as I can see, the same thing is true of all the other ways in which it is possible that my belief might be mistaken. If this is so, then the lottery paradox provides no obstacle to my knowledge in this case.[20]

This response to the lottery paradox seems to me to be on the right track. It must be conceded, however, that it is in considerable need of further development and may turn out to have problems of its own. But that is a subject for another paper.[21]

There is one other sort of response, mentioned briefly above, which the externalist might make to the sorts of criticisms developed in this paper. I want to remark on it briefly, though a full-scale discussion is impossible here. In the end it may be possible to make intuitive sense of externalism only by construing the externalist as simply abandoning the traditional idea of epistemic justification or rationality and along with it anything resembling the traditional conception of knowledge. I have already mentioned that this may be precisely what the proponents of externalism intend to be doing, though most of them are anything but clear on this point.[22]

Against an externalist position that seriously adopts such a gambit, the criticisms developed in the present paper are of course entirely ineffective. If the externalist does not want even to claim that beliefs satisfying his conditions are epistemically justified or reasonable, then it is obviously no objection that they seem in some cases to be quite unjustified and unreasonable. But, as already noted, such a view, though it may possess some other sort of appeal, constitutes a solution to the epistemic regress problem or to any problem arising out of the traditional conception of knowledge only in the radical and relatively uninteresting sense that to reject that conception entirely is also, of course, to reject any problems arising out of it. Such "solutions" would seem to be available for any philosophical problem at all, but it is hard to see why they should be taken seriously.

Notes

1   For a fuller discussion of the regress argument, including a discussion of other possible outcomes of the regress, see my paper "Can Empirical Knowledge Have

a Foundation?" *American Philosophical Quarterly* 15 (1978):1–13. That paper also contains a brief anticipation of the present discussion of externalism.

2 It could, of course, still be claimed that the belief in question was *empirically* basic, so long as both the needed justifying premises were justifiable on an *a priori* basis. But this would mean that it was an *a priori* truth that a particular empirical belief was likely to be true. In the present paper, I shall simply assume, without further discussion, that this seemingly unlikely state of affairs does not in fact obtain.

3 For criticism of this view, see the paper cited in note 1.

4 D. M. Armstrong, *Belief, Truth and Knowledge* (London, Press, 1973). Bracketed references in the text will be to the pages of this book.

5 The clearest passages are at p. 183, where Armstrong says that a belief satisfying his externalist condition, though not "based on reasons," nevertheless "might be said to be reasonable (justifiable), because it is a sign, a completely reliable sign, that the situation believed to exist does in fact exist"; and at p. 189, where he suggests that the satisfaction of a slightly weaker condition, though it does not yield knowledge, may still yield rational belief. There is no reason to think that any species of rationality or reasonableness other than the epistemic is at issue in either of these passages. But though these passages seem to me to adequately support my interpretation of Armstrong, the strongest support may well derive simply from the fact that he at no point *disavows* a claim of epistemic rationality. (See also the parenthetical remark in the middle of p. 77.)

6 Fred I. Dretske, *Seeing and Knowing* (London, 1969), chap. III. Dretske also differs from Armstrong in requiring in effect that the would-be knower also believe that the externalist condition is satisfied, but not of course that this belief be justified.

7 Goldman does this most clearly in "Discrimination and Perceptual Knowledge," *Journal of Philosophy* 73 (1976):771–91; and in "What is Justified Belief?", In G. Pappas, ed., *Justification and Knowledge: New Studies in Epistemology* (Reidel, 1979), 1–23. See also "A Causal Theory of Knowing," *Journal of Philosophy* 64 (1967):355–72, though this last paper is more concerned with the Gettier problem than with a general account of the standards of epistemic justification.

8 William P. Alston, "Two Types of Foundationalism," *Journal of Philosophy* 73 (1976):165–85; see especially p. 168.

9 Alston, "Varieties of Privileged Access," in Roderick Chisholm and Robert Swartz, *Empirical Knowledge* (Englewood Cliffs, N.J., 1973), pp. 396–9. Alston's term for this species of privileged access is "truth-sufficiency."

10 See Chisholm, *Theory of Knowledge*, 2nd edn. (Englewood Cliffs, N.J., 1977), p. 22, where Chisholm offers the following definition of the concept of a state of affairs being *self-presenting*:

h is *self-presenting* for *S* at *t* = Df *h* occurs at *t*; and necessarily, if *h* occurs at *t* then *h* is evident [i.e., justified] for *S* at *t*.

Despite the overtones of the term "self-presentation," nothing in this passage seems to require that believer have any sort of immediate awareness of the state in question; all that is required is that it actually occur, i.e., that his belief be true. On the other hand, Chisholm also, in the section immediately preceding this definition, quotes with approval a passage from Leibniz which appeals to the idea of "direct awareness" and of the absence of mediation "between the understanding and its objects," thus suggesting the non-externalist variety of foundationalism (pp. 20–21).

11 Armstrong actually formulates the criterion as a criterion of knowledge, rather than merely of justification; the satisfaction of the belief condition is built into the criterion and this, with the satisfaction of the indicated justification condition, entails that the truth condition is satisfied.

12 This assumes that clairvoyant beliefs are caused in some distinctive way, so that an appropriately complete description of Samantha will rule out the possibility that the belief is a mere hunch and will connect appropriately with the law governing her clairvoyance.

13 This further supposition does not prevent the belief about the President's whereabouts from being non-inferential, since it is not in any useful sense Norman's reason for accepting that specific belief.

14 This is the basic objection to Dretske's version of externalism, mentioned above. Dretske's condition requires that one have an analogously unjustified (though true) belief about the reliability of one's perceptual belief.

15 The only apparent answer here would be to claim that the reasonable presumption is in favor of one's having such reliable means of access, unless there is good reason to the contrary. But it is hard to see why such a presumption should be thought reasonable.

16 Mark Pastin, in a critical study of Armstrong, has suggested that ascriptions of knowledge depend on the epistemic situation of the ascriber rather than on that of the ascribee at this point, so that I am correct in ascribing knowledge to Norman so long as *I* know that his belief is reliable (and hence also that the other conditions of knowledge are satisfied), even if Norman does not. But I can see no very convincing rationale for this claim. See Pastin, "Knowledge and Reliability: A Study of D. M. Armstrong's *Belief, Truth and Knowledge*," *Metaphilosophy* 9 (1978):150–62. Notice further that if the epistemic regress problem is in general to be dealt with along externalist lines, then my knowledge that Norman's belief is reliable would depend on the epistemic situation of a further external observer, who ascribes knowledge to me. And similarly for the knowledge of that observer, etc., *ad infinitum*. I do not know whether this regress of external observers is vicious, but it seems clearly to deprive the appeal to such an observer of any value as a practical criterion.

17 Of course there are cases in which one must act, even though one has no adequate knowledge of the likely consequences; and one might attempt to defend epistemic externalism by arguing that in epistemic contexts the analogous situation *always* obtains. But there are several problems with such a response. First, to

3434

simply assume that this is always so seems to be question-begging, and the externalist can argue for this claim only by refuting all alternatives to his position. Second, notice that in ethical contexts this situation usually, perhaps always, obtains only when not acting will lead definitely to bad consequences, not just to the failure to obtain good ones; and there seems to be no parallel to this in the epistemic case. Third, and most important, the justification for one's action in such a case would depend not on the external fact, if it is a fact, that the action leads to good consequences, but simply on the fact that one could do no better, given the unfortunate state of one's knowledge; thus this position would not be genuinely a version of moral externalism, and analogously for the epistemic case.

18 I am assuming here, following Chisholm, that knowledge requires a degree of justification stronger than that required to make a belief merely reasonable.

19 I do not, alas, have any real account to offer here of the notion of *relevant similarity*. Roughly, the idea is that two possibilities are relevantly similar if there is no known difference between them that has a bearing on the likelihood that they will be realized. But this will not quite do. For consider a lottery case in which there are two tickets bearing each even number and only one for each odd number. Intuitively, it seems to me, this difference does not prevent all the tickets, odd and even, from being relevantly similar, despite the fact that it is twice as likely that an even ticket will be drawn.

20 But if this account is correct, I may still fail to know in many other cases in which common sense would say fairly strongly that I do. E.g., do I know that my house has not burned down since I left it this morning? Ordinarily we are inclined to say that we do know such things. But if it is true, as it might well be, that I also know that of the class of houses relevantly similar to mine, at least one will burn down at some point, then I do not, on the present account, *know* that my house has not burned down, however improbable such a catastrophe may be. (On the other hand, knowledge would not be ruled out by the present principle simply because I knew that certain specific similar houses, *other than mine*, have in the past burned down or even that they will in the future burn down. For I know, *ex hypothesi*, that my house is not one of those. The force of the principle depends on my knowing that at least one possibility *which might for all I know be the one I am interested in* will be realized, not just on descriptively similar possibilities being realized.)

21 This response to the lottery paradox derives in part from discussions with C. Anthony Anderson.

22 The clearest example of such a position is the Goldman's paper "Discrimination and Perceptual Knowledge," cited above, where he rejects what he calls "Cartesian-style justification" as a requirement for perceptual knowledge, in favor of an externalist account. He goes on to remark, however, that one could use the term "justification" in such a way that satisfaction of his externalist conditions "counts as justification," though a kind of justification "entirely different from the sort of justification demanded by Cartesianism" (p. 790). What is

unclear is whether this is supposed to be a purely verbal possibility, which would then be of little interest, or whether it is supposed to connect with something like the concept of epistemic rationality explicated in section I. Thus it is uncertain whether Goldman means to repudiate the whole idea of epistemic rationality, or only some more limited view such as the doctrine of the given (reference to which provides his only explanation of what he means by "Cartesianism" in epistemology).

2

THE INTERNALIST CONCEPTION OF JUSTIFICATION

Alvin Goldman

One possible aim of epistemology is to advise cognizers on the proper choice of beliefs or other doxastic attitudes. This aim has often been part of scientific methodology: to tell scientists when they should accept a given hypothesis, or give it a certain degree of credence. This *regulative* function is naturally linked to the notion of epistemic justification. It may well be suggested that a cognizer is justified in believing something just in case the rules of proper epistemic procedure prescribe that belief. Principles that make such doxastic prescriptions might thereby "double" as principles of justification.

In the first part of this paper I contrast the regulative conception of justification with another, equally tenable, conception. Then, after noting a fundamental worry about the applicability of the regulative conception, I proceed to lay it out in more detail. The regulative justificational status of a doxastic attitude for person S at time t depends upon (a) the right set of doxastic instructions and (b) the states S is in at (or just before) t.

The regulative conception per se is neutral about the right doxastic instructions. But the question naturally arises: What *makes* this or that set of instructions the *right* instructions? The rest of the paper is devoted to this question. Two approaches are identified: *externalism* and *internalism*. Internalism takes its inspiration from a perspective that has dominated epistemology since the time of Descartes. I try to show that this perspective yields no definite or adequate answer to the question posed here; it provides no adequate conception of the rightness of doxastic instructions. This leaves externalism as the only available option, and I defend its plausibility.

Parts of this paper are positive and constructive. But the bulk of the paper is negative. It tries to undermine a classical epistemological perspective by showing that it cannot answer the question: What are the right doxastic instructions? I do not myself try to answer this question. But I do end the paper on a positive note, with a sketch of a framework within which that question may be answered.

I

In "Doing The Best One Can,"[1] Holly S. Goldman distinguishes two possible functions of a moral principle. First, it can serve as an instrument for making theoretical evaluations of actions. Second, it can serve as a device that an agent can employ to guide his/her activitives. A moral principle may not be equally useful for these two purposes. For example, the standard act-utilitarian principle – an act is right if and only if it would produce at least as much net happiness as any available alternative – is perfectly suitable (which is not to say correct) as an instrument for theoretical evaluation. It specifies conditions that determine the rightness or wrongness of an action. But this principle is not entirely suitable as an action-guiding principle. At the time of action an agent may not know which act would produce the most happiness; he may not even *believe* of any particular act that it would produce the most happiness. Thus it is unclear how to use the act-utilitarian principle to guide his conduct. In an unpublished paper,[2] Goldman suggests that we need distinct principles for decision-making purposes. One possible decision-making principle that might be associated with act-utilitarianism is to choose the act with the highest subjective probability of producing the most happiness. A different decision principle that might be paired with act-utilitarianism is to choose the act that, given your subjective probabilities, has the greatest "expected" happiness. (These two principles are not equivalent. An act with a slightly higher subjective probability than any other of producing the most happiness but a non-negligible chance of producing disaster would be enjoined by the first of these principles but not necessarily by the second.) Whichever decision principle should be associated with act-utilitarianism, the general point is that there are distinct *types* of principles: one for "theoretical evaluation" and one for practical guidance of action.

The concept of epistemic justification calls for an analogous distinction between kinds of theories or principles. On the one hand, a principle of justification might specify the features of beliefs (or other doxastic attitudes) that confer epistemic status. These features may or may not be usable by a cognizer to make a doxastic choice. On the other hand, a principle of justification might be designed specifically to guide a cognizer in regulating or choosing his doxastic attitudes. Here the criteria of justification must be ones to which a cognizer can appeal in the process of making a doxastic decision. That the theoretical and regulative functions of justification principles can be distinct emerges clearly from an account of justified belief I have proposed in another paper.[3] Refinements aside, this account – which I call "Historical Reliabilism" – says that a belief is justified just in case its causal ancestry consists of reliable belief-forming processes, i.e., processes that generally lead to truth. As a theoretical specification of epistemic status, such an account is entirely suitable. But this theory or principle cannot be used by a cognizer to make a doxastic decision; nor is it so intended. First, at the time of belief a cognizer may not know, or be in a position to find out about, the causal ancestry of his belief; and a cognizer may not know, or be able to tell, whether the processes that composed this ancestry are generally reliable. Thus there is no guarantee that a cognizer can apply the Historical Reliabilist theory to his own case. Second, Historical Reliabilism simply is not a *rule* or *prescription* for choosing beliefs or other doxastic attitudes. It considers an *already formed* belief of a cognizer and says what features are necessary and sufficient for that belief to count as justified. It does not take a cognizer who is trying to decide which doxastic attitude to adopt *vis-à-vis* a given proposition and tell him what to do (doxastically speaking).

Epistemologists have been interested in theories of justification for at least two reasons. First, many have thought that a necessary condition of *knowing* a proposition is having a justified belief in that proposition. So a full analysis of knowledge requires an indication of the conditions in which belief is justified. Second, many epistemologists have been interested in "doxastic decision principles," i.e., rules for the formation of belief or other doxastic attitudes, e.g., subjective probabilities. Descartes's clearness-and-distinctness test was intended as a criterion to be used in deciding what to believe. And contemporary Bayesianism instructs cognizers to have credence functions, i.e., sets of subjective probabilities, that satisfy the axioms of the probability calculus. Many epistemologists, I believe, have conflated these two interests. They have assumed that a regulative notion of justification is the same notion of justification as the one that appears in the analysis of propositional knowledge. I think this assumption is mistaken. The best candidate for inclusion in the analysis of knowing is the Historical Reliabilist conception of justifiedness, and that notion is not a regulative one. For the purposes of the present paper, however, this issue is incidental. Here I wish to explore the idea of justification in its regulative role, whether or not it has any bearing on the concept of propositional knowledge.

I have introduced the regulative conception of epistemology by means of an analogy with ethics. It is questionable, however, whether the analogy is perfect. Ethics is largely concerned with individual actions, and actions are certainly subject to voluntary control and hence proper objects of self-guidance or regulation. But it is problematic whether doxastic states or attitudes are subject to (direct) voluntary control, and therefore problematic whether there is any point in formulating doxastic decision principles. I suspect that formation, retention, and revision of doxastic states are *not* subject to voluntary control, except perhaps in a restricted domain. Doxastic voluntarism is a dubious doctrine, however cherished it may have been by Descartes and other epistemologists. For the sake of discussion, though, let us proceed on the assumption (at least for a while) that doxastic voluntarism is true, that a cognizer can decide or choose whether to believe a given proposition at a given moment. We can then construe a principle of justification as one that instructs cognizers to adopt or retain certain beliefs (or other doxastic attitudes) in various circumstances. A principle of justification would be analogous to a moral principle that is designed to serve a regulative, or decision-making, function.

Let us be more precise about the relationship between the *justifiedness* of a belief and *doxastic decision principles* (for short, "DDPs"). We may represent a DDP as a function whose *inputs* are certain conditions of a cognizer – e.g., his beliefs, perceptual field, and ostensible memories – and whose *outputs* are prescriptions to adopt (or retain) this or that doxastic attitude – e.g., believing p, suspending judgment with respect to p, or having a particular subjective probability *vis-à-vis* p. Unless otherwise indicated, I shall here mean by "DDP" a *total* DDP, i.e., a single complete set of principles prescribing all doxastic attitudes a cognizer should have at a single time. Such a total DDP would presumably make use of a variety of different inputs, including those that pertain to perception, memory, induction, and the like.

The justificational status of believing a given proposition, say p, for cognizer S at time t presumably depends in part on the conditions S is in at, or just before, t, e.g., what evidence S possesses. But whether S is justified in believing p at t – whether S "ought," epistemically speaking, to believe p at t – also depends on the correct DDP. Assume that a unique DDP is correct, or right. Then S is justified in believing p at t if and only if the right DDP, when applied to the relevant conditions that characterize S at t, yields as output the prescription "believe p." More generally *S is justified in having doxastic attitude D vis-à-vis p at t if and only if the right DDP, when applied to the relevant input conditions that characterize S at t, yields as output the prescription* ⌜*adopt attitude D vis-à-vis p.*⌝ This general relationship constitutes the basic framework of the regulative view of justification which will be presupposed in the rest of our discussion.[1]

Given this approach to justificational status, several questions obviously become paramount. First, what are admissible sorts of input conditions for a DDP? Which states of a cognizer are relevant to the justificational status of a doxastic attitude? Second, are we right in assuming that there is a uniquely correct DDP? Third, if this assumption is correct, what *makes* a certain DDP right, or correct?

II

Let us begin with the question concerning admissible inputs. In illustrating input conditions, I mentioned various cognitive states of a person, e.g., his beliefs and ostensible memories. It is worth asking, however, why the relevant input conditions should be cognitive states, or, for that matter, why they should be *states* of the person at all. Why could input conditions not be states of the world, or the external environment? On purely formal grounds, the following seems to qualify as a DDP: "For any proposition p, if p is true, then believe p (at any time *t*)." The input conditions for this DDP are not states of the cognizer; rather, they are the truth-values of the various propositions, or the "states of the world" that make these propositions true or false. But why not allow a DDP with input conditions of this kind? Admittedly, this is an intuitively inappropriate DDP. But what exactly makes it inappropriate?

The answer is straightforward. If a DDP is to be actually *usable* for making deliberate decisions, the conditions that serve as inputs must be *accessible* or *available* to the decision-maker at the time of decision. The agent must be *able to tell*, with respect to any possible input condition, whether that condition holds at the time in question. Now if the truth-value of any random proposition is a possible input condition, a cognizer would have to be able to tell, with respect to any such proposition, whether or not it is true. This requirement is not satisfied. Hence, the general class of truths and falsehoods cannot serve as the appropriate domain (i.e., input conditions) for a DDP.

We now see why a person's current cognitive states are a plausible class of input conditions. It is plausible to hold that for such states a person *can tell*, at any moment, exactly which of them he is in at that moment. So these input conditions would satisfy the requirement of being "accessible" or "available" to the decision-maker. But what exactly do we mean in saying that a person "*can tell*" with respect to a given condition whether or not that condition obtains? Here is a reasonable answer: "For any person S and time t, if S asks himself at t whether condition C obtains at the time in question, then S will believe that condition C obtains then if and only if it does obtain then."[5]

Notice that *past* cognitive states do not satisfy this constraint. It is not true, in general, that if I ask myself at time t whether or not I was in a certain cognitive state G at an earlier time t_0, then I will believe that I was in G at t_0 if and only if I was. I may forget or misremember my past cognitive states. For this reason, cognitive *ancestry* is not among the conditions that can serve as a DDP input. Thus a "historical" theory is excluded as a *regulative* theory of justification.

It is worth exploring some other consequences of our constraint on input conditions. Epistemologists commonly include logical relationships in their epistemic rules. For example, a rule might say: "If you are justified in believing Q, and Q *logically implies* P, then believe P." One input for this rule is the obtaining of a logical implication. But according to our constraint this is not an admissible input. It is not in general true that a person *can tell*, for any propositions Q and P, whether or not Q logically implies P. It appears, then, that many favorite examples of epistemic rules may not be legitimate (portions of) DDPs.

The rule in the previous paragraph poses another question about admissible input conditions. Is the justificational status of a doxastic attitude a legitimate input condition? Is *being-justified-in-believing Q*, as opposed to merely *believing Q*, an admissible input? If we admit (regulative) justificational status as an input condition, we have a threat of circularity in our theory. The aim of specifying a class of inputs and a correct DDP is to provide a theory of justification. If (the notion of) justificational status itself appears in the input conditions, our account would seem to be circular.

The charge of circularity should not be leveled too hastily. If a recursive account of justification were given, it would be unobjectionable to have a *recursive clause* by which the justificational status of believing Q could help determine the justificational status of believing P.[6] However, such a recursive account would also need *base clauses*, and to avoid circularity these base clauses would have to specify non-justificational conditions – substantive or "factual" conditions – for justificational status. So the justificational status of believing P would ultimately be traceable to these substantive conditions, which may be viewed as the relevant inputs. Thus it is appropriate to add the following restriction to our constraint on inputs: inputs must be purely factual, non-epistemic conditions.

This is all I shall say about admissible inputs for a DDP. Let us now turn to the question of what makes something the right DDP, and whether, indeed, a uniquely correct DDP can be demanded.

III

The choice of a DDP clearly depends on the *goals* of cognition, or doxastic-attitude-formation. A very plausible set of goals are the oft-cited aims of *believing the truth* – as much truth as possible – and *avoiding error*. (Some alternative goals will be examined later.) These twin desiderata, however, tend to compete with one another. A "conservative" DDP prescribes more suspension of judgment than does a "venturesome" DDP. Greater conservatism would tend to produce less false belief, which is good, but also less true belief, which is bad. Which of two such DDPs is preferable, on the whole, is a function of how the totality of true belief is weighted as compared with the amount of error. One view would be that a single false belief outweighs a tremendous amount of truth. Another view would be that there is as much positive value in a single (modest) truth as there is negative value in a single (modest) error. For my purposes, this knotty issue can be sidestepped. The issues I wish to raise in this paper are independent of the weighting problem. So let us proceed on the assumption that *some* combination of true belief and error avoidance is what we seek in a DDP.[7]

Given the aim of true belief and error avoidance, the right DDP is apparently one that would produce optimal results in terms of true belief and error avoidance. It is the DDP that would have such optimal results in the long run for the sum-total of cognizers. Or, assuming that what is best for one (human) cognizer is best for others, the right DDP is the one that would produce optimal results for any cognizer taken singly. It is the DDP that God in his omniscience would recommend.

Unfortunately, the foregoing characterization of the right DDP ignores a crucial aspect of traditional epistemology. The foregoing conception rests on an *"externalist"* perspective: the perspective of a Godlike observer who, knowing all truths and falsehoods, can select the DDP that optimally conduces to true belief and error avoidance. Traditional epistemology has not adopted this externalist perspective. It has been predominantly *internalist*, or egocentric. On the latter perspective, epistemology's job is to construct a doxastic principle or procedure *from the inside*, from our own individual vantage point. To adopt a Kantian idiom, a DDP must not be "heteronomous," or dictated "from without." It must be "autonomous," a law we can give to ourselves and which we have *grounds* for giving to ourselves. The *objective* optimality of a DDP, on this view, does not make it right. A DDP counts as right only if it is "certifiable" *from within.*

To illustrate the point, suppose a DDP were proposed that consisted in a very, very long list of propositions to be believed: propositions about individual events and states of affairs, laws of nature, and so on. Belief in these propositions is prescribed *unconditionally*, independent of the cognitive states of the agent. In short, the input conditions for this DDP are the null set. Further suppose that all the prescribed propositions in this long list are *true.* Does that make this DDP a strong candidate for the right DDP? Not at all, according to internalism. This is a DDP that a Godlike observer might give us, not the sort we can legitimately give to ourselves. More cautiously, if we *are* in a position to give that DDP to ourselves, it must be because we have used some other, more fundamental, DDP to ascertain the relevant set of truths. It is that more fundamental DDP which ought to be proposed as the genuinely correct DDP.

The foregoing example, it must be conceded, has oddities that are irrelevant to the point at issue. The DDP in question is counterintuitive because it contains no *general* instructions, no precepts for generating new beliefs from old, no provisions for learning from experience. All these features would naturally be expected in a good DDP. For this reason, let us illustrate the internalist idea with another, more familiar, example: the problem of induction.

Assume for the sake of argument that there is a unique inductive rule that would actually be optimal for predictive puposes. (Specification of an inductive rule will probably require, to meet Goodmanian concerns, either an enumeration of projectible predicates or a set of rules of projection. Assume these are built into the rule in question.) The mere fact of optimality, however, would not be regarded by internalism as a solution to the problem of induction. According to internalism, an inductive rule is right only if we can *justify* the claim that it is optimal, i.e., only if we can *show* that it will lead to truth, or will probably lead to truth, or that it (alone) meets some weaker (e.g., Reichenbachian) test of optimality. *De facto* optimality does not satisfy the internalist. A rule that just *happens* to be optimal is not right unless we *know*, or are *justified* in believing, that it is optimal.

Thus far I have given a rather vague characterization of the internalist conception of justifiedness. In the remainder of the paper I want to explore this conception critically. I shall argue that the internalist conception is either fundamentally confused or unfulfillable. Either (A) there is no definite and acceptable set of conditions that articulate the vague idea of the internalist, or (B) although such a definite set of conditions can be specified, there is nothing – no DDP, or rule of justification – that meets these conditions. In short, what appears to be a comprehensible and attractive conception of justification melts away when examined carefully. Finally, I shall argue that externalism provides a perfectly satisfactory conception of justifiedness.

IV

The crucial question for internalism is: What is the right DDP? We shall not try to pinpoint the particular DDP that is right according to internalism (nor the one that is right according to externalism). Rather, we shall try to see whether there is a definite and acceptable set of conditions that determine what internalism would *count* as the right DDP. We can indicate the sort of condition being sought by formulating the condition appropriate to *externalism*, viz. (1):

(1)   DDP X is right if and only if: X is actually optimal.

By 'optimal' I mean, of course, optimal in producing true belief and error avoidance. As indicated earlier, the exact weighting of true belief and error avoidance is here neglected.

For reasons given above, (1) does not satisfy the internalist. What, then, *would* do so? Judging by our earlier characterization of internalism, the condition that seems to capture the internalist's conception is this:

(2)   DDP X is right if and only if: we are justified in believing that X is optimal.

There is a fatal problem with (2), however. It uses the notion of justification! As indicated previously, the aim of a theory of justification is to assign justificational status in *non-justificational* terms. In particular, the aim of a regulative theory of justification is to provide instructions concerning doxastic attitudes that do not presuppose the prior existence, or establishment, of any such prescriptions. If the (regulative) notion of justifiedness is allowed in the condition(s) for the rightness of a DDP, this requirement will clearly be violated. For the rightness of a DDP is one of the two basic components of the theory of justifiedness. In short, proposal (2) is blatantly circular, and inadmissible on purely "formal" grounds.

It will do no better to say, in place of (2), that a DDP must be "certifiable" as optimal, or that we must have "grounds" for believing it to be optimal. Terms like 'certifiable' and 'grounds' are themselves epistemic terms, roughly synonymous with 'justified'. All such terms are equally inadmissible for the purposes at hand. Unfortunately, the initial sketch of the internalist conception utilized these very terms. This suggests that (2) correctly expresses the intuitive idea behind internalism, unacceptable as that idea turns out to be. But there may be other, unobjectionable ways of fleshing out internalism. Let us explore some further possibilities.

In place of (2) we might try (3):

(3) DDP X is right if and only if: we *believe* that X is optimal.

Clearly, (3) avoids the formal problem facing (2). But is it at all plausible? I think not. Suppose we believe some particular DDP X to be optimal for (intuitively speaking) very bad reasons, or for no reasons at all. We may believe it to be optimal out of wishful thinking, sheer confusion, or mere hunch and guesswork. We may believe it to be optimal simply because it pops into our heads, or comes to us in a dream. Is internalism committed to saying, in such circumstances, that X is really right? That doxastic attitudes *ought* (epistemically speaking) to be formed in accordance with X? Surely not. Internalism presumably does not want the rightness of a DDP to be determined by sheer eccentricity, frivolous reasons, or happenstance.

These considerations are just the sorts of considerations that motivate proposal (2). But we cannot go back to (2). Is there anything similar to (2) that does not violate the formal restriction on which (2) itself founders? It may seem promising to recall that a non-regulative theory of justified belief is available: Historical Reliabilism. It may be suggested that no circularity would be involved if we used the non-regulative notion of justifiedness in our theory of the regulative notion. More important, since Historical Reliabilism is a theory formulated in non-epistemic terms, why not use the substance of this theory without employing the term 'justification' (or any of its cognates)? This would yield the following:

(4) DDP X is right if and only if: (A) we believe that X is optimal, and

(B) this belief was caused by reliable cognitive processes.

Unfortunately, (4) founders on another restriction, a restriction peculiar to internalism. The basic idea of internalism is that there should be guaranteed epistemic access to the correctness of a DDP.[8] No condition of DDP-rightness is acceptable unless we have epistemic access to the DDP that in fact satisfies the condition, i.e., unless we can tell which DDP satisfies it. The internalist's objection to externalism's condition of rightness, i.e., actual optimality, is precisely that cognizers may have no way of telling which DDP satisfies it. Internalism's *own* condition of rightness must, therefore, be such that any cognizer *can tell* which DDP satisfies it. But this restriction is not met by (4). In general, we are not in a position to tell how some belief of ours was caused; nor is it guaranteed that we can tell which of our cognitive processes are reliable and which are not.

In addition to the foregoing objections (which are conclusive enough), there are other problems with (2), (3), and (4). A problem common to all three is the use of the term 'we'. To whom does this pronoun purport to refer? To *everyone*? This implies, in the case of (3) and (4), that a DDP is right (according to internalism) only if *everyone* believes it to be optimal. But surely such universal consensus is hard to come by and unreasonable to require.

How is this difficulty to be met in any future proposal? Should 'we' be taken to refer to a *majority* of people? To a *plurality* in favor of a single DDP as compared with any other DDP? Neither of these suggestions is attractive. A more promising solution is to *relativize* DDP-rightness to a cognizer (and a time). This would yield the following analogues of (3) and (4):

(3*) DDP X is right for S at *t* if and only if: S believes at *t* that X is optimal.

(4*) DDP X is right for S at *t* if and only if: (A) S believes at *t* that X is optimal, and
(B) this belief was caused by reliable cognitive processes.

The relativization solution is a serious step that should not be taken lightly. But let us defer an examination of that issue for a moment.[9] There is still another problem that would face (3*) and (4*) as they stand, a problem related to the one that relativization was intended to solve. Relativization was intended to meet the objection that the same DDP may not be believed *by everyone* to be optimal. But we must also note that some people may not believe of *any* DDP that it is optimal. Indeed, since the notion of a DDP is an abstruse notion, unlikely to be familiar to anyone but a philosopher, it is highly probable that *most* people will not believe of any DDP that it is optimal. It will follow from (3*) and (4*) that no DDP at all will be right for the vast majority of people. This would seem to imply that no doxastic instructions govern these individuals, so that there are no doxastic attitudes that they are justified (or unjustified) in choosing. Certainly this cannot be intended by internalism. Thus what internalism needs is a condition of rightness that does not require *actual belief* by a cognizer in the optimality of some DDP.

To meet this requirement the internalist might say that DDP X is right for person S at time *t* just in case S *would* believe X to be optimal, given S's antecedent mental states. But would . . . *if what*? If S formed this belief in accordance with the right DDP? Obviously the internalist cannot say that, for it would be a flagrant circularity. What might be said, however, is that S would believe X to be optimal if S used X itself. In other words, X is right for S at *t* just in case X is *"self-prescribing"* for S at *t*. This may be written as (5):

(5)   DDP X is right for S at *t* if and only if: if X is applied to S's (relevant) inputs at *t*, X prescribes belief in ⌜X is optimal⌝.

One problem with (5) is that it may fail to meet the internalist's restriction that a cognizer should be able to tell which DDP meets the condition. If a DDP is very complex, it may be difficult to tell what it prescribes, in particular, whether or not it prescribes belief in its own optimality. A second problem is even more critical. Two or more incompatible DDPs can each satisfy (5) for the same person and time. Let Y be a DDP that, among other things, prescribes use of the "scientific method" (assuming there is a unique such method). Let Z be a DDP that, among other things, prescribes belief in accordance with ostensible revelations (rather than the scientific method). Then it may well happen that, given S's inputs at *t*, Y prescribes belief in ⌜Y is optimal⌝ and Z prescribes belief in ⌜Z is optimal⌝. According to (5), *both* Y and Z are right for S at *t*. But since they are incompatible, they will generate some incompatible doxastic prescriptions. Which of these competing prescriptions should be followed? Which should be used to assess the justificational status of S's doxastic attitudes? (5) cannot answer these questions and is therefore unacceptable.

V

Let us return now to the issue of relativization. It follows, of course, from the strategy of relativization that a DDP which is right for one cognizer may not be right for another. Is such "*epistemological relativism*" acceptable to internalism? It is clear, I think, that internalists have not generally intended any such relativism. They have usually assumed that some uniform set of doxastic principles should govern all human cognizers. Foundationalists think that foundationalism (insofar as it generates doxastic prescriptions) is right for everyone. Coherentists think that coherentism is right for everyone. Bayesians think that Bayesianism is right for everyone. So we will need some special and strong argumentation to sustain the idea that internalism should incorporate relativism.

One possible line of argumentation would attempt to draw an analogy with the distinction in ethics between *objective* and *subjective* rightness.[10] An act is said to be objectively right just in case it actually satisfies the conditions for moral rightness. An act is said to be subjectively right just in case, roughly speaking, the agent's beliefs or evidence concerning the circumstances or consequences of the act suggest that it is objectively right. Subjective rightness involves relativization to the beliefs or evidence of the agent at the time of action. Now it might be suggested that the moral status of objective rightness is analogous to the *ex*ternalist conception of DDP rightness and that the *in*ternalist conception of DDP rightness is analogous to the moral status of subjective rightness. Since the moral notion involves relativization, it is proper for the epistemic notion to involve relativization as well.

Apart from the issue of relativization, the idea of subjective rightness in ethics may hold promise of assistance in our present predicament. After all, the notion of subjective rightness in ethics is usually thought to be tolerably clear. Why not borrow its analysis for the purpose of stating conditions of DDP rightness?

Regrettably, matters are not so simple. There seem to be two basic strategies for analyzing subjective rightness in ethics: (A) Action A is subjectively right if and only if the agent *believes* of A that it is objectively right; or (B) Action A is subjectively right if and only if the agent is *justified* in believing of A that it is objectively right. We may call these the "*doxastic*" and "*epistemic*" approaches, respectively. Neither of these approaches works well when applied to our present topic. When transferred to our topic, the doxastic approach yields (3) or (3*), which proved quite unsatisfactory. (Some of the same criticisms might apply to the *moral* notion as well.) Furthermore, the epistemic approach would yield our proposal (2) (or a relativized version of (2)), which is wholly inadmissible. The moral theorist is entitled to use an epistemic notion to explicate *his* concept of subjective rightness, but *we* are not entitled to use an epistemic notion, for our *explicandum* is itself epistemic.

The ethicist's notion of subjective rightness, then, proves to have less utility for our purposes than we might hope. Still, it may help support the idea of relativization. What we need, however, is not just the analogy from ethics but a particular example that motivates this idea in the epistemic sphere. Here is an example designed to serve this purpose.

Consider two men who belong to different cultures in different historical periods. The first belongs to a prescientific or early scientific community, in which precise methods of experimentation and statistical techniques have never been dreamed of. The second belongs to a scientifically advanced culture and has personally been trained in methodological and statistical techniques. Imagine that each of these men happens to entertain the same scientific hypothesis, H, and that each has the same observational evidence that bears on H. According to the DDP believed by the first man to be optimal, H should be believed. According to the DDP believed by the second man to be optimal, H should not be believed. Now suppose each man adopts the doxastic attitude *vis-à-vis* H prescribed by his favored DDP. Is each not *justified* in adopting this doxastic attitude? In particular, the member of the prescientific culture isn't justified – at least "subjectively justified" – in adopting his doxastic attitude? After all, the sophisticated techniques of advanced science are, by hypothesis not yet invented. He can hardly be faulted for proceeding as best he can, by his own lights. Is not the DDP he uses at least "right for him?"

Although this example is plausible, it is not wholly convincing. A defender of epistemological objectivism might reply as follows. "It is admittedly *excusable* or *pardonable* for the member of the prescientific community to accept his own DDP – call it W – and for him to form the doxastic attitude prescribed by W. But to say that this is *excusable* is not to say that the resultant doxastic attitude is *justified*. A doxastic attitude is justified only if it is enjoined by proper procedure, and the description of the case presupposes that DDP W is not proper procedure, i.e., is not the right DDP. To be sure, it may be difficult for this cognizer, in his historico-cultural setting, to identify the right DDP. This is why we would not *blame* him for his doxastic act. Still, there is no need to consider him *justified* in believing H. Nor is there need to say that W is in *some* sense a 'right' DDP. The only right DDP is the objectively right DDP. Even internalism should insist on an objectively right DDP, whether or not it is equivalent to the 'optimal' DDP."[11]

I am inclined to endorse this response of the objectivist and conclude that the example in question should not impel the internalist to be a relativist. On the other hand, even if the internalist wants to be a relativist, we have not yet identified conditions that express an adequate version of internalism, either of a relativistic or a non-relativistic variety. Thus we have yet to make cogent sense of the vague intuitions that motivate internalism. Thus far internalism is a mere will-o'-the wisp.

VI

At this juncture the internalist may object that I have ignored the most obvious and straightforward way of specifying his conception. At least since the time of Descartes there has been a reasonably well-defined idea of the "*internal standpoint*" in epistemology. This is the idea of a certain epistemological *starting point*, a position from which all doxastic decisions are to be made. To make doxastic decisions, however, one needs a DDP, and so it is natural to say that the DDP must also be chosen from the same "internal" starting point. This was Descartes's own practice, for his criterion of clearness-and-distinctness was proposed and argued for from this very vantage point.[12] We have, then, a natural way of formulating the internalist's condition for the rightness of a DDP:

(6) DDP X is right if and only if: X is the proper DDP to choose if one chooses a DDP from the internal standpoint.

So formulated, internalism certainly contrasts with externalism, for there is no guarantee that the DDP properly chosen from the internal standpoint would be identical with the optimal DDP.

Is (6) a clear and definite condition for DDP-rightness? That depends on how clear and definite we can make the idea of the internal standpoint and the criteria of "proper choice." I shall argue that, however clear and definite we can make this idea and these criteria, there is no unique DDP that can be generated.[13] In short, even if (6) is a condition that satisfactorily expresses the spirit of internalism, it does not select or determine a preferred DDP. In this sense the internalist conception of a right DDP is "*unfulfillable.*"

A merely apparent difficulty for choosing a DDP from the internal standpoint is the threat of a vicious regress. The choice of a DDP requires a criterion of choice, and it might be supposed that this criterion must itself be a DDP: a meta-DDP. But how is *that* DDP to be chosen? By means of a meta-meta-DDP? And so on ad infinitum? This worry rests on a confusion. A DDP is not a proposition but a *policy* or set of conditional *prescriptions*. (*That such-and-such a DDP is optimal* is a proposition; but the DDP is not a proposition.)

Since a DDP is not a proposition, the adoption of a DDP is not the adoption of a *doxastic* attitude. Since no *doxastic* attitude is being chosen, no DDP is required. To be sure, some criterion of choice is needed, which does, as we shall see, pose problems. But the criterion in question may be a familiar decision criterion, such as maximizing expected value, not a DDP. Thus no infinite regress is launched.

A somewhat analogous problem, though, is the central problem that confronts the attempt to choose a DDP from the internal standpoint. Although the choice of a unique DDP does not require a prior (meta-) DDP, it *does* require antecedent doxastic attitudes on which to base a choice. To assess the probable consequences of this or that policy of forming physical-world beliefs, for example, one needs some doxastic attitudes toward propositions that describe typical events in the physical world and relationships between the physical world and one's mental states. But such doxastic attitudes are absent in the internal standpoint.

To clarify this point, let us be more precise about the nature of the internal standpoint. As indicated, this standpoint is supposed to be an epistemological starting point. At such a point one should be epistemologically neutral or uncommitted. More specifically, *doxastic* neutrality is required. The whole point of choosing a DDP, after all, is to license selected doxastic attitudes. Until a DDP has been properly chosen, no doxastic attitudes can be licensed, at least no doxastic attitudes toward epistemologically problematic propositions. So the internal standpoint must disallow the use of, or appeal to, prior doxastic attitudes we may happen to have. As in Rawls's "original position," the internal standpoint is a perspective in which principles must be chosen from behind a "veil of ignorance."

I said that no appeal may be made to doxastic attitudes toward epistemologically "problematic" propositions. Which propositions are problematic? Virtually all contingent propositions have generally been regarded as problematic, and doxastic attitudes toward these should certainly be barred from the internal standpoint. A possible exception is first-person-current-mental-state propositions, which are often regarded as unproblematic although they are contingent. We may allow beliefs in these propositions to be used in the internal standpoint, just for the sake of argument.[11] It is unlikely that this will substantially assist the internalist's project anyway.

The foregoing characterization of the internal standpoint is obviously modeled on Descartes's procedure. Yet Descartes himself is not sufficiently thoroughgoing. He advocates the policy of *suspending judgment* on problematic propositions at the epistemological starting point. But suspension of judgment is itself a kind of doxastic attitude. What justifies Descartes in adopting *that* attitude toward the propositions in question? He operates on the assumption that when evidence is inconclusive you should suspend judgment. But this in itself is a partial DDP, and, like any DDP, should first be argued for. Before the selection of a DDP we cannot say that the proper attitude to adopt is suspension of judgment. This is not doxastic neutrality.

It must be admitted, though, that suspension of judgment may be the best approximation to doxastic neutrality, or doxastic nullity. If you have a proposition in mind at all, how else can you avoid commitment? So let us permit the use of suspension of judgment in the internal standpoint. However, suspension of judgment must not be equated with a subjective probability of (.5). *Such* a doxastic attitude certainly would be prejudicial.

Let us now see how the absence of usable doxastic attitudes in the internal standpoint makes it impossible to choose a unique DDP. The most popular criterion of choice in decision theory is *maximizing expected value*. Suppose that this criterion is used in trying to make the choice. In the present case maximizing expected value means selecting the DDP that has the greatest expected value as measured by true belief and error avoidance. For each DDP the "expected" verific consequences of adopting it would be computed and then the DDP with the greatest expected value would be chosen. The rub, however, is that the notion of "expected" value is partly a function of *subjective probabilities*. The "expected" value of adopting a given DDP is a function of one's estimate of that DDP's leading to truth and away from error. But we have already seen that no such subjective probabilities *vis-à-vis* contingent subject matter – at least physicalistic subject matter – can be appealed to in the internal standpoint. Hence the criterion of maximizing expected value cannot be used in the internal standpoint to select a unique DDP.

A concrete example may help. Suppose you are trying to decide whether to choose a DDP that incorporates the rule: "Whenever you experience a certain sequence of sensations, believe the proposition: 'There is a doorknob before me.'" To make this decision you need an assessment of the consequences of including this rule. Will adoption of it tend to produce true beliefs or errors? What proportion of each? Unless you have a (doxastic) estimate of these outcomes, you cannot assess the expected value of this rule. But any such estimate is a doxastic attitude toward a *contingent* proposition and is therefore barred from the internal standpoint. This is so even if phenomenalism is true. Even if phenomenalism is true, any given sequence of sensations is compatible not only with there being a doorknob before you but also with, for example, your hallucinating the feeling of touching a door knob. Since the sequence of sensations is compatible with both states of affairs, an estimate of the verific consequences of adopting the rule in question will depend upon an estimate of the frequency with which you will really encounter doorknobs as opposed to merely hallucinate such encounters. But no such estimates are permitted in the internal standpoint.

My argument for the impossibility of choosing a DDP from the internal standpoint has thus far rested on a particular decision criterion: maximizing expected value. But decision theory has a larger inventory of decision rules, and some of these might dictate a choice without the indicated doxastic attitudes. Consider the criterion of maximin, for example. This criterion tells a decision-maker to choose an option (here, a DDP) whose worst possible outcome is at least as good as the worst possible outcome of any other option (DDP). Trivially, the worst outcome for a DDP that enjoins any beliefs at all is the outcome where all enjoined beliefs turn out false. So the worst outcome of a DDP that never enjoins belief at all – the skeptic's, or agnostic's, DDP – is clearly the best of the worst outcomes. Thus it might appear that maximin *would* generate the choice of a unique DDP from the internal standpoint, namely, the skeptic's DDP.

But why use the maximin criterion when choosing a DDP from the internal standpoint? Why not select, say, the maximax criterion instead? Maximax tells you to choose an option (here, a DDP) whose best possible outcome is at least as good as the best possible outcome of any other option (DDP). Obviously, maximax would generate a very different choice of DDP than maximin would, if it generates any unique choice at all.[15] Maximax would mandate a DDP that prescribes belief most liberally (indeed, profligately), since the best possible outcome of such a DDP – viz., all the enjoined beliefs being true – will be unsurpassed.

Perhaps *some* situations could dictate a preference for maximin over maximax and other situations the reverse preference. But the internal standpoint permits no preference whatever. *Ex hypothesi*, the internal standpoint contains no doxastic attitudes toward (problematic) contingent propositions, so there is no basis for either optimism or pessimism in one's choices. Without a basis for selecting a unique criterion of choice, no unique DDP can be generated from the internal standpoint.

Have I been too restrictive in excluding doxastic attitudes toward virtually all contingent propositions from the internal standpoint? Could we not so specify the internal standpoint as to admit more doxastic attitudes, even beliefs? Well, we certainly *could*, as many epistemologists have done by admitting "premises" about the uniformity of nature, or the initial credibility or reliability of memory. But on what ground may we impute such doxastic attitudes to the internal standpoint? How are we to choose the particular doxastic attitudes? Presumably the selection should not be made randomly or arbitrarily. Should we choose beliefs that are widespread among human cognizers? This would be a poor rationale, since widespread beliefs may have no claim to epistemological priority. Should we impute beliefs that strike us as epistemically sound? That sort of strategy would seem to rely on *prior* epistemic standards, some prior commitment to a DDP. But the entire rationale for inventing the internal standpoint is precisely to *choose* a DDP (for the first time!). Basing such a choice on some antecedent DDP is indeed self-defeating and invites the prospect of a vicious regress.

Some readers may not be fully convinced by my attack on the feasibility of generating a unique DDP from the internal standpoint. They might feel that recent epistemologists in the foundationalist tradition have succeeded in producing doxastic principles of the sort I have in mind (if not an entire DDP), e.g., such epistemologists as Roderick Chisholm or John Pollock.[16] Are these epistemologists not good examples of internalists, and do they not succeed in displaying the favorable prospects for internalism?

Although Chisholm and Pollock may indeed be foundationalists, I do not think they are thoroughgoing internalists *in the sense of this notion that I have specified*. Whatever the merits of their work, they do not succeed in supporting our version of internalism.

Chisholm's epistemic principles may be viewed as partial DDPs. These rules assign epistemic status to propositions, and this assignment of epistemic status is roughly equivalent to prescribing, permitting, or prohibiting belief. To say in Chisholm's terminology that a proposition is "evident" for a person is to say, roughly, that he ought to believe it. The crucial question is how Chisholm's principles are supposed to be derived. For example, Chisholm endorses the principle, "If you believe that you *perceive* something to have property F, where F is a sensible characteristic, then you ought to believe the proposition that there *is* something which has property F (before you)."[17] Chisholm would presumably be unwilling to endorse either (i) "If you believe that you *telepathize* a person to be thinking thought T, then you ought to believe the proposition that someone (else) *is* thinking thought T," or (ii) "If you believe that you '*clairvoy*' that x will happen, then you ought to believe the proposition that x *will* happen." Why is the principle concerning ostensible perception, but not the principles concerning ostensible telepathy or clairvoyance, to be endorsed? Chisholm proceeds by assuming that "we have at our disposal certain instances that the rules should countenance or permit and other instances that the rules should reject or forbid."[18] In other words, we rely on our commonsensical intuitions or judgments concerning what we know, or what the proper epis-

temic standards are.[19] This suggests that Chisholm's choice of epistemic principles rests on *prior* epistemic standards, which contravenes the idea of internalism. To put the point slightly differently, Chisholm seems to be engaged
merely in codifying or systematizing antecedent doxastic practice, at least
reflective doxastic practice. But it cannot be assumed that this practice, or the
epistemic standards it expresses, derives from the internal standpoint. There
is no guarantee, or even a hint of a guarantee, that our intuitive epistemic
judgments could have been properly chosen from the internal standpoint.
Hence nothing in Chisholm's discussion alleviates the difficulties for internalism.

Essentially the same point holds for Pollock. Pollock says that the
"basic epistemological task" is to "*spell out*" the justification conditions for
statements in different areas of knowledge.[20] This apparently means that
epistemology should elucidate the set of justification conditions (roughly,
the DDP) that we antecedently or commonsensically accept. True, Pollock
maintains that the *meanings* of our ordinary physical-object statements,
statements about the past, etc., consist in criteria of justification. But even if
this is right, it just implies that we have chosen to use words in a way
that commits us to certain justification principles (a DDP). There is no assur-
ance, however, or even the glimmer of a suggestion, that such principles
have been chosen, or could have been chosen, from the internal standpoint.
So Pollock, like Chisholm, offers no comfort to internalism as *I* have
delineated it.

VII

The epistemological difficulties of the Cartesian or egocentric position are
familiar, and the previous section only reformulates these difficulties within a
certain structure or framework. (I believe, however, that this framework makes
the problems clearer than they have sometimes been made.) In particular, it
is a familiar fact that it is difficult for the internal standpoint to license belief
in *contingent* propositions. Still, the domain of logic might seem to be a different kettle of fish. After all, it is (allegedly) an *a priori* domain. Should the internal standpoint not be able to license doxastic attitudes toward propositions of
logic? Should it not be able to generate *certain* doxastic principles (partial
DDPs), viz., principles that derive from logic?

The relative tractability of these subjects is an illusion. First let us consider
how to generate doxastic principles from logic. An initially attractive principle is this: "For any propositions Q and P, if Q logically implies P, and you

believe Q, then believe P." There are two objections to this principle. First, as Gilbert Harman points out,[21] it may be best to abandon belief in Q under these circumstances rather than adopt a belief in P. Second, this principle violates our admissibility constraint on inputs (as we pointed out in section II). People cannot in general tell infallibly whether a putative logical implication really is one or not; hence this condition cannot serve as an antecedent of a doxastic principle.

The principle might be amended to read: "If you *believe* that Q logically implies P, and you believe Q, then believe P." This meets the admissibility constraint, but it does not meet Harman's objection. In fact, Harman's point is doubly troublesome here, since it is also problematic whether you should retain your belief in the putative logical implication; perhaps *that* belief should be abandoned.

A possible further amendment is this: "If you *justifiably* believe that Q logically implies P, and you *justifiably* believe Q, then believe P." This amendment might accommodate Harman's worry, but the resulting principle can serve only as a recursive principle and it focuses our attention on the need for *base clauses* concerning logical relationships (e.g., propositions of the form "Q logically implies P"). In light of our earlier restrictions (see section II), these base clauses must specify *non-epistemic* conditions in which one should believe logical truths.

Bayesians and confirmation theorists of various persuasions have often said that every tautology or logical truth should be assigned a subjective probability of 1.0. In our framework this amounts to the principle "For any proposition p, if p is a logical truth, then believe p (or be completely certain of p)." But this violates our "can tell" constraint on inputs. Ignoring that constraint for the moment, it should be clear that this principle is misguided. In terms of our regulative conception, it says that a person is automatically *justified* in believing (indeed, being certain of) any proposition that is a logical truth. Such a principle has no appeal. It conflates the modal or logical status of a proposition with its epistemic status. Bear in mind that the logical status of a proposition is a matter, like any other, in which mistakes and confusions are possible.[22] A person who is untrained or poorly trained in logic is even more likely to make mistakes, or to fail to "grasp" or "intuit" a logical relationship when one is present. Thus there is no plausibility in saying, of any person whatever, that whenever he entertains a proposition that is a logical truth, he is justified in believing it (indeed, in being completely certain of it).

Thus far the difficulties we have canvassed concerning matters of logic are as much a problem for externalism as for internalism. But our discussion highlights two peculiar difficulties for internalism. First, we have seen that propositions of logic are epistemologically problematic. Beliefs in such propositions, therefore, cannot be allowed in the internal standpoint; they cannot be used to choose a DDP. This exacerbates the difficulty of choosing a DDP from the internal standpoint, for it is hard to *figure out* what doxastic policies to adopt if one cannot employ (beliefs in) truths of logic in one's figuring. Second, our discussion reminds us of the fact that an appropriate doxastic strategy *vis-à-vis* propositions of logic partly depends on our powers of reasoning and intuition. Well-chosen doxastic instructions should reflect the scope and accuracy of our imaginal and computational faculties. The exact nature of these powers and faculties, however, is a contingent matter, so there cannot be doxastic attitudes concerning them in the internal standpoint. This adds still another reason why no choice of doxastic principles for the domain of logic can be generated from the internal standpoint.

VIII

Internalists may object that I have not been entirely fair to them. Acknowledging the force of the difficulties I have raised, they may hasten to say that these difficulties stem largely from the assumption that true-belief-cum-error-avoidance is the proper goal of cognition. If a different goal is posited, it may be easier to choose a DDP from the internal standpoint.

Is there a plausible alternative goal? One classical candidate is *coherence* among doxastic attitudes. Coherence is a notoriously ambiguous concept, though. One version interprets it as *consistency*: a set of beliefs is coherent if and only if the propositions believed are logically consistent. A set of subjective probabilities is coherent if and only if they conform to the probability calculus. It has often been pointed out, however, that mere consistency (in either form) is an implausibly modest goal. It is too easy (relatively speaking) to obtain a merely consistent set of beliefs. Furthermore, it is unclear on this view why scientists and scholars regard the accumulation of additional evidence, and performance of new tests and experiments, as worthwhile intellectual enterprises. If mere consistency is our aim, new evidence and experiments are irrelevant. We can retain consistent beliefs with as sparse an evidence-base as you please. Evidently, we gather more evidence because more evidence (we assume) will contribute to greater truth-acquisition and/or error-avoidance.

Other forms of coherence have been advanced, *explanatory* coherence being the leading example. The notion of explanatory coherence, though, is far from clear.[23] Furthermore, it is hard to see why it should be regarded as the goal of cognition unless best explanatory hypotheses are likely to be *true*. So it is truth once again that surfaces as the fundamental cognitive desideratum.

Other candidate goals may be mentioned briefly. Peirce regarded the aim of inquiry as the "fixation" of belief, by which he meant the formation of belief in such a fashion that subsequent change is avoided. But why should mere fixity of opinion be sought? Besides, it is too easy a goal to meet, at least if doxastic voluntarism is true. One kind of DDP that meets this goal is a DDP that instructs cognizers to retain beliefs they have held in the past. Unfortunately, there are many different total DDPs that would contain this instruction. There is no way to choose from these DDPs, since they all meet the specified goal. This shows that the goal is too weak.

Another candidate desideratum out of the pragmatist tradition is the goal of "relieving agnosticism." Isaac Levi's treatment renders this equivalent to the goal of maximizing belief "content."[24] But Levi couples this with the goal of error-avoidance, and this again introduces an element that internalism finds difficult to handle. It is clear, moreover, that content-maximization by itself is an implausible *exclusive* desideratum. A DDP could promote this goal by prescribing belief in every proposition, including contradictory propositions, which is radically counter-intuitive. Nor is it plausible to couple content-maximization with mere inconsistency-avoidance. There are indefinitely many consistent-but-detailed sets of possible beliefs. Which of these should be chosen? There would be no criterion of selection from these sets on the basis of this twofold goal.

I conclude that truth-acquisition and error-avoidance is the best candidate for the goal of cognition (or doxastic-attitude formation). Postulation of this goal does indeed pose problems for internalism, but that reflects ill on internalism, not on the goal.[25]

IX

We have surveyed numerous attempts to articulate the vague idea that underlies internalism. Most of these attempts proved unsatisfactory. When we finally formulated a condition that did not seem palpably inadequate, i.e., (6), we found good reason to believe that no unique DDP[26] could be generated from this condition. There seems, then, to be no way of fulfilling internalism's conception of the right DDP. Should we conclude that internalism is a mirage, a conception that beckons to us with no real prospect of satisfaction? Many epistemologists would shrink from this conclusion, since it would leave nothing but externalism to satisfy our need for a theory of justification. But I shall argue that we should be thoroughly content with externalism, that it offers everything one can reasonably expect (if not everything one has always wanted) in a theory of justification.

One objection to externalism is its failure to *guarantee* epistemic access to the optimal DDP, the DDP that externalism says is right. But this fact should not be confused with the claim that the optimal DDP is necessarily *in*accessible. Nothing in the conception of an optimal DDP precludes the possibility of successful identification of the optimal DDP. Furthermore, since two distinct total DDPs can share a large proportion of instructions, the uniquely optimal DDP may be approximated to a greater or lesser extent by numerous sub-optimal DDPs. We may get "close" to the optimal DDP, even if we do not get every detail exactly right. And if we regulate our doxastic attitudes in accordance with a slightly sub-optimal DDP, we may still "do" almost everything correctly, i.e., justifiably; for the great majority of our doxastic attitudes may conform with the right (= optimal) DDP as well as with our approximation to it.

Still, at any given time, we may not be in possession of the right DDP. Can this be reconciled with people's common practice of rendering epistemic appraisals? Certainly it can. People's appraisals of doxastic attitudes as justified or unjustified reflect only their *beliefs* about justifiedness, not the *facts* of justifiedness. When Smith judges Jones's belief to be justified (in the regulative sense), this indicates that Smith *believes* that Jones's belief accords with the right DDP. It does not mean that Jones's belief *does* accord with the right DDP, nor even that Smith is *justified* in believing that it so accords (though doubtless Smith *thinks* that he is justified).

However, many people have great confidence in their epistemic appraisals. Can this be reconciled with the externalist conception, which makes the right DDP difficult to identify? Part of the answer is that ordinary people have no inkling of the theoretical problems and difficulties and may therefore have *misplaced* confidence in their appraisals. With increased sophistication, some of this confidence may fade. The same is true of moral judgments. The mere fact that ordinary people often have great confidence in their moral judgments hardly shows that the correct moral standard (assuming there is one) is easily accessible. The common man's confidence in his moral appraisals may be misplaced.

But do not philosophers, logicians, and statisticians often have great confidence in their epistemic appraisals, which are not so readily dismissible as misplaced? Yes, but many of these appraisals are *negative*, and it is much easier to *fault* a piece of reasoning, or a conclusion, than it is to sustain one. If you can see that a certain pattern of thought will lead systematically to error, you can plausibly conclude that some other pattern of thought is better, and hence that the conclusion in question is not licensed by the optimal DDP. You can do all this without pretending to know exactly what the optimal DDP *is*.

Finally, even *positive* epistemic appraisals do not imply putative knowledge of the *total* optimal DDP. Saying that a certain doxastic attitude accords with the optimal DDP does not suggest that you can specify that DDP, any more than saying that a certain act conforms with (fails to violate) the criminal code implies that you can specify the details of that code in its entirety.

What is most perturbing about externalism, however, may be something entirely different. Suppose that the actually optimal DDP can be found only with difficulty and effort. *What are we supposed to do in the meantime?* How should we form our doxastic attitudes? How should we search for the optimal DDP? Which (meta-) DDP should we use in the search procedure?

The first point to note is that internalism faces the very same problems. Whatever the internalistically right DDP is supposed to be, we could not rely on its falling to us from heaven. We should probably have to work to get it. The same questions, then, arise: how should we form our doxastic attitudes in the meantime? and which DDP should we use in searching for the internalistically right DDP? These worries do not create a special presumption against externalism, since they are of equal significance for internalism.

Furthermore, there is an important reason why these questions and worries probably have no application, either to externalism or to internalism. This point rests on the probable falsity of doxastic voluntarism, at least the radical version of this doctrine which says that doxastic attitudes can *only* be chosen, that they cannot be formed by non-deliberative processes. On the contrary, there are native, or constitutional, doxastic processes that generate beliefs independently of our will and independently of the deliberate selection of a DDP. Perceptual processes automatically produce representations that, unless inhibited by other cognitions, serve as beliefs. Similarly, we are all ground-level inductivists. Expectation based on past experience is part of our animal heritage. Thus we do have means of forming doxastic attitudes before choosing doxastic *principles*. Native doxastic *habits* render the selection of doxastic *principles* not strictly necessary. When we do come to choose doxastic principles, this choice may be based on beliefs formed by antecedent doxastic habits. No meta-DDP is required.

Indeed, a stronger argument can be made. Not only is it *possible* for the choice of a doxastic principle to be based on doxastic habit; it is *necessary*. If every choice of a DDP rests on doxastic attitudes that result from a prior DDP choice, there would be an infinite regress of DDP choices. Such an infinite regress is impossible (at least physically impossible). So if there are any DDP choices at all, they must rest, ultimately, on doxastic habits.

This conclusion jibes with the most plausible reconstruction of how doxastic principle choices come to be made. At the start a creature forms beliefs from automatic, preprogrammed doxastic processes; these beliefs are largely about its own immediate environment. At a later stage of development, at least in a sophisticated creature, beliefs are formed about its own belief-forming processes. The creature comes to believe that certain of its belief-forming processes often lead to error and that others are more reliable. This kind of belief can arise as follows. The creature predicts a certain event, i.e., believes it will occur. The creature then observes its non-occurrence, i.e., believes it has failed to occur. If the creature remembers the earlier belief, it can conclude that the earlier belief was false, hence that the process which generated it is (somewhat) unreliable. These beliefs presuppose, of course, that the creature has a conception of truth and falsity. This need not be a philosophical *theory* of truth but merely a rudimentary conception thereof. (Such a conception would seem to go hand-in-hand with a conception of belief, since believing a proposition is believing it to be true.) Once the creature distinguishes between more and less reliable belief-forming processes, it has taken the first step toward doxastic appraisal. It can then introduce a (non-regulative) notion of *justifiedness*; beliefs are justified if and only if they are produced by (relatively) reliable belief-forming processes. The creature can also begin doxastic self-criticism, in which it proposes *regulative* principles to itself.[27] On the assumption that doxastic states are at least partly subject to deliberate decision, the creature can formulate and endorse DDPs that might avert errors or biases in its native processes.

What is noteworthy in this reconstruction is that the notion of justifiedness, especially the regulative notion, is a late arrival. It does not appear until the creature already has beliefs and a conception of truth. This reverses the scenario that internalism tends to foster. Internalism encourages the idea that the choice of a DDP should antecede all belief, that we must first select a *criterion* of truth – a principle for deciding which propositions are true – before we form any beliefs. But if my description of how things actually go is correct, this order is reversed. Beliefs come before the selection of a DDP. Upon reflection, it is hard to see how things *could* go otherwise, given the kind of creature we are.

If the foregoing discussion is right, the answers to our earlier questions are straightforward. We do have a means of forming doxastic attitudes prior to our (initial) choice of a DDP: we have our native, preprogrammed doxastic processes. Similarly, there is a straightforward answer to what we should do in trying to identify the optimal DDP. At first we should (and must) use our constitutional doxastic habits. Once these habits generate the choice of a DDP, that DDP should be used (together with the habits which it does not wholly displace) to form any new views about the optimal DDP.

Actually it is an open question whether *any* doxastic processes can be deliberately influenced. If all doxastic processes are, in Hume's terminology, "permanent and irresistible," then the entire conception of a DDP has no application whatever. A middle ground is possible, though. *Some* doxastic processes may operate independently of the will and may not be modifiable by voluntary means: *other* doxastic processes may be subject to reflective and voluntary direction. In this case – which is the most convenient one for present purposes – there would be points of application for DDPs, but there would also be automatic processes that operate prior to the appearance of reflective choice in the doxastic domain.

Notice that even if the *doxastic* domain does not admit of voluntary intervention, there is still scope for deliberate self-guidance in the intellectual sphere. There are doubtless other events or states – distinct from doxastic states themselves – that can be voluntarily controlled and have indirect influence on doxastic attitudes. The search for evidence (e.g., deployment of the sensory apparatus in purposefully selected directions) and the search for, or attention to, hypotheses on deliberately chosen topics are examples of voluntary processes that have a major impact on our beliefs. So even the falsity of *doxastic* voluntarism would not undermine the regulative orientation of epistemology.[28] However, we might have to substitute the idea of a CDP – a *cognitive* decision principle – for that of a DDP – a *doxastic* decision principle.

The perspective advanced in our recent discussion has salient points of contact with epistemological "*contextualism*," e.g., the version of this approach adopted by W. V. Quine. Quine emphasizes that there is no point of cosmic exile.[29] We have to start, epistemologically speaking, from the beliefs we have at a given time. Similarly, Karl Popper emphasizes that rational inquiry can consist only in criticism of antecedently held belief. We do and must start from an uncritically held body of opinion, or mental structure.[30] The same view is expressed by C. S. Peirce: ". . . there is but one state of mind from which you can 'set out,' namely, the very state of mind in which you actually find yourself at the time you do 'set out' – a state in which you are laden with an immense mass of cognition already formed, of which you cannot divest yourself if you would . . .".[31]

My contextualism, however, is only a view at the *meta-theoretical* level. It only answers the question: How should we go about choosing a criterion of justifiedness, i.e., a DDP? My answer to *this* question is entirely neutral with respect to the specific criterion of justifiedness that should ultimately be chosen, i.e., the optimal DDP. That DDP could turn out to be some sort of *"foundationalist"* DDP. Its belief-prescriptions might reflect the idea that there is a special class of propositions that should be believed quite independently of other beliefs and from which all other beliefs should be inferred. I do not mean to *endorse* this sort of foundationalism. I cite it only to illustrate the point that, whereas Quine, for example, is a thoroughgoing opponent of foundationalism, my own *two-leveled* theory allows more room for epistemological flexibility. On the meta-level – "How can we try to identify the right DDP?" – I take a contextualist position. But on the basic level – "Which DDP is the right DDP?" – any answer is viable (in principle).[32]

The reader may feel that this very flexibility is a weakness of my discussion. If I have not specified the right DDP, or even the general form of the right DDP (foundationalist, coherentist, etc.), what has been accomplished? Two important things, I believe, have been accomplished. First, we have elucidated the general idea of a regulative conception of justifiedness and shown how justificational status, so conceived, depends upon (a) the cognizer's current states and (b) the right DDP. Second, we have articulated the only tenable conception of DDP-rightness (externalism) and disposed of an illusory rival conception (internalism) that traditional epistemology suggests. We have thereby provided two fundamental building blocks of any fully detailed regulative epistemology, at least any regulative epistemology that seeks to guide *doxastic* choices.

Notes

Some of the ideas in this paper germinated during research that was sponsored by the John Simon Guggenheim Foundation and the Center for Advanced Study in the Behavioral Sciences. For many helpful suggestions and criticisms I am indebted to Holly Goldman, Louis Loeb, and Terence Horgan.

1 In A. I. Goldman and J. Kim, eds., *Values and Morals* (Dordrecht, 1978). See p. 194.
2 "Moral Decision Principles."
3 "What is Justified Belief?," in George S. Pappas, ed., *Justification and Knowledge* (Dordrecht, 1979).

4   One general problem with this approach is the assumption of a uniquely correct
     DDP. Suppose instead that two or more DDPs are *"tied"* for best and that some
     of these make conflicting prescriptions. In particular, suppose one DDP tells S
     to believe proposition p and another tells S to disbelieve it. Which doxastic atti-
     tude *vis-à-vis* p is S justified in adopting? The solution is to say that a cognizer is
     justified in having doxastic attitude D *vis-à-vis* p at *t* if and only if there is *at least
     one best* DDP that prescribes D *vis-à-vis* p at *t*. This is tantamount to saying that
     a cognizer is justified in adopting D *vis-à-vis* p just in case he is *permitted* to have
     D *vis-à-vis* p and that he is permitted to have D *vis-à-vis* p if at least one best DDP
     prescribes it. This is indeed quite plausible. In fact, apart from the problem of
     multiply correct DDPs, there is much to be said for linking justifiedness with a
     permission to adopt the indicated doxastic attitude rather than a *prescription* to do
     so. Even a single DDP may contain permissions as well as prescriptions and
     prohibitions, and it is plausible to say that a doxastic attitude is justified if it is
     permitted.
         For purposes of simplicity, however, I am going to bypass these issues. First, I
     shall link justifiedness to what is prescribed rather than to what is permitted.
     Second, I shall generally assume that there is a uniquely right DDP. More pre-
     cisely, I shall ignore the problem of "ties." In later discussion when I *do* admit
     the possibility of there not being a uniquely correct DDP, I shall have in mind
     not the possibility of ties but the possibility of correctness being relativized to
     different cognizers.

5   Is this explication of "can tell" too strong? Admittedly, it may be controversial
     whether even current mental states meet the requirement as formulated. In all
     likelihood, such states as *stored* beliefs, especially the *totality* of one's stored beliefs,
     do not satisfy this constraint. But we can live with such consequences. The reg-
     ulative conception need not try to decide precisely which states (if any) satisfy its
     constraint on inputs. This would only have to be decided by anyone seeking to
     use, or *apply*, the regulative conception. For simplicity I am just assuming that a
     variety of current cognitive states do satisfy the constraint.
         Still, we can entertain the prospect of weakening the explication in the text.
     But something like it seems needed. A principle cannot be a genuine decision-
     principle unless a person can actually be guided by it, i.e., act in conformity with
     it. He must be able to bring it about that he executes an output-prescription when
     and only when the corresponding input-condition is fulfilled. To do this, it seems,
     he must have the power to tell, or detect, when each input condition (antecedent
     of a principle) is or is not fulfilled.

6   More precisely, we are not interested in a recursive "account" of justification but
     in a recursive DDP, i.e., a recursive set of doxastic principles. The consequent of
     a doxastic principle will not be something of the form "you are justified in believ-
     ing Q," but rather something like "believe Q." Hence, perhaps a better schema
     for an inductive (or recursive) member of a recursive set of principles would be
     this: "If, given your present inputs, this DDP instructs you to believe Q, and Q
     bears such-and-such a relation to P, then believe P."

7   The indicated goal may bias the choice of a DDP in favor of "belief"-principles as opposed to "subjective-probability"-principles. To avoid this bias we could elaborate the goal by giving positive value to assignments of subjective probabilities greater than .5 to truths and negative value to assignments of subjective probabilities greater than .5 to falsehoods. In the remainder of our discussion, however, I shall ignore this complication.

8   It is part of the regulative conception in general – hence common to both externalism and internalism – that a cognizer must be able to tell which *input* conditions obtain. But here we are discussing *DDP-rightness*, not input conditions. The regulative conception *per se* imposes no requirement of epistemic access to the right DDP. It merely says that a doxastic attitude is justified if it is prescribed by the DDP that is *in fact* right, whether or not the cognizer knows it is right. Internalism goes further by seeking to make it a condition of a DDP *being right* that a cognizer can know or tell that it is right (or optimal).

9   If relativization is permitted, we need a slight amendment in the basic relationship between justifiedness and DDP-rightness. That relationship would then be formulated as follows: S is justified in having doxastic attitude D *vis-à-vis* p at *t* if and only if the right DDP (*or the DDP that is right for S at t*), when applied to the relevant input conditions that characterize S at *t*, yields as output the prescription ⌜adopt attitude D *vis-à-vis* p⌝.

10   For a distinction between objective and subjective justification in epistemology, see John L. Pollock, "A Plethora of Epistemological Theories," in Pappas, ed., *Justification and Knowledge*. It is arguable that Keith Lehrer's view in *Knowledge* (London, 1974) is a form of subjectivism or relativism. On the other hand, it might be construed as a kind of non-relativistic coherentism.

11   A more difficult case is proposed by Holly Goldman. Suppose that a cognizer uses the right DDP – call it R – to decide which DDP is right, and R prescribes belief in the *false* proposition that DDP W is right. Then this cognizer is *justified* in believing that W is right. (Suppose also that W prescribes belief in its being right.) Now suppose he considers whether to believe proposition p, and W prescribes belief in p. On the other hand, R prohibits belief in p. Is the cognizer justified in believing p? According to the basic structure of the regulative approach (see section I), he is not so justified, since the right DDP does not prescribe belief in p. On the other hand, there is a strong temptation to say that he *is* justified in believing p. After all, he is justified in believing that he is justified in believing p, and it is an attractive principle that if one is justified in believing that one is justified in believing p (JJp), then one is justified in believing p (Jp). However, we are not forced to accept this principle, and an epistemological objectivist is well advised not to accept it.

12   However, it is not clear that all traditional epistemologists have tried to *select* a DDP from the internal standpoint. Many have simply presupposed some (inadequately specified) DDP and explored the question whether this DDP, when applied to the internal standpoint, prescribes our commonsensical beliefs, e.g., belief in the external world. Thus, what I am here calling "internalism" may not

correctly describe most historical epistemology. Nonetheless, if epistemology accepts the doxastic regulative enterprise, the selection of a DDP is absolutely central, and criteria for the rightness of a DDP are equally crucial. Once this problem is posed, it seems consonant with the epistemological tradition to suggest that DDP-rightness be judged from the internal standpoint.

13 Indeed, there is not even a *small group* of DDPs that can be picked out as best.

14 It might be thought that the regulative conception itself automatically confers special status on first-person-current-mental-state propositions, for the regulative conception (RC) presupposes that cognizers can infallibly form beliefs about their own current mental states. We should avoid misunderstanding, however. The RC just lays down a *constraint* on input conditions (the antecedents of DDPs), i.e., that they must meet the "can tell" requirement. The RC does not say which *specific* conditions meet this requirement, if any. *I* claimed that, plausibly, a person's cognitive states – at least many such states – meet this requirement. But the RC per se makes no commitment on this point. In any case, even if it is *true* that such-and-such mental states meet this requirement, it does not follow that beliefs in propositions describing these states should be allowed in the internal standpoint. These propositions may still be epistemologically problematic.

15 It is doubtful that maximax would select a unique DDP. There are infinitely many incompatible DDPs that prescribe equally profligate belief-formation. The best outcomes of each of these will be equally good.

16 See Roderick M. Chisholm, *Theory of Knowledge* (Englewood Cliffs, N.J., first edition, 1966, second edition, 1977) and John L. Pollock, *Knowledge and Justification* (Princeton, 1974).

17 The formulation here includes some rewording of my own.

18 Chisholm, *Theory of Knowledge*, first edition, p. 24.

19 See ibid., second edition, p. 16.

20 Pollock, *Knowledge and Justification*, p. 21.

21 Gilbert Harman, *Thought* (Princeton, 1973), p. 157.

22 This is stressed by Hume, among others. See *A Treatise of Human Nature*, book I, part IV, section I.

23 See Lehrer, *Knowledge*, chap. 7.

24 Isaac Levi, *Gambling with Truth* (New York, 1967).

25 Still another possible goal is the satisfaction of needs or desires. But it is not easier for internalism to generate a DDP for this goal than for the goal of true-belief-cum-error-avoidance. Indeed, need or desire satisfaction will depend heavily upon truth-acquisition and error-avoidance.

26 Or even any small set of best DDPs.

27 I do not mean to imply here that the non-regulative conception of justifiedness must temporally precede the regulative conception.

28 This point is also made in "Epistemics: The Regulative Theory of Cognition," *The Journal of Philosophy*, 75, no. 10 (October 1978):509–23.

29 W. V. Quine, *Word and Object* (Cambridge, Mass., 1960), p. 275.

30 Karl Popper, *Objective Knowledge* (Oxford, 1972), pp. 71–2.

31 Justus Buchler, ed., *Philosophical Writings of Peirce* (New York, 1955), p. 256.

32 One might think that the regulative conception (RC) is biased in favor of foundationalism. Is it not committed to the idea that we have infallible access to our own cognitive states? And is this idea not peculiar to foundationalism? Two comments are in order. First, as indicated in notes 5 and 14 above, the RC does not say *which* states of a person, if any, have this special status. It merely lays down a *constraint* on inputs. Second, it is not true that infallible access to cognitive states is a thesis peculiar to foundationalism. Coherentism is committed to the same sort of thesis. In particular, it is committed to the assumption that we can tell what our own current *beliefs* are. Unless we can tell what (all) our current beliefs are, we cannot tell whether they satisfy the requirement of coherence (whatever exactly this requirement is), nor can we adjust our beliefs to meet that requirement.

3

INTERNALISM AND EXTERNALISM IN EPISTEMOLOGY

William P. Alston

One hears much these days of an epistemological distinction between "internal" and "external." It is often found in discussions of reliabilism in which the critic accuses the reliabilist of violating "internalist" restrictions on justification and of resting content with justification that is "external" to the subject's perspective.[1] But just what distinction is this (are these)? That is not so clear.

As just intimated, those who wield the distinction intend to be contrasting different views on what can confer justification or on what can convert mere true belief into knowledge. The main emphasis has been on justification, and we will continue that emphasis in this paper. In all these discussions it is the internalist position that lays down constraints; the externalist position *vis-à-vis* a given internalist position is simply the denial that the internalist constraint in question constitutes a necessary condition of justification. Thus our attempts at clarification can be confined to the internalist side.

As the name implies, an "internalist" position will restrict justifiers to items that are *within* something, more specifically, within the subject. But, of course, not everything that is "within" a knowing subject will be admitted as a possible justifier by an internalist. Physiological processes within the subject, of which the subject knows nothing, will not be allowed. Then just where, how, or in what sense, does something have to be "in the subject" in order to pass the internalist test?

Two quite different answers are given to this question in the literature. First there is the idea that in order to confer justification something must be within the subject's "perspective" or "viewpoint" on the world, in the sense of being something that the subject knows, believes, or justifiably believes. It must be something that falls within the subject's ken, something of which the subject has taken note. Second there is the idea that in order to confer justification something must be accessible to the subject in some special way, e.g., directly accessible or infallibly inaccessible. We shall explore each of these versions in detail, noting alternative formulations of each, exposing unclarities and incoherences, and seeking to develop the strongest form of each position. We shall consider what can be said for and against each version, and we shall explore their interrelations. Finally we shall make some suggestions concerning the most reasonable position to take on these issues.

I

Let's begin by considering the first form of internalism. In the essay already cited, BonJour, in discussing the view that there are "basic beliefs", has this to say.

> Thus if basic beliefs are to provide a suitable foundation for empirical knowledge, . . . then that feature, whatever it may be, in virtue of which an empirical belief qualifies as basic, must also constitute an adequate reason for thinking that the belief is true. And now if we assume, plausibly enough, that the person for whom a belief is basic must *himself* possess the justification for that belief if *his* acceptance of it is to be epistemically rational or responsible, and thus apparently that he must believe *with justification* both (a) that the belief has the feature in question and (b) that beliefs having that feature are likely to be true, then we get the result that this belief is not basic after all, since its justification depends on these other beliefs.[2]

The specific conclusion here is that there can be no basic beliefs, no beliefs that are justified otherwise than on the basis of other beliefs. But that is not our present concern. We are interested in the constraint on justification invoked by BonJour to arrive at this result. That is the requirement that "that feature, whatever it may be, in virtue of which an empirical belief qualifies as basic", that is, that feature by virtue of which it is justified, must be justifiably believed by the subject to attach to that belief if the belief is to be thereby justified. That is, the justifying feature must be part of his "perspective on the world", must be known or justifiably believed by him to obtain if it is to do its justifying work.

BonJour continues to employ this same understanding of internalism in characterising the opposed externalist position.

> But according to proponents of the view under discussion, the person for whom the belief is basic need not (and in general will not) have any cognitive grasp of any kind of this reason or of the relation that is the basis for it in order for this basic belief to be justified; all these matters may be entirely *external* to the person's subjective conception of the situation.[3]
>
> When viewed from the general standpoint of the western epistemological tradition, externalism represents a very radical departure. It seems safe to say that until very recent times, no serious philosopher of knowledge would have dreamed of suggesting that a person's beliefs might be epistemically justified simply in virtue of facts or relations that were external to his subjective conception.[4]

Again, in "A Rationale for Reliabilism" Kent Bach writes as follows.

> Internalism requires that a person have "cognitive grasp" of whatever makes his belief justified.[5]

And in "The Internalist Conception of Justification" Alvin Goldman writes:

> Traditional epistemology has not adopted this externalist perspective. It has been predominantly *internalist*, or egocentric. On the latter perspective, epistemology's job is to construct a doxastic principle or procedure *from the inside*, from our own individual vantage point.[6]

All this would suggest the following formulation of internalism.

(1)   Only what is within the subject's "perspective" can determine the justification of a belief.

Let's call this version of internalism "perspectival internalism" (henceforth "PI").

PI needs some refinement before we are ready to consider what can be said for and against it. First, we have been specifying the subject's "perspective" disjunctively as what the subject "knows, believes, or justifiably believes". It will make a considerable difference what choice we make from between these alternatives. For the present let's proceed in terms of justified belief. At a later stage of the discussion we will explicitly consider the three alternatives and justify this decision. This gives us the more specific formulation:

(2)   Only the justified beliefs of the subject can determine what further beliefs of that subject are justified.

(2) may seem to smell of circularity, but there can be no definitional circularity, since the internalism we are discussing is not concerned with defining "justified"; it is merely laying down one constraint on the provision of justification. There are, of course, well known problems with making all justification depend on other justified beliefs, and we shall attend to these in due course.

Next we need to consider the way in which the perspective *determines* the justification of belief. But first a terminological matter. BonJour's formulation is in terms of a "feature" of the belief by which it is justified. Sometimes this is the most natural construal, as when we think of beliefs about ones current conscious states as being justified by virtue of the fact that they, the beliefs, are incorrigible, or by virtue of the fact that they, the beliefs, are "self-warranted". However it is usually more natural to think of the justification of a belief as stemming from its relation to some state of affairs other than itself, as when a belief is justified by virtue of being based on adequate evidence or reasons, or by virtue of arising from a certain sensory experience. To be sure, these ways of talking are mutually translatable. By a well known grammatical trick we can always take a belief's relation to some external justifying state of affairs to be a property of the belief. And, contrariwise, we can take the fact that belief B is incorrigible to be the state of affairs that justifies it. Hence I shall feel free to use now one construal, now the other, as seems most natural in the particular context. However I will most often speak in terms of justifying *facts* or *states of affairs* and will refer to them as "justifiers".

Let's return to the issue concerning the way in which the perspective determines justification. In the first quotation from BonJour he allows any sort of fact, not just other justified beliefs of the subject, to be a justifier, provided the subject has certain justified beliefs concerning it and its relation to the initial belief. A justifier for a perceptual belief that there is a tree in front of one, can be, e.g., a sensory experience from which that belief sprang. In that case, the belief would be justified by the experience (or by its origin from the experience) only if S justifiably believes that the belief sprang from that experience and that this origin is sufficient for justification. On this version the perspective determines justification by determining what can justify what; but it allows items outside the perspective (items other than justified beliefs of that subject) to function as justifiers.[7]

Here and elsewhere in the paper the following distinction will be useful. A belief is *mediately (indirectly)* justified provided it is justified by virtue of its relations to other justified beliefs of the subject that provide adequate support for it. In such cases the belief is justified by the *mediation* of those other beliefs. If it is justified in any other way it will be said to be *immediately (directly)* justified. In terms of this distinction, the view embodied in the first quotation from BonJour rules out *purely* immediate justification, justification by something other than other justified beliefs of the subject *alone*, since it holds that an experience can justify a belief only if the subject has certain justified beliefs about the experience and its relation to the belief; but it is hospitable to mixed justification, in which both other justified beliefs *and* something else are required for justification.[8] However there is or can be a version of PI that is more radically opposed to immediate justification, one that would "perspectivize" justifiers more thoroughly, by holding that only justified beliefs can *be justifiers*. On this version what justifies a perceptual belief is not the experience itself, or actual origin from the experience, but the justified belief that the experience has occurred or that the belief originated from it.

We have made the distinction between these versions hang on what is allowed to count as "a justifier". In the perceptual case both versions require a justified belief that the relevant experience occurs, but they differ as to whether the experience itself can function in a justifying role. But this might be thought a trivial verbal difference, having to do only with where we draw the line between what is doing the justifying, and the conditions under which it is enabled to do so. What difference does it make where that line is drawn? On both views both "the justifier" and "the conditions that must obtain if it is to be a justifier" figure essentially in the conditions that are necessary for the belief in question to be justified. Why does it matter how we divide that set of conditions into what *does* the justifying and what *enables* it to do that justifying?

I agree that the division is not of any great importance. Nevertheless there is an important difference between the versions. For BonJour's version, in allowing the experience itself into the necessary conditions for justification, under whatever rubric, is imposing a condition for the justification of the perceptual belief over and above those imposed by the more radical alternative. Put it this way. Both versions alike hold that S is justified in believing that p (that there is a tree in front of one) only if S is justified in believing that S has experience E. But BonJour imposes the additional requirement that S *have* the experience; i.e., he requires that the supporting belief be *true*. And this can be seen to mark a decisive superiority of the more radical alternative. We are dealing with a case in which S's belief that s/he has experience E provides him/her with an adequate reason for the perceptual belief. (If more justified beliefs on S's part, about normality or other background conditions, are required for this, let them be included also.) Otherwise the case would fall short of justification by reason of the insufficiency of the alleged ground and we would never get to the problems raised by the internalism-externalism distinction. But if I do justifiably believe that I am having E, and if that constitutes a sufficient reason for my supposing that p, that is surely enough for my being justified in believing that p. To require that my supporting beliefs be *true* might be appropriate if we were laying down requirements for knowledge, but it is clearly too strong a requirement for justification. If, e.g., I am justified, to as high degree as you like, in supposing that my car is in my garage, then I am surely *justified* in denying that it is parked in front of the bank, even if, unbeknownst to me, someone had removed it from my garage and parked it in front of the bank. Thus BonJour's version represents something of an overkill.[9] Let's codify the preferred version.

(3)   The only thing that can justify S's belief that p is some other justified beliefs of S.

Next let's note a respect in which (3) needs broadening. Recall the important notion of *prima facie* justification. One is *prima facie* justified in believing that p provided that one is so situated that one will be (unqualifiedly, all things considered, *ultima facie*) justified in believing that p, provided there are no sufficient "overriding"[10] considerations. Thus in a normal perceptual situation in which I take myself to see a tree in front of me I am thereby *prima facie* justified in believing that there is a tree in front of me; but this justification can be overridden by abnormalitites in the situation, e.g., sensory malfunctioning of various sorts. Now consider what a PI internalist should say about the conditions under which a *prima facie* justification is overthrown. Does the mere existence of a sufficiently serious malfunctioning suffice? Or would the subject have to know or be justified in believing that this was the case? Clearly it is the second alternative that is in the spirit of PI. Just as the mere fact that a belief was produced in a highly reliable manner cannot justify it, so the mere fact that a belief was generated in an unreliable fashion cannot serve to discredit the belief. In both cases justification, or the lack thereof, depends on how the situation appears within my perspective, i.e., on what I know or justifiably believe about it. If and only if I have sufficient reason to think there to be something fishy about this case of perception, will *prima facie* justification be overthrown. And, indeed, most epistemologists have taken this line about what overrides *prima facie* justification, even where they haven't also accepted (3) as a constraint on justification.[11] Thus we should add overriders to the scope of (3). In the interest of concise formulation let us introduce the term "epistemizer" to range over anything that affects the justification of a belief, positively or negatively. We can then reformulate (3) as:

(4)   The only thing that can epistemize S's belief that p is some other justified belief(s) of S.

Now we are in a position to return to the choice between knowledge, belief, and justified belief in the specification of the subject's perspective. To deal with this properly we must note that (4) places severe restrictions on a theory of justification by implying that only *mediate* justification is available. Let's call any theory of justification that recognizes only mediate justification a discursive theory. Whether there are other varieties depends on how narrowly the boundaries of coherentism are drawn, and there is wide variation on this. For the present let's think of coherentism widely, as ranging over any discursive theory.

Next let's distinguish between "positive" and "negative" coherence theories. John Pollock introduced the distinction as follows.

There are two kinds of coherence theories. On the one hand, there are coherence theories which take all propositions to be prima facie justified. According to those theories, if one believes a proposition, P, one is automatically justified in doing so unless one has a reason for rejecting the belief. According to theories of this sort, reasons function primarily in a negative way, leading us to reject beliefs but not being required for the justified acquisition of belief. Let us call these negative coherence theories. The other kind of coherence theory (a positive coherence theory) demands positive support for all beliefs.[12]

In other words, on a positive coherence theory a belief is justified only if it stands in the right relation to justifiers. On a negative coherence theory a belief is justified unless it stands in the wrong relation with overriders. What makes them both coherence theories is that in both cases the epistemizers must be drawn from the subject's propositional attitudes.

Now let's go back to the various sorts of propositional attitudes that might be supposed by PI to make up the subject's perspective: beliefs, justified beliefs, knowledge. In formulations (2), (3), and (4) we chose *justified belief* without explaining or justifying that choice. I now turn to that task.

First what about the decision between knowledge and justified belief? Here the point is that the more modest constraint is called for. Suppose that I am justified in believing that my car is in the garage, since I left it there this morning and have been away from the house since, no one else has a key to the house or garage, and the neighborhood is remarkably free of crime. In the afternoon I see a car that looks like mine in the parking lot of a bank, but believe that it isn't mine, on the grounds of my car's being in my garage. Suppose further that my car has been stolen and this is my car, so I didn't *know* that my car was in the garage even though I was justified in believing this. I am surely justified in believing that the car in the parking lot is not mine, even though the basis for this belief is something I am justified in believing but do not know. Cases like this indicate that it is sufficient for a belief to be a justifier that it be justified; it is not also required that it count as knowledge.

But what about the alternative between any beliefs on the one hand, and only justified beliefs on the other? It may seem that we can settle this issue in the same way. Suppose I merely believe that my car is in the garage, just because that is where I normally expect it to be when I don't have it with me; but I am not justified in believing this. On the contrary, I took it to a repair shop to be worked on yesterday; when I believe that it is in my garage I have temporarily forgotten about this incident, even though I am quite capable of remembering it and have been remembering it except for this temporary lapse. Again I take my car's being in my garage as a reason for supposing that the car I see in the·bank parking lot is not mine. Here it is quite clear that I am not justified in this latter belief by virtue of basing it on an unjustified belief. On the contrary, the fact that I am quite unjustified in supposing my car to be in my garage shows that I don't become justified in some further belief by virtue of basing it on that belief. More generally, it seems that beliefs cannot acquire justification by being brought into relation with unjustified beliefs. One belief cannot "transfer" to another belief a justification it does not possess.

This last argument is, I believe, conclusive for what we might call "local" mediate justification, justification of a particular belief by the evidential or other logical relations in which it stands to one, or a few, other beliefs. Justification can be transferred "locally" only by beliefs that already have it. But the more common sort of discursive theory is a "holistic" coherence theory, one which takes a given belief to be justified, at least in the last analysis, not by its relations to a very few other beliefs "in the vicinity", but by the way in which it fits into some very large system of beliefs. Since the term "coherence theory" derives from the idea that a belief is justified if and only if it "coheres" with such a total system, it will be most natural to restrict the term "coherence theory" to holistic theories. The obvious choice for the system with which a belief must cohere in order to be justified is the totality of the subject's current beliefs. Thus on the most usual sort of coherence theory the subject's "perspective" by reference to which the justification of any particular belief is to be assessed consists of the subject's beliefs, without any further restriction to justified beliefs. Indeed, there could not be such a restriction. For on the kind of (pure) coherence theory we are now considering a belief is or is not justified just by its relations to the whole of the subject's beliefs. Apart from that coherence with *all* the subject's beliefs there are no justified beliefs to serve as a reference class. Hence by the time the totality of beliefs has been segregated into justified and unjustified it is too late to use the former class as a touchstone to determine whether a given belief is justified. That determination has already been made. Of course, if at a future time the subject has some new beliefs, we can at that time assess their justificatory status, and this determination will be made after the earlier demarcation of the justified from the unjustified beliefs. But that doesn't change the verdict. At that future time, by the terms of the theory, a given belief (new or old) is justified solely on the basis of its coherence with the total set of beliefs the subject has at that time. And so for a pure coherence theory PI should be formulated as follows.

(5)   Only the total set of S's beliefs at t can function as a epistemizer at t.[13]

Since I find pure coherence theories quite unsatisfactory for a variety of reasons, I might seek to rule out (5) on those grounds. But in this paper I did not want to get into *substantive* epistemological issues like those concerning the opposition between foundationalism and coherentism. This paper is designed to be restricted to meta-epistemological issues concerning basic epistemological concepts, their explication, interrelations, and suitability for one or another purpose. Thus I shall just point out that the internalism-externalism dispute is mostly carried on by thinkers who believe in local mediate justification. Hence we will ensure maximum contact with that debate if we focus on (4) rather than (5) in the ensuing discussion.

One more point must be laid on the table before we turn to the consideration of what can be said in support of PI. Go back to the initial quotation from BonJour; we have not yet squeezed it dry. There BonJour requires for the justification of S's putatively basic belief that S justifiably believe not only that the belief have the "feature" in question but also *that beliefs having that feature are likely to be true.* When we come to the main argument for PI we will see the rationale for this additional higher level requirement. For the moment we need only note its general character. It is clear that BonJour imposes *this* requirement just because he takes truth conducivity to be required for, as we might say, *justificatory efficacy.* Earlier in the essay he had written that "the distinguishing characteristic" of epistemic justification is "its internal relation to the cognitive goal of truth" (p. 54). Elsewhere BonJour has laid it down that it is essential to a justifier to be "truth conducive".[11] Thus this additional requirement is really a requirement to the effect that the subject be justified in supposing not only that the putative justifier obtains but also that it be efficacious, that it have what it takes to justify the belief. But he can't come right out and say that. Consider his situation if he were to try. Formulate the additional requirement as: *S justifiably believes that the possession of that feature suffices to justify the belief*. But BonJour is committed to deny this; his specific contention is that no feature of a belief can be sufficient to justify the belief; the subject must also have certain justified beliefs about that feature.[15] Then how about requiring that the possession of that feature is part of what confers justification on this belief? But we want the requirement to be more specific than that. The two justified beliefs are also part of what confers justification on the belief in this situation, but a different part. We want to specify what part the feature is contributing to the justification. That is what BonJour is attempting to do with his requirement that S be justified in believing that the feature is probabilifying, that by virtue of having this feature the belief is likely to be true. That will do the job, on the assumption that probabilification is just what it takes for justificatory efficacy. But this is controversial. In fact, other internalists have been in the forefront of denying just this claim.[16] Thus it appears that if we are to give an adequate formulation of this higher level requirement we must commit ourselves to some highly controversial assumption as to what is required for justification, some highly controversial assumption in substantive epistemology.

Fortunately there is a coward's way out, since we are working with (4), which restricts us to purely mediate justification, rather than with BonJour's versions. On (4) the only justifiers are other justified beliefs of the same subject. Hence the way in which any justifier has to be related to a belief in order to do its job is to provide "adequate support" or "adequate evidence", to be an "adequate reason". No doubt, it is both obscure and controversial what is required for one belief (or the propositional content thereof) to constitute an adequate reason or to provide adequate support for another. But leaving all this aside, and taking cover behind the criterion-neutral term "adequate", we can put the additional, higher-level requirement just by saying that S must justifiably believe that the justifying belief(s) provide adequate support for the justified belief.[17] Tacking this on to our canonical formulation we get:

(6)   Only S's justified beliefs can epistemize S's belief that p, and then only if S justifiably believes that the other justified beliefs in question

provide adequate support for p (or for something else, in the case of overriders).

II

We have now explicated PI sufficiently to consider what can be said in its favor. That consideration will lead to further refinements. First let's consider what defense is offered by BonJour in "Externalist Theories of Empirical Knowledge." The main effort there is devoted to an attack on reliability theories, utilizing an example of alleged clairvoyance. It is stipulated that the subject has a reliable capacity for determining the disposition of distant objects on no apparent basis. BonJour first argues that if the person has adequate reason for supposing that a belief thus formed is false, or that her clairvoyance is not reliable, then she is not justified in the clairvoyant beliefs, even though they are formed reliably. But, as BonJour acknowledges, this shows only that the subject's justified beliefs do have a bearing on what other beliefs are justified, not that they are the only thing that have this bearing. Next, he more boldly argues that in the case in which the subject has no reasons for or against the reliability of her powers or the truth of the belief (whether or not she believes that the powers are reliable), she is not justified in holding the beliefs, however reliable her clairvoyant powers are in fact. However these "arguments" simply consist in BonJour's displaying his intuitions in opposition to those of his opponent. A couple of quotations will give the flavor.

> We are now face-to-face with the fundamental – and seemingly obvious – intuitive problem with externalism: *why* should the mere fact that such an external relation (the reliability of the faculty) obtains mean that Norman's belief is epistemically justified, when the relation in question is entirely outside his ken?
>   One reason why externalism may seem initially plausible is that if the external relation in question genuinely obtains, then Norman will in fact not go wrong in accepting the belief, and it is, *in a sense*, not an accident that this is so. But how is this supposed to justify Norman's belief? From his objective perspective, it *is* an accident that the belief is true.[18]

This is more like an appeal to PI than a support for that restriction. There are, as we shall see, some germs of a more substantial argument in BonJour, but they will need developing.

Nor are we helped by a rather common argument for PI that stems from a confusion between the *activity* of justifying a belief and the *state* of a belief's being justified. Here is a good sample.

> In whatever way a man might attempt to justify his beliefs, whether to himself or to another, he must always appeal to some belief. There is nothing other than one's belief to which one can appeal in the justification of belief. There is no exit from the circle of one's beliefs.[19]

Of course, if I am to carry out the *activity* of justifying a belief I must provide an argument for it; I must say something as to why one should suppose it to be true. And to do this I must employ other beliefs of mine. In saying what reasons there are for supposing that p I am expressing other beliefs of mine, and contextually implying that I am justified in accepting them. But this all has to do with the activity of *justifying* a belief, *showing* it to be justified. From the fact that I can *justify* a belief only by relating it to other beliefs that constitute a support, it does not follow that a belief can *be justified* only by its relations to other beliefs. Analogously, from the fact that I cannot justify my expenses without saying something in support of my having made them, it does not follow that my expenses cannot *be justified* unless I say something in support of my having made them. Indeed, we all have innumerable beliefs that are commonly taken to be justified but for which we never so much as attempt to produce reasons. It might be argued with some show of plausibility that one can be justified in believing that p only if it is *possible* for one to justify that belief; but I cannot imagine any remotely plausible argument for the thesis that I can be justified in believing that p only if I *have justified* that belief. Hence the point made by Lehrer about justifying leaves completely intact the possibility that one might *be justified* in a belief by something other than one's other beliefs.

We will have to make the same judgment on an analogous argument from what is involved in *deciding* what to believe. Here is a version by Pollock.

> In deciding what to believe, we have only our own beliefs to which we can appeal. If our beliefs mutually support our believing P, then it would be irrational for us not to believe P and hence belief in P is justified. There is no way that one can break out of the circle of his own beliefs.[20]

Again, even if this shows that I can have no basis other than my own beliefs for a *decision* as to what to believe, it falls far short of showing that nothing can *justify* a belief except other beliefs. For there is no reason to suppose that the only justified beliefs are those the subject *decided* to adopt.

Even though, as will appear in the fullness of time, I am no advocate of PI, I feel that I can improve on the recommendations for that view that can be found in the writings of its supporters. Here is what I take to be the strongest argument for it. I have gleaned the basic idea for this line of argument from various sources, but the development of it is my own.[21]

"First let's note that the fact that q can enter into the justification for S's believing that p only in the guise of S's being justified in believing that q. Consider the popular idea that what justifies me in beliefs about my own current conscious states is that such beliefs are infallible, i.e., are such that I couldn't mistakenly form such a belief. But how could that fact justify those beliefs unless I were cognizant of the infallibility? If I am unaware of their infallibility, and they have no other justification, am I not proceeding *irresponsibly* in forming such beliefs? Just as the mere fact that X is about to attack me will not justify my striking X unless I have good reason to suppose that he is about to attack me, so the mere fact that current feeling beliefs are infallible can't justify me in accepting them unless I at least have good reason to regard them as infallible. *Pari passu*, the mere fact that I am being appeared to treely cannot render me justified in believing that there is a tree in front of me, unless I am justified in believing that I am being appeared to treely. If I am unaware of the existence of the warrant conferring fact then, for me, it is just as if it did not exist. How can a fact of which I take no account whatever have any bearing on what it is *permissible* for me to do, in the way of action or of belief? Thus it would seem that my being justified in believing that q is at least a *necessary* condition of q's playing a role in justifying my belief that p.

But it is also a sufficient condition. Provided I am justified in believing that beliefs about current feelings of the subject are infallible, what more could be required to legitimate those beliefs? Even if they are not in fact infallible, how can that prevent its being *permissible* for me to accept them? If, so far as I can tell, there are facts that strongly support the supposition that p, then surely it is *all right* for me to give my assent to p. What more could be *demanded* of me? I have done all I can. What the actual facts are over and above what I am most justified in believing is something I cannot be held *responsible* for. Once I have marshalled all the cognitive resources available to me to determine the matter I have, in my body of justified beliefs, the closest approximation I can make to the actual facts. That is the best I have to go on, and it would be quite unreasonable to suggest that I *ought* to be going on something else instead. What I am justified in believing provides sufficient as well as necessary conditions for the justification of further beliefs."[22]

How does this line of argument go beyond simply displaying internalist (PI) intuitions? It does so by grounding those intuitions in a particular conception of justification, one that makes epistemic justification a matter of the subject's normative situation, a matter of how the subject's believing that p stands *vis-à-vis* relevant intellectual norms, standards, obligations, duties, and the like. If S's believing that p is *not* in contravention of relevant intellectual obligations, then it is *permissible* for him to believe that p, he cannot be rightly *blamed* for doing so, it is *all right* for him to hold that belief, he is *in the clear* in so believing. Let's call this a "deontological" conception of epistemic justification. The argument just presented exhibits the PI constraint as flowing from *what justification is*, as thus conceived. Since whether I am justified in believing that p depends on whether I could rightfully be blamed or held to account for so believing, then what is crucial for whether I am justified is the way the relevant facts appear from my perspective; justification depends on what the relevant facts are like, *so far as I can tell*. For that is what is crucial for whether I can be blamed for my belief. If and only if my belief is adequately supported *so far as I can tell*, I cannot be blamed for the belief.[23]

Elsewhere I have explored the deontological conception and contrasted it with the very different "strong position" (SP) conception, as well as distinguishing various versions of each.[24] Roughly speaking, to be SP justified in believing that p is to believe that p in such a way as to be in a strong position thereby to attain the truth and avoid error. It is to believe that p in a "truth conducive" way. It is for one's belief to have been formed in such a way or on such a basis that one is thereby likely to be believing correctly. Note that each conception omits the crucial emphasis of the other, thereby implicitly denying it to be necessary for justification. Freedom from blameworthiness, being in the clear as far as one's intellectual duties are concerned, is totally ignored by the "strong position" theorist. So long as one forms one's belief in a way that is well calculated to get the truth, it is of no concern how well one is carrying out intellectual duties. Conversely, the deontologist has nothing to say about truth conducivity.[25] So long as I am not violating any intellectual duties I am "in the clear" in believing that p, whatever my chances for truth. This is not to say that each side denies the importance of what is crucial for the other. The deontologist need not be indifferent to the truth, nor need the "strong position" theorist be uninterested in intellectual duties. But they differ on how these admittedly important matters relate to epistemic justification.

To get a properly rounded picture we should also note a way in which truth conducivity does typically enter into deontological theories of justification. Even though truth-conducivity does not enter into the meaning of "justified" for the deontologist he is likely to give it a prominent place when

he comes to spell out the content of our most important intellectual obligations. Such theorists typically hold that our basic intellectual obligation is to
so conduct our cognitive activities as to maximize the chances of believing
the true and avoiding believing the false.[26] Thus even though one may be
deontologically justified without thereby being in a favorable position to get
the truth, if our basic intellectual obligation is to maximize truth and mini-
mize falsity one cannot be deontologically justified in a belief unless one is
believing in such a way that, so far as one can tell, is well calculated to reach
the truth.

Now we can see that just as the deontological conception supports a PI
restriction, so an SP conception supports its denial. It is obviously not con-
ceptually necessary that one comes to believe that p in a truth conducive way
only if that belief is well supported by other justified beliefs of the subject. It
is clearly possible that there are ways of being in a strong position in one's
beliefs other than by basing those beliefs on other justified beliefs. Plausible
examples of such other ways are not far to seek. Perceptual beliefs about the
physical environment, e.g., that the lilies are blooming in the garden, are based
on the subject's sensory experience, on the way in which things sensorily
appear to one. Furthermore let's make the plausible supposition that one does
not typically form beliefs about how one is being sensorily appeared to; the
sensory appearance directly gives rise to the belief about the environment. It
is not that one says to oneself, even rapidly, implicitly, or below the level of
consciousness, "I am having a visual experience of such and such a sort; therefore the lilies are blooming in the garden". No such inference typically takes
place, for the premises for such inferences are rarely made objects of belief.
Finally, let's make the plausible assumption that our perceptual belief forming
mechanisms are generally reliable, at least for the sorts of perceptual beliefs
we typically form, in the sorts of situations we typically encounter. Granting
all this, perceptual belief formation constitutes massive support for the thesis
that one can form beliefs in a reliable, truth conducive, manner, without
basing them on other justified beliefs.

Beliefs about ones current conscious states provide even stronger support.
It is very plausible to suppose that we have a highly reliable (some would even
say infallible) mechanism for the formation of such beliefs. And yet it would
be extremely implausible to suppose that these beliefs are formed or held
on the basis of reasons. What would such reasons be? It may be suggested
that my reason for supposing that I feel sleepy at the moment is that I do
believe this and that such beliefs are infallible. But many persons who form
such beliefs do not even have the relevant concept of infallibility, much less
typically believe that such beliefs are infallible whenever they come to believe

such things. Once again we have reason to suppose that beliefs can satisfy the SP conception of justification without satisfying the PI constraint on justification.

Next let's note that the argument we have given for PI supports both the lower level and the higher level requirement laid down in (6). The "lower level requirement" is that the belief that p *be* adequately supported by other justified beliefs of the subject, and the "higher level requirement" is that the subject justifiably *believe that* these other justified beliefs provide adequate support for the belief that p. We have been emphasizing the way in which the argument establishes the lower level requirement, but it also lends powerful support to the higher level requirement. For suppose that my belief that p is based on other justified beliefs of mine and, let's suppose, these other justified beliefs provide adequate support for the belief that p. But suppose further that I do not justifiably believe that these other beliefs do provide adequate support. In that case, so far as I can tell, I do not have within my perspective adequate support for p. Would I not be proceeding irresponsibly in adopting the belief that p? Couldn't I properly be held accountable for a violation of intellectual obligations in giving my assent to p under those conditions? Therefore if I am to be in the clear in believing that p, the belief must not only be based on other justified beliefs of mine; I must also be justified in supposing those beliefs to provide sufficient support for the belief that p.

That shows that the higher level belief is necessary for justification. We can now proceed to argue that it, together with the lower level requirement, is sufficient. The crucial question here is whether it is also necessary for justification that the other justified beliefs do in fact provide adequate support, that their propositional contents are indeed so related as to make the one an adequate reason for the other. A consideration of conditions of blame, being in the clear, etc., will support a negative answer. For if, going on what I know or justifiably believe about the world, it is clear to me that other justified beliefs of mine adequately support the belief that p, what more could be required of me? Even if I am mistaken in that judgment I made it in the light of the best considerations available to me. I can't be held to blame if I proceed in the light of the best reading of the facts of which I am capable. Hence a *justified belief* that I have adequate support is all that can rightfully be imposed in the way of a higher level requirement.

Now that we have a two level PI internalism-externalism contrast, there is the possibility of being an internalist on one level and an externalist on another. The two parties disagree both over what can be a justifier and over that by virtue of which a particular item justifies a particular belief. A particularly live possiblity of a compromise is an internalism as to what can justify and an externalism as to what enables it to justify. One could be a PI internalist about justifiers by virtue of recognizing only mediate justification, but insist that my belief that p is justified by its relations to my belief that q if and only if q does in fact provide adequate support for p. At the end of the paper we shall advocate a similar mediating position, though the internalist component will not be the PI brand.

Now let's consider a way in which what is supported by our argument for PI differs from the formulation of PI with which we have been working. We have represented the deontologist as maintaining that whether S is justified in believing that p is solely a function of what other justified beliefs S has. But that cannot be the whole story. Consider a case in which, although the sum total of the justified beliefs I actually possess provide an adequate basis for the belief that p, that would not have been the case had I been conducting myself properly. If I had looked into the matter as thoroughly as I should have, I would be in possession of effective *overriders* for my evidence for p, and my total body of evidence would not have given sufficient support for the belief that p. Here the belief that p *is* adequately supported by the perspective on the world that I actually have, and I justifiably believe that it is; but nevertheless I am not in the clear in believing that p, not justified in the deontological sense.

These considerations show that PI must be modified if it is to be supported by a deontological conception of justification. It must include a codicil to the effect that overriders that the subject does not possess, but would have possessed had s/he been conducting him/herself as s/he should have been, also can serve to epistemize beliefs.[27] PI now becomes:

(7)   Only S's justified beliefs can epistemize S's belief that p, and then only if S justifiably believes that those other justified beliefs provide adequate support for S's belief that p; but overriders that S should have had but didn't can cancel out justification provided by the preceding.[28]

Going back once more to our argument for PI, I now wish to point out that it utilizes a special form of a deontological conception of justification that is limited in ways that render it either totally inapplicable, or at least severely limited in application.

First it utilizes a concept of justification that assumes beliefs to be under direct voluntary control. The argument takes it that one is justified in believing that p if and only if one is not to blame *for believing that p*, if and only if *in that situation this was a belief that one was permitted to choose*. All this talk has application only if one has direct voluntary control over whether one believes that p at a given moment. If I lack such control, if I cannot believe or refrain from believing that p at will, then it is futile to discuss whether I am *permitted* to believe that p at t or whether I would be *irresponsible* in choosing to believe that p at t. And it seems that we just don't have any such control, at least not in general. For the most part my beliefs are formed willy-nilly. When I see a truck coming down the street I am hardly at liberty either to believe that a truck is coming down the street or refrain from that belief. Even if there are special cases, such as moral or religious beliefs, where we do have pin point voluntary control (and even this may be doubted), it is clear that for the most part we lack such powers.[29]

Not only does the argument in question presuppose direct voluntary control of belief. It considers the requirements for justification only for those beliefs that are acquired by an explicit, deliberate choice. For it arrives at the PI constraint by pointing out that only what I am cognizant of can be taken account of in my *decision* as to whether to believe that p. "If I am unaware of their infallibility, . . . am I not proceeding irresponsibly in *forming* such beliefs?" "If, so far as I can tell, there are facts that strongly support the supposition that p, then surely it is all right for me to give my assent to p." But this fact, that only what I am cognizant of can affect the permissiblity of my choice, will imply a *general* constraint on justification only if justification is confined to beliefs that are *chosen* by a deliberate voluntary act. But even if beliefs are *subject to* direct voluntary control that control need not always be exercised. One can hold that it is always in principle possible to choose whether to believe a given proposition without thereby being committed to the grossly implausible supposition that all our beliefs are in fact acquired by an explicit choice. Even overt actions that are uncontroversially under voluntary control, such as tying ones shoelaces, can be, and often are, performed habitually. Likewise, even if beliefs are as subject to direct voluntary control as tying ones shoelaces, beliefs are often acquired willy-nilly. Even if we are always capable of voluntarily controlling our perceptual belief formation, e.g., we rarely do so. Hence a concept of epistemic justification that is confined to beliefs acquired by deliberate choice covers only a small part of the territory.

Third, it follows from the point just made that the argument utilizes a concept of justification that evaluates a belief solely in terms of its original acquisition, for the argument has to do with what can determine the permissiblity of the *choice* of a belief. But it is often noted by epistemologists that the epistemic status of a belief may change after its acquisition, as the subject comes to acquire or lose support for it. Suppose that after coming to believe that Susie is quitting her job, on the basis of no evidence worthy of the name and hence unjustifiably, I come into possession of adequate evidence for this supposition; let us further suppose that this new evidence now functions as the basis for my belief. In this case my belief comes to be justified *after* its acquisition. Thus a concept of justifiably *acquired* belief is at best only a part of an adequate concept of justified belief.

To be sure, it is not difficult to modify this very restrictive concept, so as to make it more generally applicable. Let's begin by showing how the direct voluntary control assumption can be dropped. It is uncontroversial that our beliefs are under *indirect* voluntary control, or at least subject to influence from our voluntary actions. Even if I can't effectively decide at this moment to stop believing that Reagan is inept, I could embark on a regimen that is designed to improve my assessment of Reagan, and it might even succeed in time. With this possibility of indirect influence in mind, we can reconstrue "intellectual obligations" so that they no longer attach to believings and abstentions therefrom, but to actions that are designed to influence our believings and abstentions. Reinterpreted in this way the argument would be that whether we are justified in believing that p at t would depend on whether prior to t we had done what could reasonably be expected of us to influence that belief. The difference between these two understandings may be illustrated as follows. Suppose that my belief that there is life outside our solar system is inadequately supported by the totality of my justified beliefs. On the direct voluntary control interpretation I have an effective choice, whenever I consider the matter, as to whether to keep believing that or not. It is my duty to refrain from believing it since it is not adequately supported by my "perspective"; since I continue to believe it in defiance of my duty I am doing something that is not permitted; my belief is not justified. But the matter sorts out differently on the "indirect voluntary control" construal. It is recognized that I lack the capacity to discard that belief at will; at most I have the ability to make various moves that increase the chances of the belief's being abandoned. Hence so long as I am doing as much along that line as could reasonably be expected of me, I can't be faulted for continuing to have the belief; and so it is justified. On either of these interpretations, whether my belief is justified is a function of how things appear in my perspective rather than of how they are in actual fact. So long as life outside the solar system is improbably relative to what I am justified in believing, then my belief is unjustified unless (on the indirect control version) my best efforts have failed to dislodge it.

Next consider how we can lift the other restrictions. We can confine this discussion to the direct control version, since on the indirect control version there was no reason to impose them in the first place. Let's first take the restriction to explicitly chosen beliefs. On the direct control version we can say that the belief is justified provided that it was acquired on such a basis that if the agent had chosen to adopt the belief on that basis he could not have been blamed for doing so. In other words, where the belief, or its furtherance, was not explicitly chosen we can evaluate it, on the deontological conception, by considering whether its basis is such that if it or its furtherance was chosen on that basis the agent would have been in the clear in so choosing.

Now let's see how to lift the restriction to the original acquisition of the belief, and extend the concept to the evaluation of one's continuing to believe that p at times after its original acquisition. Once again the crucial move is to consider what would be the case if we were to make a choice that we did not in fact make. For one thing, we can consider what the judgment would be on my coming to believe this if the belief were voluntarily adopted on the basis of this evidence I possess at present (and analogously for the indirect control version). Or, closer to home, we could consider the possiblity that I should now explicitly raise the question of whether to retain the belief, in the light of the evidence I now possess, and should come to a decision to retain it. In that case would I be in the clear in making that decision? If so I am now justified in retaining the belief.

It is time to take our bearings with respect to these increasingly proliferating variations in a deontological concept of justification. To keep complexity within manageable bounds, I shall formulate a version that is designed to take care both of habitually formed beliefs and post-acquisition influences on justifications. I shall formulate this both in a direct control and an indirect control version.

(8)   Direct control version. One is justified in believing that p at t if and only if either (a) in choosing at t to adopt or retain the belief that p one was not violating any intellectual obligations, or (b) one's belief that p at t has such a basis that if one were to decide, in the light of that basis, to retain one's belief that p, one would not be violating any intellectual obligations in so doing.

(9)   Indirect control version. One is justfied in believing that p at t if and only if one's believing that p at t does not stem from any violations of intellectual obligations.

Thus it is not difficult to concoct distinctively deontological conceptions of justification that avoid the severe limitations of the concept employed by the argument for PI. But what sort of argument for PI can be constructed on the basis of these alternative conceptions?

The first point is that no case at all can be made for PI on the basis of the indirect control version. According to (9), justification is a function of certain features of the causal history of the belief. Was that history such that if the subject had lived up to his/her intellectual obligations in the past then s/he would not have believed that p? This is not a "perspectival" matter. The justified beliefs of the subject do not play any crucial role in determining whether or not that condition was satisfied. It is matter of what actually went on, rather than a matter of how what went on is represented in the subject's viewpoint. Thus (9) supports an externalist position on justification; at least it supports the externalist contrast to PI. Of course we could try to "perspectivize" (9). Any condition for anything that is in terms of what the facts actually are can receive a "perspectival" modification, transforming it into a condition that the facts be represented in a certain way in the subject's perspective. So modified (9) would become:

(10)   S is justified in believing that p if and only if S's belief that p did not, so far as S can tell, stem from S's violations of intellectual obligations.

But (10) is wildly permissive. We rarely have reason to think that one of our beliefs stems from intellectual transgressions. To know about the causal history of beliefs takes research, and we rarely engage in such research. Hence we have very few beliefs about the causal history of our beliefs. And so practically all beliefs, no matter how shoddy or disreputable, will be justified on this criterion. The prospects for support for PI from an indirect control version of a deontological conception are vanishingly small.

Things do not look much rosier from the perspective of (8). According to (8) a belief can be justified on the basis of anything whatsoever, not just other justified beliefs of the subject, provided that one would be in the clear, vis-a-vis one's intellectual obligations if one were to consider whether to retain the belief in the light of that basis. If one were to engage in such a consideration one would, of course, be choosing to retain the belief on the basis of other justified beliefs, in particular the belief that that basis obtains. That is the situation envisaged by the restrictive concept employed in the original argument for PI. But the extended concept differs from that precisely by not making the actual obtaining of such a situation necessary for justification. It recognizes that a belief can be justified even if one never does make any decision with respect to it on the basis of what one justifiably believes about its basis. Hence on this modified deontological concept a belief could be justified by being based on some experience, even if the subject in fact has no beliefs about that experience. What is supported by (8) is a denial rather than an affirmation of the PI constraint.

Thus it appears that we have a significant argument for PI only if we utilise a concept of justification that cannot be seriously defended as generally applicable, a concept according to which the justification of beliefs is solely a matter of whether a belief is *chosen* in such a way that this choice does not involve any dereliction of intellectual duty. But we cannot seriously suppose that justified beliefs are restricted to those that are *chosen* in that way, even if some are. Insofar as we are working with an even minimally defensible concept of justification, the argument for PI dissipates.

When we consider the higher level requirement embodied in (7), things look even worse. (7) implies that I will be justified in believing that p on the basis of my justified belief that q only if I am justified in supposing that the latter belief provides adequate support for the former. One reason this darkens the prospects for PI is that it is doubtful that we satisfy that condition very often. Just how often it is satisfied depends on what it takes to be justified in beliefs like that, and that is not at all clear. One thing that is clear for the PI advocate, however, is that to be justified such a belief will have to be mediately justified, since that is the only kind of justification PI recognizes. We will have to have sufficient reasons for supposing that *the belief that q adequately supports the belief that p* if we are to be justified in that higher level belief. How often do we have such reasons? Not very often, I would suggest. Perhaps the following will suffice to indicate the difficulties. Consider perceptual beliefs. If my perceptual belief that it is raining outside is to be mediately justified, this will presumably be on the basis of a justified belief that I am having certain visual experiences, plus perhaps (depending on the requirements we adopt) justified beliefs about the normality of the situation.[30] Now to have adequate reasons for supposing that reasons like that are sufficient support for a perceptual belief about one's environment is to be in the position that many great philosophers have labored to get themselves into when they have wrestled with the problem of how to infer facts about the external world from facts about the sensory experiences of the individual percipient. And even if some philosophers have solved that problem, which I am strongly inclined to deny, it is quite clear that the overwhelming majority of the population is not in possession of any such solution. For a second illustration, consider the point that in order for some non-deductive evidence to be adequate support for a given belief (so that this latter belief is justifiably held) there must be no other justified beliefs of mine that serve to defeat the *prima facie* support provided by the first-mentioned evidence. Suppose that my reason for supposing that Ray will be in his office today is that today is Wednesday and Ray has a fixed disposition to work in his office on Wednesdays. However I have temporarily forgotten that Ray told me last week that he will be out of town on Wednesday of this week. When that justified belief of mine is added to the picture the total evidence no longer adequately supports the supposition that Ray will be in his office today. This means that I can be justified in supposing that my belief that q renders my belief that p justified only if I am justified in supposing that there is nothing else I am justified in believing such that when that is added to q the conjunction does not adequately support p. And it is difficult to be justified in any claim concerning what is or is not present in the totality of ones justified beliefs.

Thus it is dubious that the higher level requirement of PI is very widely satisfied. If that is required for justification not many people are justified in many beliefs. But there is an even more serious difficulty with the requirement. It engenders an infinite regress. If in order to be justified in believing that p, I must be justified in believing that my reason, q, adequately supports p, the justification of this later belief requires the justification of a still higher level belief. That is, if r is my reason for supposing that q adequately supports p, I can be justified in supposing that q adequately supports p only if I am justified in supposing that r adequately supports **q adequately supports p**. And my justification for this last belief includes my being justified in a still higher level belief about adequate support. Given PI, I cannot be justified in any belief without simultaneously being justified in all the members of an infinite hierarchy of beliefs of ever ascending level.

Let's make sure we fully appreciate the character of this difficulty. The view that all justification is mediate itself gives rise to a much more widely advertised regress, this one stemming from the lower level requirement that a given belief can be justified only by its relation to another justified belief. The same is true of the justification of this supporting belief; i.e., it can only be justified by its relation to still another justified belief; and so on ad infinitum. The standard coherentist response to this difficulty is to opt for a circle of justification, rather than an infinite regress, and then to switch from local to holistic justification. I find this response quite inadequate, but this is not the place to go into that. Instead I want to stress the difference in the difficulty entailed by the higher level regress. The preference for a circle over an infinite set is of no avail here. Since there is a regress of *levels* we are foreclosed from doubling back. No adequate support-belief at an earlier stage will serve to do the job required at a later stage because it will have the wrong content. At each stage what is required is a justified belief to the effect that the "reason for" relationship *at the immediately previous stage* is an adequate one; and no earlier beliefs of that sort in the hierarchy will have been concerned with that particular "reason for" relationship. Hence there is no alternative here to an infinite regress. And, needless to say, it is highly doubtful that any of us is in possession of such an infinite hierarchy of "adequate support" beliefs.

III

PI has not emerged in strong shape from our examination. Let's turn now to the second construal of an internalist constraint on justification, and see if it fares any better. This second construal has to do with the kind of access we can have to justifiers. The general idea is that possible justifiers are restricted to items to which we have a specially favored access. This special access is variously specified as direct, incorrigible, and obtainable just by reflecting. We have already seen Goldman, in "The Internalist Conception of Justification", identifying internalism with PI. Here is an AI formulation from the same essay.

> The basic idea of internalism is that there should be guaranteed epistemic access to the correctness of a DDP. No condition of DDP-rightness is acceptable unless we have epistemic access to the DDP that in fact satisfies the condition, i.e., unless we can tell which DDP satisfies it. The internalist's objection to externalism's condition of rightness, i.e., actual optimality, is precisely that cognizers may have no way of telling which DDP satisfies it. Internalism's *own* condition of rightness must, therefore, be such that any cognizer *can tell* which DDP satisfies it.[31]

Another person we cited as a source of PI, Kent Bach, also brings AI into the picture in "A Rationale for Reliabilism".

> Internalism . . . treats justifiedness as a purely internal matter: if p is justified for S, then S must be aware (or at least be immediately capable of being aware) of what makes it justified and why.[32]

The parenthetical phrase formulates the AI alternative to the PI formulation outside the parentheses.

However I have found the most elaborate developments of this conception in epistemologists who do not actually employ the "internalism" label. Thus R. M. Chisholm, in a well known passage, lays it down that whenever we are justified in a belief we can determine by reflection what it is that so justifies us.

We presuppose, second, that the things we know are justified for us in the following sense: *we* can know what it is, on any occasion, that constitutes our grounds, or reason, or evidence for thinking that we know.

In beginning with what we think we know to be true, or with what, after reflection, we would be willing to count as being evident, we are assuming that the truth we are seeking is "already implicit in the mind which seeks it, and needs only to be elicited and brought to clear reflection".[33]

Carl Ginet gives a more elaborate statement of this version of internalism

Every one of every set of facts about S's position that minimally suffices to make S, at a given time, justified in being confident that p must be *directly recognizable* to S at that time. By 'directly recognizable' I mean this: if a certain fact obtains, then it is directly recognizable to S at a given time if and only if, provided that S at that time has the concept of that sort of fact, S needs at that time only to reflect clear-headedly on the question of whether or not that fact obtains in order to know that it does.[31]

In the interest of securing a definite target let's focus on the version of special access internalism that requires *direct* access for justifiers, construed along Ginet's lines. I shall refer to this second construal of internalism as "access internalism" (hereinafter "AI").

Our next order of business should be to consider the relation between the two internalisms. Now that we have completed the laborious process of explicating and refining our conception of PI we are at last in a position to do this. Are the two conceptions importantly different? Just how are they related? Can one be subsumed under the other? Does one imply the other?

First let's consider the possibility that PI is a special case of AI. Is the restriction of justifiers to the subject's viewpoint a special case of a restriction of justifiers to what is directly accessible? Only if ones own perspective is directly accessible, and this does not seem to be the case. The sum total of my justified beliefs cannot be depended on to spread themselves before my eyes on demand, not even that segment thereof that is relevant to a particular belief under consideration. I may know something that provides crucial evidence for p and yet fail to realize this even on careful reflection. We need not invoke Freudian blockages to illustrate this, though they are relevant. It may be that the sheer volume of what I know about, e.g., ancient Greek philosophy, is too great for my powers of ready retrieval; or some of this material may be so deeply buried as to require special trains of association to dislodge it. We are all familiar with cases in which something we knew all along failed to put in an appearance when it was needed to advance a particular inquiry. And, remembering our last modification of PI, still less is it the case that *what I would be justified in believing had I been behaving as I ought* is readily available on reflection.

Thus an item may pass the PI test without passing the AI test. PI is not a special case of AI. How about the converse? Is the restriction to the directly accessible just a special case of the restriction to the subject's justified beliefs and knowledge? Only if nothing other than my knowledge and justified beliefs is directly accessible to me. But that is clearly not the case. My feelings and other conscious experiences are directly accessible if anything is. And even if it were true, as I see no reason to suppose it to be, that I cannot have a conscious experience without knowing that I do, still the experience is distinguishable from the knowledge of the experience. Hence an item can pass the AI test without passing the PI test. This is what makes it possible for partisans of AI like Chisholm and Ginet to recognize immediate justification and to escape coherentism.

Thus PI and AI look quite independent of one another. But surely they must be closely related in some way. Otherwise how can we understand the fact that they are so persistently lumped together under the "internalism" label? And in fact on closer inspection we can see an interesting connection. We can think of AI as a broadening of PI. Whereas PI restricts justifiers to what the subject already justifiably believes (or, in the modified version, to that plus some of what the subject would justifiably believe under ideal conditions), AI enlarges that to include what the subject *can* come to know just on reflection. It is clear that any item that passes the AI test is something that is readily assimilable into the subject's viewpoint, just on reflection. AI, we might say, enlarges the conception of the subject's perspective to include not only what does in fact occur in that perspective (and what should occur), but also what *could* be there if the subject were to turn his attention to it.

Next let's turn to what can be said in support of AI. We have seen that PI is most plausibly supported on a deontological conception of justification, and the AI constraint has also been defended on the same conception. Here we are fortunate to have an explicit statement of the argument from Carl Ginet.

Assuming that S has the concept of justification for being confident that p, S *ought* always to possess or lack confidence that p according to whether or not he has such justification. At least he ought always to withhold confidence unless he has justification. This is simply what is meant by having or lacing *justification*. But if this is what S ought to do in any possible circumstance, then it is what S *can* do in any possible circumstance. That is, assuming that he has the relevant concepts, S can always tell whether or not he has justification for being confident that p. But this would not be so unless the difference between having such justification and not having it were always directly recognizable to S. And that would not be so if any fact contributing to a set that minimally constitutes S's having such justification were not either directly recognizable to S or entailed by something directly recognizable to S (so that its absence would have to make a directly recognizable difference). For suppose it were otherwise: suppose that some part of a condition minimally sufficient for S's being justified in being confident that p were *not* entailed by anything directly recognizable to S. Then S's position could change from having such justification to lacking it without there being any change at all in what is directly recognizable to S. But if there is no change in directly recogizable features of S's position, S cannot tell that his position has changed in other respects: no matter how clearheadedly and attentively he considers his position he will detect no change. If it seemed to S before that he had justification for being confident that p then it must still seem so to him. So this sort of justification would be such that it would not always be possible for its subject to tell whether or not he possessed it, which is contrary to what we noted is an obvious essential feature of justification. So there can be no such justification. That is, there can be no set of facts giving S justification for being confident that p that has an essential part that is neither directly recognizable to S nor entailed by something directly recognizable to S.[35]

Note that the conclusion of this argument is not quite the same as the AI thesis I previously quoted from Ginet. According to that thesis, every part of a justifier must be directly recognizable; but the argument purports to show only that a justifier must be either this or *entailed* by what is directly recognizable. Ginet may feel that the additional disjunct makes no significant difference, but this is not the case. One may not be able to spot everything that is entailed by what is directly recognizable; the disjunctive conclusion leaves open the possibility of justifiers that are not wholly identifiable from what is directly recognizable. However I shall suppress this difficulty in the ensuing discussion. For the sake of simplicity I shall consider the thesis in the simpler form, bringing in the second disjunct only where it is specially relevant to the point under consideration.

I have said that Ginet argues from a deontological conception of justification, but this may not be obvious from his formulation of the argument. I shall try to make it more obvious. But first let's note that Ginet explicitly lays out such a conception.

> One is *justified* in being confident that p if and only if it is not the case that one ought not to be confident that p: one could not be justly reproached for being confident that p.[36]

This concept does not explicitly appear in the argument, but it is just below the surface. Ginet uses this concept to define the concept of *having a justification* that he employs in the argument.

> I shall take "S has justification for being confident that p" . . . to mean S is in a position such that if he is, or were to be, confident that p then he is, or would be, justified in being so.[37]

We then get "is justified in being confident that p" defined deontologically as in the previous quotation. Thus the concept used in the argument is, so to say, the first derivative of a deontological conception. It is the concept of having what it takes to be justified in the deontological sense if one will only make use of those resources.

Before entering into a critical scrutiny of the argument, let's note some of its features, with special attention to the points we were making concerning the argument for PI. First, the argument should, by rights, apply to overriders of prima facie justification as well as to justifiers. Consider that done. Second, Ginet is obviously presupposing direct voluntary control of belief. Since "in any possible circumstance", "S *ought* always to possess or lack confidence that p according to whether or not he has such justification", this is something that "S *can* do in any possible circumstance". It is always possible for S to stop and consider any actual belief of his, or any candidate for belief, and bring it about then and there that he does or does not adopt or continue to hold the belief according as he has or lacks sufficient justification for it.[38] It is not so clear whether Ginet's concept of justification applies only to beliefs that are acquired by a deliberate choice, and then only in terms of what is true at the moment of acquisition. Let's suppose that he is only assuming the ever present possiblity of a deliberate choice between adopting (continuing) a belief and refraining from doing so, and that to be justified in believing that p is to be so situated that if one were, in that situation, to choose to believe that p (or continue to do so) one could not be blamed, on intellectual grounds, for that choice.

It will help us to critically evaluate Ginet's argument if we exhibit its skeleton.

1   S ought to withhold belief that p if s/he lacks justification for p.[39]
2   What S ought to do S can do.
3   Therefore, S can withhold belief wherever S lacks justification.
4   S has this capacity only if S can tell, with respect to any proposed belief, whether or not S has justification for it.
5   S can always tell us this only if justification is always directly recognizable.
6   Therefore justification ia always directly recognizable.

This bare bones rendition should make it apparent where the argument goes astray. It is at step 5. Step 5 claims that S can tell whether he has justification for a belief only if it is directly recognizable by him whether he does or not. But why should we suppose this? Ginet, in company with almost all contemporary epistemologists, wisely avoids holding that one can know only what is evident to one on simple reflection and what is entailed by that. We know many things only because we have reasons for them in the shape of other things we know, and these reasons are not always deductively related to what they support. Thus direct recognition is only one way to acquire knowledge. Why should we suppose that only this way is available for knowing about justification? That would have to be argued. In the absence of any such argument we are at liberty to deny that justification can always be spotted just by reflection. The argument leaves standing the possibility that S might, in various instances, come to know in some other way whether he has a justification for p.

Consider the ethical analogy that is inevitably suggested by Ginet's argument. There is an exactly parallel argument for the thesis that the justification of actions is always directly recognizable. But that is clearly false. Often I have to engage in considerable research to determine whether a proposed action is justified. If it is a question of whether I would be justified in making a certain decision as department chairman without consulting the executive committee or the department as a whole, I cannot ascertain this just by reflection, unless I have thoroughly internalized the relevant rules, regulations, by-laws, and so on. Most likely I will have to do some research. Would I be legally justified in deducting the cost of a computer on my income tax return? I had better look up the IRS regulations and not just engage in careful reflection. The situation is similar with respect to more strictly moral justification. Would I be morally justified in resigning my professorship as late as April 12 in order to accept a position elsewhere for the following fall? This depends, *inter alia*, on how much inconvenience this would cause my present department, what faculty resources there are already on hand for taking up the slack, how likely it is that a suitable temporary replacement could be secured for the coming fall; and so on. There is no guarantee that all these matters are available to me just on simple reflection. Why should we suppose, without being given reasons to do so, that the justification of beliefs is different in this respect?

Let's remember that in the argument we quoted Ginet supported his position by a *reductio* that runs as follows.

1   Suppose that some part of a justification were not entailed by what is directly recognizable to S.
2   Then S's position could change from having such justification to lacking it without there being any change in what is directly recognizable to s.
3   But then S cannot tell that his position *vis-à-vis* justification has changed.
4   Therefore if S can always tell what his justificatory situation is, no part of a justification can fail to be directly recognizable.

This argument, in step 3, presupposes a strong foundationalism according to which any knowledge I can have is based on what is directly recognizable to me, and this could well be contested. But even if we go along with this, the argument is unsound. The trouble is in 2, in the assumption that *anything* not entailed by the directly recognizable can change with no change in what is directly recognizable. To assume this is to assume that the non-directly recognizable is effectively reflected in what is directly recognizable only if the former is entailed by the latter. For if there are other modes of reflection, then a change in the former will sometimes be mirrored in a change in the latter, even when the former is not *entailed* by the latter. For convenience of exposition, let's lump together everything that is not entailed by anything directly recognizable by me as "the world." It is certainly the better part of reason to recognize that much of the world is not adequately reflected in what *I* can directly recognize; if that were not the case I would be in an immeasurably stronger epistemic position than is the lot of humanity. But to suppose that the world beyond my direct recognition *never* reveals itself in what I can directly recognize would be subversive of the very type of foundationalism this argument presupposes. For in that case the foundations would ground no knowledge of anything beyond themselves except by way of logical deduction. And I am sure that Ginet does not want that. If then a change in "the world" is sometimes reflected in changes in the directly recognizable, why suppose that this is not the case with respect to justification?

Put the matter another way. All that Ginet can extract from his strong foundationalist assumption, his deontological concept of justification, and the "ought implies can" principle, is that it is always possible to determine *from* what is directly recognizable to the subject whether the subject is justified in a certain belief. But that does *not* imply that what does the justifying is itself directly recognizable, or is entailed by what is directly recognizable. It only implies that either it has this status *or* it can be ascertained on the basis of what is directly recognizable.[10]

However, Ginet's argument can easily be transformed into an argument for a more moderate form of AI. To begin with the other extreme, suppose we formulate AI just as the view that to be a justifier an item must be epistemically accessible in some way to the subject. It is not *impossible* for the subject to acquire that bit of knowledge (or justified belief). It does seem that Ginet's argument would establish that much accessibility, granted his premises. If I ought to do something that requires knowing the answer to a certain question, it must be *possible* for me to get that answer.

But what is the significance of this result? What does this constraint exclude? It excludes factors that are in principle unknowable by human beings; but it is dubious that any of the parties to the discussion are disposed to suggest justifiers that satisfy that description. The putative justifiers that internalists typically wish to exclude are items other than beliefs and experiences of the subject. BonJour's clairvoyant subject in "Externalist Theories of Empirical Knowledge" is representative of the disputed territory. This person in fact has clairvoyant powers but has neither any understanding of what is going on nor any good reasons for supposing that these powers are reliable. So far as he can tell, the beliefs simply occur to him, and he is, strangely enough, irresistibly constrained to accept them. What shall we fasten on as the strongest candidate for a justifier here? There are no beliefs or experiences on which the clairvoyant beliefs are based. Let's say that if anything justifies them it is their resulting from the exercise of reliable clairvoyant powers. The subject knows nothing of such powers. But is it *impossible* that he should discover them and discover that they are reliable? I see no reason to suppose that. He might ascertain this just by discovering that these strange beliefs about distant places that apparently just popped into his mind out of nowhere are invariably true. It appears, then, that the requirement of being knowable somehow is too weak to be of much interest.

Perhaps there is a mean between the extremes that is both of some significance and still not too strong to be supportable. We might try requiring knowability, not just on reflection at the moment, but at least without a great deal of research. Admittedly this is quite vague. The vagueness may be reduced by bringing in the notion of what could reasonably be expected in the way of time and effort devoted to searching out the justifiers. These expectations might differ from case to case, depending on the kind of justifiers that would be required, the capacities and initial position of the subjects, and so on. If a belief is based on experience, we would naturally expect the subject to ascertain that right off the bat. If, on the other hand, a belief is based on a large and complex body of evidence, we would not expect the subject to be able to survey all that in a moment. And so on. We might dub this intermediate conception "reasonably immediate accessibility".[11] Although this may seem a more reasonable requirement than Ginet's, and although it obviously is less restrictive, this increase in modesty has not purchased any greater support by Ginet's line of argument. I can't see that an "ought implies can" principle supports a "reasonably immediate accessibility" any more than it supports a direct recognizability. In the absence of further reasons to the contrary, all that would seem to be required by the principle is knowability in some way or other.

We should also consider whether a Ginet-like argument can be mounted on the basis of an indirect control version of a deontological conception of justification. In a word, NO. Ginet's argument depends on the point that knowledge is required to carry out intellectual obligations. But on the indirect control version intellectual obligations do not attach to believing or refraining from believing. Hence the knowledge needed to carry out these obligations is not knowledge of whether there is a justification for some particular belief.

Now let's turn to the question of a higher level extension of AI. It is clear that the AI constraint, like the PI constraint, can be imposed on various levels. We saw that the basic argument for PI equally supported the first and second level constraints. It supported both the claim that a justifier had to be a justified belief, and the claim that one justified belief can justify another only if the subject is justified in the higher level belief that the first belief does adequately support the second. What about the argument for AI? Ginet does not use his argument to support a higher level extension. As noted earlier, he does impose a higher level PI constraint on mediate justification, but he associates no higher level constraint of any kind with his AI position. He takes AI to require only that *justifiers* be directly recognizable, not that it be directly recognizable that they posses justificatory efficacy. And yet his argument supports a higher level AI requirement just as strongly, or weakly, as the lower level requirement. This can be seen as follows. Suppose that the sorts of things that can count as justifiers are always accessible to me, but that it is not always accessible to me which items of these sorts count as justifications for which beliefs. I have access to the justifiers but not to their justificatory efficacy. This will take away my ability to do what I am said to have an obligation to do just as surely as the lack of access to the justifiers themselves. To illustrate, let's suppose that experiences can function as justifiers, and that they are accessible to us. I can always tell what sensory experiences I am having at a given moment. Even so, if I am unable to tell what belief about the current physical environment is justified by a given sensory experience, I am thereby unable to regulate my perceptual beliefs according as they possess or lack experiential justification. Knowing what the facts are doesn't suffice for enabling me to regulate my behavior accordingly; I also have to know the significance of these facts for what I ought to do. Thus the "ought implies can" argument supports the higher level requirement to just the extent to which it supports the lower level requirement.

Thus AI, too, has higher-level troubles. The trouble is not nearly as severe as its PI analogue. For one thing, what is required here is not actual higher level knowledge (justified belief) about justification, but only the capacity to obtain it. Thus we are not required to attribute to all subjects an absurdly inflated body of actual knowledge about the conditions of justification. Second, for the same reason we are not faced with nasty infinite regresses or hierarchies. Since to be justified in believing that p, S need not actually justifiably believe that the alleged justifier is fitted to do its job, but only be capable of ascertaining this, we are not committed to an actual infinite hierarchy of such justified beliefs. Nevertheless there are serious questions as to whether even a modest AI higher level requirement is not too severe. The requirement implies that state of affairs, A, cannot justify me in believing that p unless I am capable of determining that A is a genuine justification for a belief that p. But how many subjects are capable of this? Indeed, there are substantial grounds for scepticism about the possibility of anyone's having adequate reasons for claims about justification. The grounds I have in mind concern the specter of epistemic circularity, the danger that, e.g., any otherwise promising argument for a principle laying down conditions under which perceptual beliefs are justified will have to use perceptual beliefs among its premises. I have considered this problem elsewhere and have concluded that, despite the pervasive presence of epistemic circularity in such arguments, it is possible to be justified in beliefs about the conditions of justification.[12] But even if that rather optimistic conclusion is justified, it still seems that many subjects are not capable of acquiring adequately justified beliefs concerning what justifies what. To go into this properly we would have to decide what it takes for the justification of such beliefs, and there is no time for this lengthy investigation in this paper. Let me just say that it seems eminently plausible that beliefs about what justifies what would have be justified by reasons (not directly justified), and it would seem that such reasons are directly accessible to few, if any of us.

All this suggests limiting AI to the lower level. Something can function as a justifier only if it is (fairly readily) accessible, but in order to function as a justifier it is not necessary that its justificatory efficacy be likewise accessible. At some point we must rely on things just *being* a certain way, without its also being the case that we do or can assure ourselves that they are that way. And this would seem to be the proper place to draw that line. We shall return to this possibility in the last section. For now, let's sharpen the issue by recalling the fact that a reliability account of justification (S is justified in believing that p if and only if S's belief that p was reliably produced) is often attacked on the grounds that justification could not be lost by a loss of reliability, so long as the situation is the same, *so far as we can tell*. Consider a possible world that is indistinguishable from the actual world so far as we can tell, but in which a Cartesian demon has rigged things so that our perceptual beliefs concerning external physical objects are all false, since there are no such objects. Since such a world is indistinguishable (by us) from our world, we would have just as much justification for our perceptual beliefs there as we actually do. But *ex hypothesi* those beliefs would not be reliably formed. Hence reliability is not necessary for justification. Here are some snatches of such an argument from an essay by Richard Foley. (The demon world is called "w".)

If we are willing to grant that in our world some of the propositions S perceptually believes are epistemically rational, then these same propositions would be epistemically rational for S in w as well. After all, world w by hypothesis is one which from S's viewpoint is indistinguishable from this world. So, if given S's situation in this world his perceptual belief p is rational, his belief p would be rational in w as well.

Even if, contrary to what we believe, our world is world w, it still can be epistemically rational for us to believe many of the propositions we do, since the epistemic situation in world w is indistinguishable from the epistemic situation in a world which has the characteristics we take our world to have. The point here is a simple one. In effect, I am asking you: aren't some of the propositions you believe epistemically rational for you to believe? And wouldn't whatever it is that make those propositions epistemically rational for you also be present in a world where these propositions are regularly false, but where a demon hid this from you by making the world from your viewpoint indistinguishable from this world (so that what you believed, and what you would believe on reflection, and what you seemed to remember, and what you experienced were identical to this world)?[13]

In each of these passages the fact that we cannot distinguish w from the actual world is taken to imply that whatever justifies a certain belief in the one world will ipso facto justify that same belief in the other world. This argument presupposes an AI internalist constraint on both levels. For suppose AI put constraints only on what can count as a justifier, not also on what has justificatory efficacy for which beliefs. In that case the reliablist would remain free to claim that although the same putative justifiers (of perceptual beliefs) are present in the two worlds, they do justify perceptual beliefs in the actual world but not in w, since their production of perceptual beliefs is reliable in the actual world but not in w. If and only if justificatory efficacy were subject to an AI constraint would this be impossible, as Foley claims. If, on the other hand, one follows my suggestion that we adopt an accessibility constraint only on the lower level, we can recognize that a state of affairs, A, can justify a belief that p in one possible world and not in another, even though we can't tell any difference between the two worlds.

IV

The upshot of the paper is that existing forms of internalism are in serious trouble. Both PI and AI run into severe difficulties over their higher level component, but if we try shearing off that component we lose such support as has been provided them. That support is less than impressive in any case. The only arguments of any substance that have been advanced proceed from a deontological conception of justification and inherit any disabilities that attach to that conception. Indeed, PI gains significant support only from the most restrictive form of a direct voluntary control version of that conception, one that is, at best, of limited application to our beliefs. As for AI, the arguments in the literature that are designed to establish a direct recognizability version markedly fail to do so. And it is not clear that a more moderate form of AI can be developed that will be both well supported by these arguments and strong enough to have any cutting edge.

Thus internalism has not emerged in strong shape from this examination. It looks as if no sort of internalist constraint can be justified, and hence that an unrestricted externalism wins the day. However I do not believe that so extreme a conclusion is warranted. I am convinced that the considerations advanced in this paper show that existing versions of internalism are untenable, and that such arguments as have been advanced for them fail to establish any form of that position. And yet I am inclined to suppose that a suitably modest form of AI internalism can be supported, though in a very different way from any employed by the internalists we have been discussing. If any readers have persevered this far, I will not further test their patience by embarking on a full dress development and defense of this suggestion, but I will just indicate what I have in mind.

Earlier I indicated that what I called a strong position (SP) conception of justification does not support any sort of internalist restriction. One can believe that p in such a way as to be in a strong position to acquire the truth whether or not that belief is supported adequately by other of one's justified beliefs (PI), and whether or not one has strong epistemic access to the grounds for the belief. In my "Concepts of Epistemic Justification" I have argued for the superiority of the PS conception over any kind of deontological conception. Thus, so far as these options for a concept of justification are concerned, pure externalism reigns supreme. Nevertheless I do not take this to be the last word. Even if internalist intuitions cannot be supported by the most basic features of the concept of justification, they may have a certain validity on their own, as an independent contribution to the concept. Let's once more consider "out of the blue" reliable modes of belief formation. Let's say that when I am suddenly seized with apparently irrational convictions concerning the current weather in some distant spot, these convictions always turn out to be correct. If there is nothing to justification other than believing in such a way as to be in a strong position to acquire the truth, then we should say that I am justified in those convictions. And yet we are loath to admit this, at least before I become aware of the reliability of this mode of belief formation. (After I become aware of this I have an adequate reason for the convictions, and this should satisfy any internalist scruples.) Why this reluctance? What is missing? What is missing, of course, is any basis or ground that S *has, possesses*, for his belief, anything that he can point to or specify as that which gives him *something to go on* in believing this, any *sign* or *indication* he has that the belief is true. Wherever nothing like this is involved, we feel uneasy in taking S's belief to be *justified*. Thus it looks as if there is a basic, irreducible, requirement of *epistemic accessibility of ground for the belief* that attaches to our concept of epistemic justification.[11] For reasons we have rehearsed at some length, let's take the accessibility required to be of the relatively modest sort that we earlier called "reasonably immediate accessibility".

Can this requirement be derived from other features of the concept? It certainly cannot be derived from an SP conception, and we have seen that such support as it gleans from a deontological conception would bring fatal difficulties with it, even if such a conception were viable for epistemology. I am inclined to think that the requirement is a fundamental constituent of our concept of epistemic justification, though I do not take that to imply that there can be no sort of explanation for its presence. I will conclude by briefly adumbrating what I take to be responsible for this internalist feature of the concept.

My suggestion is that the background against which the concept of epistemic justification has developed is the practice of critical reflection on our beliefs, the practice of the epistemic assessment of beliefs (with respect to the likelihood of their being true), the challenging of beliefs and responses to such challenges. To respond successfully to such a challenge one must specify an adequate ground of the belief, a ground that provides a sufficient indication of the truth of the belief. It would, of course, be absurd to suggest that in order to be epistemically respectable, laudatory, or acceptable (justified) a belief must have actually been put to such a test and have emerged victorious. In suggesting that the concept has developed against the background of such a practice the idea is rather that what it is for a belief to be justified is that the belief and its ground be such that it is in a position to pass such a test; that the subject has what it takes to respond successfully to such a challenge.[15] A justified belief is one that *could* survive a critical reflection. But then the justifier must be accessible to the subject. Otherwise the subject would be in no position to cite it as what provides a sufficient indication that the belief is true. This, baldly stated, is what I take to be the explanation of the presence of an AI internalist constraint in the concept of epistemic justification. Further development of this suggestion must await another occasion.

Notes

1 See e.g., Laurence BonJour, "Externalist Theories of Empirical Knowledge", *Midwest Studies in Philosophy*, Vol. V (1980).
2 BonJour, "Externalist Theories", p. 55.
3 p. 55.
4 p. 56.
5 The *Monist*, Vol. 68, no. 2 (April, 1985), p. 247.
6 *Midwest Studies in Philosophy*, Vol. V (1980), p. 32. Later in this essay Goldman considers what conditions should be laid down for the acceptance of a *doxastic decision principle* (DDP). A DDP is a "function whose *inputs* are certain conditions of a cognizer – e.g., his beliefs, perceptual field, and ostensive memories – and whose *outputs* are prescriptions to adopt (or retain) this or that doxastic attitude . . ." (p. 29) Here is what he takes to be "the condition appropriate to *externalism*":

   (1)   DDP X is right if and only if: X is *actually* optimal.

Whereas the first shot at formulating an appropriate condition for internalism is the following.

(2)   DDP X is right if and only if: we are *justified* in believing that X is optimal. (pp. 33–4)

7   Note that in the passage quoted above Kent Bach says that "internalism requires that a person have 'cognitive grasp' of whatever makes his belief justified". This too would seem to allow that what makes the belief justified could be an item of any (suitable) sort, provided the person has a "cognitive grasp" of it.

8   Thus although in that passage BonJour is arguing against the existence of "basic beliefs", i.e., immediately justified beliefs, the argument, if successful, will rule out only *purely* basic beliefs. It will not rule out beliefs a part of whose justification consists in something other than justified beliefs of the same subject.

9   What I am calling "BonJour's version" does not represent his considered position, which is more like the other version. However the former is suggested by the passage under discussion. Perhaps BonJour was led into it there because he was arguing with a partisan of immediate knowledge who claims that a certain non-belief is sufficient for the justification of a certain belief. Having no reason to deny that the non-doxastic state of affairs obtains, BonJour simply confined himself to alleging that even if it does obtain, the subject will also have to be justified in believing that it obtains.

10   I shall use "overrider" for something that cancels out a *prima facie* justification. Unlike some theorists I shall refrain from using "defeater" for this purpose, saving that term (though not using it in this paper) for a fact the mere holding of which prevents a true, overall justified belief from counting as knowledge.

11   Thus principle (B) in R. M. Chisholm, *Theory of Knowledge*, 2nd edn. (Englewood Cliffs, NJ: Prentice-Hall, Inc., 1977) runs as follows.

(B)   For any subject S, if S believes, without ground for doubt, that he is perceiving something to be F, then it is beyond reasonable doubt for S that he perceives something to be F.

And "ground for doubt" is explained as follows.

(D4.3)   S believes, *without ground for doubt*, that p = Df (i) S believes that p and (ii) no conjunction of propositions that are acceptable for S tends to confirm the negation of the proposition that p. (p. 76)

The PI constraint comes in by requiring "grounds for doubt" that consists in propositions that are "acceptable" for the subject, in order that the *prima facie* justification of perceptual beliefs be overthrown.

12   "A Plethora of Epistemological Theories", in George S. Pappas, ed., *Justification and Knowledge* (Dordrecht: D. Reidel Pub. Co., 1979), p. 101.

13   To be sure, there are more alternatives than the ones we have mentioned. In his book, *Knowledge* (Oxford: Clarendon Press, 1974), Keith Lehrer pumps for a coherence theory in which the test of justification is coherence, not with the actual set of beliefs of the subject but with what Lehrer calls the subject's "corrected doxastic system", that subset "resulting when every statement is deleted which describes S as believing something he would cease to believe as an impartial and distinterested truth-seeker". (p. 190)

14   "Can Empirical Knowledge Have a Foundation?", *American Philosophical Quarterly*, 15, 1 (Jan., 1978), p. 5.

15   Of course the "feature" could be so specified that it included the subject's justified beliefs about another feature. But then it would be this latter features with respect to which BonJour is requiring the justified beliefs, and the point would still hold.

16   See, e.g., Richard Foley, "What's Wrong with Reliabilism?", *The Monist*, Vol. 68, no. 2 (April, 1985).

17   This requirement for mediate justification is embraced by many epistemologists who do not advocate (4) with its denial of any immediate justification. See, e.g., Carl Ginet, *Knowledge, Perception, and Memory* (Dordrecht: D. Reidel Pub. Co., 1975), pp. 47–9.

18   BonJour, "Externalist Theories", p. 63.

19   Keith Lehrer, op. cit., pp. 187–8.

20   Pollock, "A Plethora of Epistemological Theories", p. 106. This does not represent Pollock's overall view.

21   This argument may be thought of as a development of BonJour's suggestion that the subject must "possess the justification" for the belief "if *his* acceptance of it is to be epistemically rational or responsible". ("Externalist Theories . . .", p. 55.)

22   Note that what this argument supports is a *positive, local justification* version of PI. But precisely parallel arguments can be given for other versions. For the suggestion of such an argument for a *negative, local justification* version, see the quotation from Wolterstorff in the following footnote. For an argument for a mere belief version, whether local or holistic, see Pollock's "A Plethora of Epistemological Theories", p. 109.

23   Here are some adumbrations of this argument. ". . . on the externalist view, a person may be ever so irrational and irresponsible in accepting a belief, when judged in light of his own subjective conception of the situation, and may still turn out to satisfy Armstrong's general criterion of reliability. This belief may in fact be reliable, even though the person has no reason for thinking that it is reliable . . . But such a person seems nonetheless to be thoroughly irresponsible from an epistemic standpoint in accepting such a belief, and hence not justified, contrary to externalism." (BonJour, "Externalist Theories . . .", p. 59.) Here is

another adumbration, this time from the standpoint of a negative coherence theory that holds a belief to be justified provided one has no sufficient reason for giving it up. "If a person does not have adequate reason to refrain from some belief of his, what could possibly oblige him to give it up? Conversely, if he surrenders some belief of his as soon as he has adequate reason to do so, what more can rightly be demanded of him? Is he not then using the capacities he has for governing his beliefs, with the goal of getting more amply in touch with reality, as well as can rightly be demanded of him?" (Nicholas Wolterstorff, "Can Belief in God Be Rational?", in Alvin Plantinga and Nicholas Wolterstorff, eds., *Faith and Rationality* (Notre Dame, IN: University of Notre Dame Press, 1983), p. 1963. Note the crucial occurrence in these passages of terms like "irresponsible", "oblige", and "rightly demanded". Both these authors, as well as other PI internalists, note the parallel between what is required for epistemic and for ethical justification. In both cases, it is argued, what is required is that the belief or the action be the one to adopt, so far as one can tell from one's own viewpoint on the world.

24 "Concepts of Epistemic Justification", *The Monist*, Vol. 68, no. 2 (Jan., 1985). For other developments of the deontological conception see Ginet, *Knowledge, Perception, and Memory*, Wolterstorff, "Can Belief in God Be Rational", and M. B. Naylor, "Epistemic Justification", 1978, unpublished.

25 BonJour is an exception in trying to combine features of the two conceptions. On the one hand, he argues for PI from a deontological conception of justification. On the other hand, as we have seen, he presupposes the truth-conductivity of justification in formulating his higher-level requirement.

26 Thus Wolterstorff: "Locke assumes – rightly in my judgment – that we have an obligation to govern our assent with the goal in mind of getting more amply in touch with reality." Wolterstorff, "Can Belief in God Be Rational?", p. 145.

27 There are other ways in which a subject's epistemic situation might have been different from what it actually is had the subject been doing a better job of carrying out his/her intellectual obligations. In particular, the subject might have had justifiers that s/he does not actually possess. However it is not at all clear that this and other differences from the actual situation have the same bearing on justification as the lack of overriders that one should have had. Consider a case in which if I had been attending to the matter as I should have I would have had justified beliefs that adequately support the belief that Jones is untrustworthy. As things actually stand I do not have adequate reasons for supposing that. Here, going on the justified beliefs I actually have, we would have to say that I would not be justified in believing that Jones is untrustworthy. But nor does it seem that that judgment would be reversed by the consideration that I would have had adequate support had I been conducting myself properly. Surely we don't want to say that the thing for me to do is to adopt that belief *in the absence of sufficient reasons*, whatever would have been the case had I been satisfying my intellectual obligations.

28   At a few points in the preceding exposition the need for this qualification was
     more or less evident. Thus at one point I represented the deontologist as saying
     that the justification of a given belief depends on the "best representation of the
     world of which I am currently capable". I have also used such phrases as "one's
     best judgment of the facts" and "so far as one can tell". All of these phrases
     point to the "ideal viewpoint" rather than to the actual viewpoint. The best rep-
     resentation of the world of which I am currently capable may not be the repre-
     sentation I actually have. There will be a discrepancy provided, as is usually the
     case to some extent, I have not made full use of my opportunities for ascertain-
     ing relevant features of the world. The importance of overriders that a subject
     ought to have but doesn't is well brought out by Wolterstorff, "Can Belief in God
     Be Rational?", pp. 165–6.
29   For a discussion of this issue see my "Concepts of Epistemic Justification".
30   If this latter sort of reason is required, that constitutes a serious stumbling block,
     for it seems that we are rarely justified in any such belief, unless the requirements
     for justification are set very low. But that is not our present concern.
31   Goldman, "The Internalist Conception of Justification", p. 35. Remember that
     a DDP is, roughly, a principle that declares certain beliefs to be justified under
     certain conditions. Therefore the requirement that there be maximal epistemic
     access to a DDP is an AI analogue of what we were calling the "higher level
     requirement" component of PI. Interestingly enough, when it comes to a high
     accessibility "lower level requirement" with respect to justifiers, "input to the
     DDP" in Goldman's lingo, Goldman lays this down on his own, with no hint
     that it is required by internalism as contrasted with externalism. "If a DDP is to
     be actually *usable* for making deliberate decisions the conditions that serve as
     inputs must be *accessible* or *available* to the decision-maker at the time of decision.
     The agent must be *able to tell*, with respect to any possible input condition,
     whether that condition holds at the time in question." (p. 30) He even spells this
     out in such a way that it is *infallible* access that is required. "But what exactly do
     we mean in saying that a person 'can tell' with respect to a given condition
     whether or not that condition obtains? Here is a reasonable answer: 'For any
     person S and time t, if S asks himself at t whether condition C obtains at the
     time in question, then S will believe that condition C obtains then if and only if
     it does obtain then.'" (31).
32   K. Bach, "Rationale for Reliabilism", p. 250. Cf. p. 252.
33   Chisholm, *Theory of Knowledge*, p. 17. The quotation is from C. I. Lewis, *Mind
     and the World Order*. It should be acknowledged that in a later essay Chisholm
     states this assumption only for "some of the things I am justified in believing".
     See "A Version of Foundationalism", *Midwest Studies in Philosophy*, Vol. V (1980),
     p. 546.
34   *Knowledge, Perception, and Memory* (Dordrecht: D. Reidel Pub. Co., 1975), p. 34.
35   Ginet, *Knowledge, Perception, and Memory*, p. 36.
36   Ginet, *Knowledge, Perception, and Memory*, p. 28.
37   Ginet, *Knowledge, Perception, and Memory*, p. 28.

38 In "Contra Reliabilism", *The Monist*, Vol. 68, no. 2 (April, 1985), Ginet defends this assumption against objections from myself. Note that Ginet's argument could easily be recast in an "indirect voluntary control" form. Instead of premising that it is always possible to decide whether or not to believe, or to continue believing, that p in the light of the presence or absence of a sufficient justification, one can hold instead that it is always possible to decide whether to do various things to encourage or discourage belief that p, in the light of the presence or absence of a sufficient justification. The direct recognizability of justifiers will be as strongly supported by this version as by the original version.

39 Ginet recognizes that we are intellectually obligated to refrain from believing that p in the absence of justification, but he wisely holds back from claiming that we are obligated to believe that p wherever we have a justification. The presence of justification gives me a *right* to believe, but I am not obliged to exercise that right; I have a choice as to whether or not to do so. It seems plausible to hold, e.g., that I am justified in believing everything that is entailed by my justified beliefs. But an infinite set of beliefs is so entailed. Thus if I were obligated to believe everything for which I have a justification I would be in a pretty pickle. Ginet's recognition of this point is evinced by his modifying "S *ought* always to possess or lack confidence that p according to whether or not he has such justification" to "At least he ought always to withhold confidence unless he has justification".

40 We could also attack the direct accessibility form of AI by pointing to the fact that not all commonly recognized justifiers satisfy the contraint. Remember that when we were considering the relations of PI and AI we pointed out that one cannot, in general, retrieve all relevant justified beliefs of oneself just on reflection.

41 Note that all these accessibility requirements, of whatever degree of stringency, can be thought of as related to PI in the same way. Any item that is epistemically accessible to S can be thought of as potentially an item in S's perspective on the world. Hence any sort of AI can be thought of as a broadening of PI to include potential additions to the perspective, as well as its present constituents.

42 See my "Epistemic Circularity", forthcoming in *Philosophy and Phenomenological Research*.

43 Richard Foley, "What's Wrong with Reliabilism?", *The Monist*, Vol. 68, no. 2 (April, 1985). See also Carl Ginet, "Contra Reliabilism", ibid.

44 Since I do not find any like tendency to withhold the concept of justification when the justificatory efficacy of the ground is not readily accessible to the subject, I am not saddled with the burden of a higher level accessibility constraint.

45 One indication that this is the right way to think about justification is the fact that we find it incongruous to apply the concept to beings that are incapable of critical reflection on their beliefs. The question of whether a dog is *justified* in supposing that his master is at the door is one that does not seem to arise. There are, to be sure, problems as to just how this restriction is to be interpreted. It

seems clearly all right to apply the concept to human beings that have little skill at the game of challenge and response. The applicability to small children is less clear, but note that in both these cases we are dealing with beings that belong to a species many members of which are capable of critical reflection a full blooded form.

4

How Internal Can You Get?

Hilary Kornblith

There has been a debate of late among epistemologists concerning the proper form of a theory of justification. The debate is between those who see themselves as internalists about justification and those who see themselves as externalists about justification. Precisely what it means to be either an internalist or an externalist is itself a matter of debate. In this kind of situation, where the very content of a position becomes an issue, one does well to go back to motivations; one needs to ask why it is that anyone ever defended a version of the position at issue. Only then can one understand what the issues really are.

My focus in this paper will be on internalism. I want to ask, among other questions, why anyone ever wanted to be an internalist and what it is that internalism is supposed to achieve. But one cannot, I think, approach these questions directly. One must first have a specimen internalist on the table, so to speak. I will thus begin by examining some features of Laurence BonJour's defense of internalism in *The Structure of Empirical Knowledge*. I choose BonJour's book as a starting point because among its many virtues are its pellucid style and its well-defined motivation. One could not ask for a better entree into the issues which separate internalists from externalists.

In spite of my great admiration for BonJour's book, I find myself in agreement with very little of it. I will isolate one central point of disagreement, surrounding what BonJour calls the Doxastic Presumption. By examining the role which this Presumption plays in BonJour's book, I hope to expose some serious difficulties for BonJour's form of internalism and, at the same time, to cast some light on the limitations of any possible internalist position.

1

BonJour defends a coherence theory of justification. Such theories typically hold that an agent's belief is justified just in case that belief coheres with the rest of the agent's beliefs. Having motivated just such an account of justification, BonJour comments,

> What we must now ask is whether and how the fact that a belief coheres in this way is cognitively accessible to the believer himself, so that it can give *him* a reason for accepting the belief. (101)

BonJour's demand that the fact of coherence be cognitively accessible to the agent seems reasonable, for it is hard to see how facts beyond the agent's ken can serve as reasons *for that agent*. The fact that Ronald Reagan lives in the White House may provide some objective reason for believing that he is President, but it does not provide me with reason for believing that he is President unless the fact is one of which I am aware. It is observations such as these which motivate BonJour's demand for cognitive accessibility. Moreover, it is the requirement of cognitive accessibility which gives birth to internalism. We shall need to examine this notion of cognitive accessibility with some care later, but for now I wish merely to see how it functions in shaping BonJour's brand of coherentism.

Thus far, BonJour requires that if an agent is to be justified in her belief, that belief must cohere with the rest of her beliefs, and this fact must be cognitively accessible to her. This will lead to still further requirements:

> if the fact of coherence is to be accessible to the believer, it follows that he must somehow have an adequate grasp of his total system of beliefs, since it is coherence with this system which is at issue. (102)

Moreover, as BonJour notes,

> Most proponents of coherence theories seem, surprisingly enough, either to take the believer's grasp of his own system of beliefs for granted, or simply to ignore the issue of whether their envisaged coherentist justification is accessible to the believer himself. (102–3)

Here, I believe, BonJour displays a far more subtle understanding of the coherence theory than anything previously available in the literature. If part of one's motivation for adopting a coherence theory is the desire strictly to obey the requirement of cognitive accessibility, then one cannot duck the issue of the accessibility of an agent's beliefs.[1] It is a virtue of BonJour's account that he takes this issue seriously.

One obvious move for a coherentist to make at this point is to suggest that an agent's understanding of the contents of her beliefs is itself justified by way of coherence. But BonJour rejects this move.

> it is beyond any doubt viciously circular to claim that the metabeliefs which constitute the believer's grasp of his system of beliefs are themselves justified by virtue of their coherence with that system. (102)

Instead, BonJour suggests that the agent's understanding of her own beliefs occupies a special role in the epistemological enterprise.

> since the basic unit of justification for a coherence theory is an entire system of beliefs, . . . the raising of an issue of empirical justification *presupposes* the existence of some specifiable *system* of empirical beliefs – or rather, . . . of *approximately* that system; the primary justificatory issue is whether or not, under the presumption that I do indeed hold approximately the beliefs which I believe myself to hold, those beliefs are justified. (103)

On BonJour's view, the question which gives rise to the epistemological enterprise is this: given that you have at least roughly the beliefs you take yourself to have, what makes you justified in holding those beliefs? This question presumes that one has at least a rough and ready grasp of the contents of one's beliefs, and this is what BonJour calls the Doxastic Presumption. One cannot even begin the epistemological enterprise without making this Presumption. It is forced on us. We must make this Presumption if we are to raise epistemological questions at all.

It is BonJour's internalism which raises the issue of our understanding of the contents of our beliefs, for without the requirement of cognitive accessibility, the question of an agent's grasp of her system of beliefs would not have been raised. In order to resolve this issue, BonJour is forced to make the Doxastic Presumption, for the Presumption cannot be justified by appealing to its coherence with one's other beliefs without vicious circularity. Nevertheless, BonJour argues, the Doxastic Presumption is not one which he alone is required to make; rather, such a Presumption is implicated in the entire epistemological enterprise. Questions about justification do not even make sense, according to BonJour, unless one has already made the Doxastic Presumption.

2

The Doxastic Presumption, then, is just this: at least most of an agent's beliefs about the beliefs she has – BonJour calls these the agent's metabeliefs – must be true. When put in this form, the Doxastic Presumption should be reminiscent of a claim Sydney Shoemaker made in *Self-Knowledge and Self-Identity*, that at least most of an agent's sincerely asserted memory statements must be true, and it should also be reminiscent of arguments which Normal Malcolm attributed to Wittgenstein (see the essays collected in Malcolm 1963), that most of our beliefs about the external world must be true. The principles of Shoemaker and Malcolm have been widely criticized as verificationist,[2] and so it is natural to wonder whether BonJour's Doxastic Presumption might not itself be subject to the same criticism.

The charge of verificationism would be better supported if BonJour claimed that the Doxastic Presumption is true, but he makes no such claim. Indeed, BonJour acknowledges that if he were to claim that the Doxastic Presumption is true, he could only do so on verificationist grounds, which he rejects (105). BonJour therefore acknowledges that he has no answer to a certain "unusual" form of scepticism, namely scepticism about our access to our own beliefs. BonJour is forthright in acknowledging the consequences of this failure.

> What the discussion leading up to the Doxastic Presumption shows is precisely that a coherence theory of empirical justification cannot, in principle, answer this form of scepticism; and this seems to me to count in favor of the sceptic, not against him. (105)

On BonJour's view, someone who is sceptical about our access to our beliefs simply cannot be answered.

What then is the force of the Doxastic Presumption once this concession is made? BonJour presents three different reasons for thinking that the Presumption has a great deal of force nonetheless.

First,

> Certainly it would be a very unusual brand of scepticism which would challenge whether my belief B is justified by raising the issue of whether I do in fact accept B, the normal sceptical claim being precisely that certain beliefs which are in fact held are nonetheless unjustified. (81)

Here BonJour is claiming that this brand of scepticism is of quite a different and more contrived form than the usual brand of scepticism. So those who are interested in responding to the most significant variety of scepticism need not be worried here.

Second,

> there can obviously be no objection to asking what follows about the justification of the rest of my beliefs from the presumption that my representation of my own system of beliefs is approximately correct. (106)

Surely we must grant that if BonJour can show that simply by making this assumption he can show the rest of our beliefs to be justified relative to it, he has accomplished a great deal.

Finally, and most important,

> Epistemic reflection . . . *begins* from a (perhaps tacit) representation of myself as having (approximately) such and such a specific system of beliefs; only relative to such a representation can questions of justification be meaningfully raised and answered. (104)

Here, of course, is BonJour's strongest claim for the force of the Doxastic Presumption: questions of justification cannot meaningfully be raised without making the Doxastic Presumption. Those who refuse to make the Presumption must cease talking about justification at all. Those who raise issues about justification thereby commit themselves to the Presumption.

3

I do not believe that BonJour is correct about the status and force of the Doxastic Presumption. I will argue that the kind of scepticism associated with rejecting the Doxastic Presumption is not at all unusual, and, indeed, that it is continuous with other forms of scepticism. There is no more reason to be sanguine about our access to our own beliefs than there is to be sanguine about our access to the external world. But I wish to argue for far more than this. Doubts about the powers of introspection do not constitute a bizarre sceptical hypothesis. Instead, there is currently very good psychological evidence to suggest that we ought to be especially cautious about claims for the reliability of introspection. Moreover, the doubts I have about the powers of introspection are not a product of some general scepticism; I have no serious doubts at all about our knowledge of the external world.

In the course of raising my doubts about introspection, I hope to show, as well, that one may certainly reject the Doxastic Presumption without thereby undermining one's right to talk about justification. The Doxastic Presumption is not implicated in all talk about justification. It has no special epistemic status at all.

I want to begin my discussion of these issues by asking why it is that BonJour's Doxastic Presumption takes the form it does. In particular, why is the Presumption so qualified as to require only that our access to our beliefs be approximately correct? Why shouldn't we ask what follows from the supposition that our access to our beliefs is perfect, instead of asking what follows from the supposition that our access to our beliefs is very good? So let us consider the claim that all of our meta-beliefs – our beliefs about what beliefs we have – are true, and let us call this claim the Presumptuous Presumption. Why does BonJour take the weaker Doxastic Presumption as his starting point rather than the stronger Presumptuous Presumption?

This question is easily answered. The principle difficulty with the Presumptuous Presumption is that it is obviously false. There are, of course, possibilities of self-deception. Anyone who has read even a bit of Freud may be put in such a cognitive state as reasonably to wonder whether some of her meta-beliefs might be false. BonJour is well aware of such possibilities, and he recognizes that the question of the justification of some of our meta-beliefs may be highly non-trivial. Regarding such beliefs he says that, "the issue of their justification can be raised and answered in particular, relatively confined cases which are for some reason especially problematic" (105). Once BonJour acknowledges this point, however, he is no longer in a position to claim that scepticism about introspective access is "a very unusual brand of scepticism".

Consider the opening of Descartes' *Meditations*. Descartes points out that he has frequently made mistakes about the external world, and this leads him to ask whether it is possible that all of his beliefs about the world are mistaken. The very fact that he has made mistakes at all makes Descartes alive to the possibility of mistake. Being a realist about the external world, he realizes that facts about the external world are radically independent of facts about his beliefs, and this leads him to ask whether he might not be completely out of touch with the world as it really is.

Someone who is a realist about belief, and who has been reading Freud, might be led by a similar chain of reasoning to doubt her access to her own beliefs. Certainly she will be aware that she has made mistakes about her beliefs in the past. Being a realist about belief, she will hold that facts about her beliefs are radically independent of her beliefs about her beliefs. As a result, she will be led to wonder whether she might not be radically out of touch with her own mental states, and, in particular, with her beliefs.

So scepticism about introspective access to our beliefs is continuous with scepticism about sensory access to the external world. Both have their source in realism. Being a realist, BonJour cannot deny the coherence of either kind of scepticism. More important, however, he cannot attempt to drive a wedge between these two forms of scepticism and claim that one of them is somehow more fundamental than the other.

What of BonJour's claim that a sceptic about introspective access must cut herself out of the epistemological enterprise? I see no reason to think that the kind of scepticism I have just described deprives one of the possibility of forming epistemological questions. The sceptic I have described is led to her scepticism by recognizing the possibility of error in her beliefs about her own mental states. She therefore raises the question, which she at least provisionally finds herself unable to answer, whether she is radically out of touch with her beliefs. This question about the extent of our contact with some aspect of reality is, I take it, a paradigm of the epistemological enterprise. Our sceptic can perfectly well formulate this question, even after she has embraced her scepticism.

BonJour, of course, is concerned about whether such a sceptic can formulate questions about justification in particular, and I assume that his reason for thinking that the sceptic about introspection cannot formulate such questions is that, on BonJour's conception of justification, justifying one's beliefs requires the appeal to other beliefs. In depriving herself of the possibility of such appeals, the introspective sceptic undercuts the possibility of justification. But even if we allow this, this does not show that our sceptic is unable to formulate her question; it shows only that she cannot answer it. And this hardly cuts her off from the epistemological enterprise. It surely does not deprive her questions of their meaning.

If I am right, then, BonJour's attempt to show that the Doxastic Presumption is implicated in the epistemological enterprise is mistaken. One can meaningfully ask epistemological questions, and even questions about justification, after one has rejected the Doxastic Presumption. This is a small point, however. For one might still hold that, although the status of the Doxastic Presumption is not quite as strong as BonJour claims, it still has some privileged epistemic status.[3] We must therefore turn now to the question of the epistemic status of the Doxastic Presumption. I will argue that although there is a grain of truth of be found in BonJour's claim about the presumptions of the epistemological enterprise, what remains of the Doxastic presumption is not enough to support internalism.

4

As Quine has argued, scepticism has its roots in the progress of science. Science shows us quite vividly the falsity of our earlier beliefs, and it is through the recognition of this possibility that scepticism gets a footing. In the case of scepticism about the powers of introspection, the relevant science is psychology, and ever since Freud we have been given vivid illustrations upon which sceptical doubts may feed. Much recent work on introspection goes far beyond the Freudian cases of motivationally driven mistakes, illustrating ways in which we may go wrong which are more nearly akin to visual illusions than they are to self-deception.

It is impossible to provide a review of the literature on introspection here, or even a review of that part of the literature which has the most direct bearing on epistemology.[1] I will instead be content to summarize some of the more important results of this literature, having argued for these claims elsewhere (Kornblith, 1989, 1993). I wish to present an account of the epistemological importance of our introspective access to our mental states and processes which sheds some light on the epistemic status of the Doxastic Presumption.

Let me begin with a few brief comments about perception. Our perceptual apparatus provides us with a ready source of information about the world. The success and speed of our perceptual mechanisms are achieved by processes which are tailored to contingent features of the world. We are able to perceive objects so readily because our perceptual processes have a built-in tendency to assume the presence of medium-sized physical objects with relatively well-defined boundaries. By the same token, this tendency leads us to make errors in situations where conditions are atypical. The visual illusions reveal the presuppositions of our perceptual apparatus. They also show us its limitations, and the respects in which atypical environments may mislead us.

There is reason to think that introspection, at least at this level of description, works in much the same way. We are able reliably to gain information about our internal states at the cost of assuming certain standard conditions. When conditions are non-standard we tend to make errors. Our speed and reliability are a product of the fact that there are certain kinds of conditions which typically obtain; our errors are a product of the fact that these conditions do not always obtain. The patterns in our errors reveal to us the presuppositions of our introspective faculty.

None of this suggests that introspection in unreliable. Indeed, on the contrary, it suggests that the introspective faculty is reliable; it tends to provide us with accurate information about our mental states.[5] This account also suggests that there will be certain conditions under which we should be especially suspicious of the deliverances of introspection, just as there are certain conditions under which the deliverances of perception are unreliable.

What implications does this have for the Doxastic Presumption? If I am right, the Doxastic Presumption is very likely true; our beliefs about our beliefs are probably at least approximately true. But on my account, the Doxastic Presumption is a very high-level empirical discovery. It does not have any privileged epistemic status. Psychological experimentation might have revealed that it was false. Instead of revealing that there are blindspots in our ability to introspect our mental states, psychological experimentation might have revealed very substantial and widespread unreliability. Fortunately, this is not the case. But the manner in which we have come to recognize the truth of the Doxastic Presumption shows that it has no previleged epistemic status at all.[6]

The situation with our meta-beliefs is much like the situation with common sense. Could what passes from common sense turn out to be false? Certainly there are many cases in which the progress of science has shown us that common sense was in error. Could all of what currently passes for common sense be mistaken? There seems no a priori reason why not. Just as science has overthrown important parts of common sense, any particular bit of common sense might be overthrown by further scientific progress. Indeed, all of what currently passes for common sense could be rejected by some future science. The route from our current understanding of the world to this future science would be one in which common sense is destroyed piece-meal, rather than all at once, but common sense certainly could be forced to make further and further concessions to science until nothing is left of common sense at all. Such a possibility cannot be ruled out a priori.

Even if science can eventually undermine common sense, the fact remains that science begins with common sense. Where else, after all, could science begin? It is in this observation that the grain of truth in the Doxastic Presumption is to be found. BonJour holds that the Doxastic Presumption must be made for as long as one wishes to engage in epistemological inquiry. At the same time, BonJour repeatedly states that epistemological inquiry must *begin* with the Doxastic Presumption (pp. 104, 105, 127), and this suggests a weaker position. One might suggest merely that epistemological inquiry begins in the assumption of approximate access to one's beliefs, although this assumption may subsequently be rejected with the progress of inquiry, without thereby undermining the very enterprise of inquiry.

I do believe that the Doxastic Presumption has this latter, weaker status. Inquiry must begin with such an assumption, although the assumption is defeasible without thereby defeating the enterprise of inquiry. But even here there are significant differences between the weakened version of BonJour's position and my own. For BonJour claims that the Doxastic Presumption has some special epistemological status; there is something distinctive, on BonJour's position, about the role our access to our beliefs plays in episte-mology. But much as I think that the epistemological enterprise cannot get off the ground without tentatively making the Doxastic Presumption, I believe that this is merely a special case of a much stronger presumption which must be made. I will call this the Presumption of Epistemic Access.

BonJour rightly claims that epistemological inquiry cannot begin without taking our meta-beliefs at face value; we must begin by assuming that our grasp of our cognitive system is at least approximately correct. The Quinean position I favor is just that inquiry cannot begin without taking all of our beliefs at face value; we begin by assuming that all of our beliefs are at least approximately correct. This is not to say, of course, that we hold even this claim of approximate truth to be incorrigible – that we hold it immune from revision. On the contrary, we hold none of our beliefs immune from revision in the face of the progress of inquiry. But unless our cognitive faculties which give rise to spontaneous beliefs put us on the right track, knowledge is surely impossible. This is true not only of the faculty of introspection, which gives us access to our mental states, but of our sensory faculties as well, which provide us with our access to the external world. Unless our sensory faculties give rise to beliefs about the world which are in some sense on the right track, we can never hope to obtain knowledge of the world through any kind of internal adjustment of our beliefs.

The Presumption of Epistemic Access is the presumption that our cogni-tive faculties put us on the right track toward truth. The practical import of making this presumption is that it allows us to take the beliefs with which we begin inquiry at face value. Only against such a background can inquiry get off the ground. Once we are in the midst of such inquiry, however, we can meaningfully and fruitfully question the truth of the presumption. It always makes sense to ask whether our cognitive faculties do indeed put us on the track of the truth, and it is, moreover, a question which we may make progress toward answering.

The progress of inquiry not only gives us a fuller and more coherent picture of the world, but it also gives us a fuller and more coherent picture of our place in the world and our ability to understand it. We may usefully ask how it is that our faculties allow us to know the world, given what we take the world to be like. It is part of the measure of the success of science that it gives rise to such questions and allows us to answer them. A coherent picture of the world which did not allow us to explain how we were able to know it would pose puzzles which would threaten to undermine that account of the world. An account of the world cannot be fully embraced without an account of how we are able to come by such an account.

BonJour denies that the kind of "justification from within" that I have just sketched could really constitute justification in the case of one's grasp of one's own beliefs. Although BonJour allows that the achievement of such a circular justification "is not by any means a trivial result", he insists that it "is not equivalent to . . . being positively justified" (138). But if I am right in insisting that the Doxastic Presumption is just a special case of the Presumption of Epistemic Access, then BonJour's concession here requires a full-scale concession to scepticism. If the presumption of our access to our beliefs is on a par with the presumption of our access to everything else, then one must either allow that the kind of justification from within which I have described is genuine justification, or one must be sceptical about the possibility of any kind of justification at all. Our access to our own beliefs cannot be singled out for special treatment.

The position I favor is a non-sceptical one, but I need not insist on that here. Rather, what I do wish to insist upon is that our meta-beliefs have no special status. The Doxastic Presumption is reasonable only to the extent that it is read as a special case of the Presumption of Epistemic Access. And if this is so, our beliefs about our beliefs have no privileged epistemological role to play at all.

5

At this point, I wish to return to the issue which separates internalists from externalists, and place the foregoing remarks in a broader context.

It was BonJour's insistence that an agent's reasons be "cognitively accessible to the believer himself" (101) which led us into the discussion of the Doxastic Presumption, and it is in this requirement of cognitive accessibility that his internalism consists. The requirement of cognitive accessibility is just the requirement that an agent's reasons somehow be internal to that agent. When introducing BonJour's position, I passed over this requirement of cognitive accessibility lightly. I now want to single it out for more careful attention.

Just what does the requirement of cognitive accessibility amount to? BonJour does not tell us directly, but his application of the requirement is revealing. On one natural account, something is cognitively accessible to us just in case we are in a position reliably to gain information about it. On such an account, those who are not sceptics will hold that facts about the external world are cognitively accessible to us. But this cannot be what BonJour has in mind, because he uses the requirement that an agent's reasons be cognitively accessible to her to drive us away from talk about the external world, and, instead, to talk about features of the agent's mind – in particular, to talk about the agent's beliefs.

This is, of course, a familiar epistemological move, and there is a familiar epistemological position which would motivate such a move. If, with Descartes, one holds that our access to the mind is direct and incorrigible, and that our access to the external world is indirect and corrigible, then it is natural to reserve talk of cognitive access, or perhaps, direct cognitive access, for the kind of special access we have to the contents of our minds. On such a view, the privileged access we have to the contents of our minds serves as a foundation on which knowledge of the external world is to be built. In spite of the fact that BonJour is a coherence theorist, his epistemological position does have this much similarity with the Cartesian view: there is a foundation of beliefs about the contents of one's own mind – in BonJour's case, beliefs about one's beliefs – and a superstructure which includes everything else.[7]

The only problem with providing BonJour with this motivation is that he rejects the Cartesian premise; he does not believe, as we have seen, that we are incorrigible about the contents of our own minds. But without this motivation, it is hard to see why BonJour should read the otherwise reasonable requirement of congitive accessibility as requiring a move inward, toward talk of one's mental states. BonJour's internalism seems terribly unmotivated.

The fact is that once one gives up the claim of incorrigible access to one's mental states, even an agent's mental states are at a certain epistemic remove from her. Like the "external" world, an agent's mental states are external to her beliefs about them. Thus, in giving up the claim of incorrigible access, BonJour gives up the possibility of going internal. There no longer is a mental realm to which one has the required cognitive access. Alternatively put, there is no longer a reason to deny that one has the relevant kind of access to the "external" world, for the epistemological contrast between internal and external evaporates. One simply has reasonably good but not perfect access to all the facts there are. Some of them are about oneself and others are not, but there is no difference here epistemologically.

On my view, then, internalism would be properly motivated only if one accepted the Cartesian claim of incorrigible access. Since the Cartesian claim is, as BonJour recognizes, false, we should reject internalism. If I am right about this, however, why has internalism seemed so attractive, even to those such as BonJour, who reject the Cartesian premise which motivates it? If the account I give of internalism is to have any plausibility at all, I must be able to answer this question.

Internalism remains attractive even to those who reject the Cartesian premise, I believe, because in rejecting the Cartesian premise one makes facts about justification external to the agent. In rejecting the possibility of incorrigible access, one is forced to allow that, whatever justification may consist in, the facts about justification and one's beliefs about justification may differ. What this means is that one may be justified in a belief, and yet one may, at the same time, reasonably believe that one is not so justified. By the same token, one may be unjustified in one's belief, and, at the same time, be justified in believing that one is so justified. Rejecting the notion of incorrigibility means that even here there is room for a failure of fit between justified belief and the truth. Even here, there may be a gap between appearance and reality.

In saying that an agent's belief is unjustified, we are holding that agent responsible for her belief. Yet there seems something terribly unfair about holding an agent responsible for her belief and claiming that she is unjustified in that belief if we allow at the same time that the agent is justified in believing that she is justified in believing it. It is the desire to eliminate this possibility that leads people to insist that justification is a matter "internal to the agent". But of course even facts internal to the agent are epistemically external once one rejects the Cartesian premise. So the desire to eliminate the apparent unfairness cannot be realized without embracing the claim of incorrigibility.

Justification is thus, whatever else it may be, a matter external to agents. The realization that there may be a gap between what an agent is justified in believing and what she is justified in believing that she is justified in believing may cause us to distance the concept of justification from that of blame. Alternatively, it may force us to recognize that we legitimately may be blamed for things for which, by our lights, we should not be blamed. My own solution to this problem is to opt for the latter alternative. This does not leave much room for an internalist account, but this, I believe, is as internal as we can get.

Notes

I have received helpful comments on this paper from Steven Luper-Foy, David Shatz, and especially Derk Pereboom.

1   This is just one of the issues raised here; the other is the accessibility of the coherence relation. I discuss this issue briefly in my "Naturalizing Rationality" (1986)

and at greater length in my *Inductive Inference and Its Natural Ground*, 1993. I argue that the relation of coherence cannot be cognitively accessible in relevant respects, because it gives rise to problems of computational intractability.

2   See, for example, the discussion in Stroud 1968.

3   Indeed, I believe that this is the position BonJour really should defend, for his very strong claim that questions about justification are meaningless unless one makes the Doxastic Presumption does not sit well with his rejection of verificationism.

4   But see, for example, Nisbett and Wilson 1977, Nisbett and Ross 1980; and Wilson 1985.

5   This is not to say that it is reliable for all purposes. Indeed, I have argued elsewhere, in my "Introspection and Misdirection" 1989, that there are epistemologically important purposes for which introspection is unreliable.

6   My summary of the conclusions of the literature on introspection presents a picture which is quite a bit rosier than many of the psychologists in the field would themselves endorse. My reasons for this are two-fold. First, as I have argued elsewhere, many of the experimenters in this field have concentrated on the mistakes to which we are liable to the exclusion of our successes. On my view, the comparison with the literature on visual illusions is especially revealing. No one would suggest on the basis of our susceptibility to visual illusion that our perceptual mechanisms are unreliable. Second, I have tried to err on the side of a rosy picture here in fairness to BonJour and to avoid exaggerating my differences with him. Far more important than the question of the truth of the Doxastic Presumption is the question of its epistemic status. I should point out again, however, that although I believe introspection to be, on the whole, reliable, I am very sceptical of the epistemological purposes to which many writers attempt to put it. See note 5.

7   BonJour notes this point about the foundationalist structure of his view on 146–7.

References

BonJour, Laurence: 1985, *The Structure of Empirical Justification*, Harvard University Press, Cambridge.

Kornblith, Hilary: 1983, "Justified Belief and Epistemically Responsible Action", *Philosophical Review* 92, 33–48.

Kornblith, Hilary: 1985, "Ever Since Descartes", *The Monist* 68, 264–76.

Kornblith, Hilary: 1986, "Naturalizing Rationality", in P. Hare and N. Garver (eds.), *Naturalism and Rationality*, Prometheus Books, Buffalo, pp. 115–33.

Kornblith, Hilary: 1989, "Introspection and Misdirection", *Australasian Journal of Philosophy* 67, 410–22.

Kornblith, Hilary: 1993, *Inductive Inference and Its Natural Ground*, MIT Press, Cambridge.

Malcolm, Norman: 1963, *Knowledge and Certainty*, Cornell University Press, Ithaca.

Nisbett, Richard and Lee Ross: 1980, *Human Inference: Strategies and Shortcomings of Social Judgment*, Prentice-Hall, Englewood Cliffs, New Jersey.

Nisbett, Richard and Timothy Wilson: 1977, "Telling More Than We Can Know: Verbal Reports on Mental Processes", *Psychological Review* 84, 231–59.

Quine, W. V. O.: 1969, *Ontological Relativity and Other Essays*, Columbia University Press, New York.

Shoemaker, Sydney: 1963, *Self-Knowledge and Self-Identity*, Cornell University Press, Ithaca.

Stroud, Barry: 1968, "Transcendental Arguments", *Journal of Philosophy* 65, 241–56.

Wilson, Timothy: 1985, "Self-Deception Without Repression: Limits on Access to Mental States", in Mike Martin (ed.), *Self-Deception and Self-Understanding*, University Press of Kansas, Lawrence, pp. 95–116.

5

Understanding Human Knowledge in General

Barry Stroud

The philosophical study of human knowledge seeks to understand what human knowledge is and how it comes to be. A long tradition of reflection on these questions suggests that we can never get the kind of satisfaction we seek. Either we reach the skeptical conclusion that we do not know the things we thought we knew, or we cannot see how the state we find ourselves in is a state of knowledge.

Most philosophers today still deny, or at the very least resist, the force of such reflections. In their efforts to construct a positive theory of knowledge they operate on the not-unreasonable assumption that since human perception, belief, and knowledge are natural phenomena like any other, there is no more reason to think they cannot be understood and explained than there is to think that digestion or photosynthesis cannot be understood and explained. Even if there is still much to be learned about human cognition, it can hardly be denied that we already know a great deal, at least in general, about how it works. Many see it now as just a matter of filling in the details, either from physiology or from something called "cognitive science." We might find that we understand much less than we think we do, but even so it would seem absurd simply to deny that there is such a thing as human knowledge at all, or that we can ever understand how it comes to be. Those traditional skeptical considerations, whatever they were, therefore tend to be ignored. They will be refuted in any case by a successful theory that explains how we do in fact know the things we do.

It would be as absurd to cast doubt on the prospects of scientific investigation of human knowledge and perception as it would be to declare limits to our understanding of human digestion. But I think that what we seek in epistemology – in the philosophical study of human knowledge – is not just anything we can find about how we know things. We try to understand human knowledge in general, and to do so in a certain special way. If the philosophical investigation of knowledge is something distinctive, or sets itself certain special or unique goals, one might question whether those goals can really be reached without thereby casting any doubt on investigations of human knowledge which lack those distinctive philosophical features. That is what I shall try to do. I want to raise and examine the possibility that, however much we came to learn about this or that aspect of human knowledge, thought, and perception, there might still be nothing that could satisfy us as a philosophical understanding of how human knowledge is possible.

When I say nothing could satisfy us I do not mean that it is a very difficult task and that we will never finish the job. It *is* very difficult, and we *will* never finish the job, but I assume that is true of most of our efforts to understand anything. Rather, the threat I see is that once we really understand what we aspire to in the philosophical study of knowledge, and we do not deviate from the aspiration to understand it in that way, we will be forever unable to get the kind of understanding that would satisfy us.

That is one reason I think skepticism is so important in epistemology. It is the view that we do not, or perhaps cannot, know anything, and it is important because it seems to be the inevitable consequence of trying to understand human knowledge in a certain way. Almost nobody thinks for a moment that skepticism could be correct. But that does not mean it is not important. If skepticism really is the inevitable outcome of trying to understand human knowledge in a certain way, and we think it simply could not be correct, that should make us look much more critically at that way of trying to understand human knowledge in the first place. But that is not what typically happens in philosophy. The goal itself is scarcely questioned, and for good reason. We feel human knowledge ought to be intelligible in that way. The epistemological project feels like the pursuit of a perfectly comprehensible intellectual goal. We know that skepticism is no good; it is an answer, but it is not satisfactory. But being constitutionally unable to arrive at an answer to a perfectly comprehensible question is not satisfactory either. We therefore continue to acquiesce in the traditional problem and do not acknowledge that there is no satisfactory solution. We proceed as if it must be possible to find an answer, so we deny the force, and even the interest, of skepticism.

What we seek in the philosophical theory of knowledge is an account that is completely general in several respects. We want to understand how any knowledge at all is possible – how anything we currently accept amounts to knowledge. Or, less ambitiously, we want to understand with complete generality how we come to know anything at all in a certain specified domain.

For example, in the traditional question of our knowledge of the material bodies around us we want to understand how we know anything at all about any such bodies. In the philosophical problem of other minds we want to understand how any person ever comes to know anything at all about what is going on in the mind of any other person, or even knows that there are any other minds at all. In the case of induction we want to understand how anyone can ever have any reason at all to believe anything beyond what he himself has so far observed to be true. I take it to be the job of a positive philosophical theory of knowledge to answer these and similarly general questions.

One kind of generality I have in mind is revealed by what we would all regard as no answer at all to the philosophical problem. The question of other minds is how anyone can know what someone else thinks or feels. But it would be ludicrous to reply that someone can know what another person thinks or feels by asking a good friend of that person's. That would be no answer at all, but not because it is not true. I *can* sometimes find out what someone else thinks by asking his best friend. But that would not contribute to the solution to the philosophical problem of other minds. We are not simply looking for a list of all the ways of knowing. If we were, that way of knowing would go on the list. But in fact we seek a more inclusive description of all our ways of knowing that would explain our knowledge in general.

What is wrong with that particular way of knowing the mind of another is not that it is only one way among others. The trouble is that it explains how we know some particular fact in the area we are interested in by appeal to knowledge of some other fact in that same domain. I know what Smith thinks by knowing that Jones told me what Smith thinks. But knowing that Jones told me something is itself a bit of knowledge about the mind of another. So that kind of answer could not serve as, nor could it be generalized into, a satisfactory answer to the question how we know anything at all about any other minds. Not because it does not mention a legitimate way of knowing something about the mind of another. It does. Coming to know what Smith thinks by asking Jones is a perfectly acceptable way of knowing, and it is a different way of getting that knowledge from having Smith tell me himself, or from reading Smith's mail. There is nothing wrong with it in itself as an explanation. It is only for the general philosophical task that it is felt to be inadequate.

The same holds for everyday knowledge of the objects around us. One way I can know that my neighbor is at home is by seeing her car in front of her house, where she parks it when and only when she is at home. That is a perfectly good explanation of how I know that fact about one of the things around me. It is a different way of knowing where my neighbor is from seeing her through the window or hearing her characteristic fumblings on the piano. But it could not satisfy us as an explanation of how I know anything at all about any objects around me. It explains how I know something about one object around me – my neighbor – by knowing something about another object around me – her car. It could not answer the philosophical question as to how I know anything about any objects around me at all.

The kind of generality at stake in these problems takes its characteristic philosophical form when we come to see, on reflection, that the information available to us for knowing things in a particular domain is systematically less than we might originally have thought. Perhaps the most familiar instance of this is the *First Meditation* of Descartes,[1] in which he asks about knowledge of the material world by means of the senses. It apparently turns out on reflection that the senses give us less than we might have thought; there is no strictly sensory information the possession of which necessarily amounts to knowledge of the material world. We could perceive exactly what we perceive now even if there were no material world at all. The problem then is to see how we ever come to get knowledge of the material world on that sensory basis.

In the case of other minds we find on reflection that the only evidence we can ever have or even imagine for the mental sates of other people is their bodily behavior, including the sounds coming out of their mouths, or even the tears coming out of their eyes. But there is no strictly physical or behavioral information the possession of which necessarily amounts to knowledge of another person's mind or feelings. With induction the general distinction is perhaps even more obvious. The only reason we could ever have for believing anything about what we are not observing at the moment is something we have observed in the past or are observing right now. The problem then is how any knowledge of strictly past or even present fact amounts to knowledge of, or reasonable belief in, some unobserved or future fact.

These apparently simple, problem-generating moves come right at the beginning of epistemology. They are usually taken as so obvious and undeniable that the real problems of epistemology are thought to arise only after they have been made. In this paper I simply assume familiarity with them and with how easily they work. They are the very moves I think we eventually must examine more carefully if we are ever going to understand the real source of the dissatisfaction we are so easily driven to in philosophy. But for now I am concerned with the structure of the plight such reflections appear to leave us in.

If we start by considering a certain domain of facts or truths and ask how anyone could come to know anything at all in that domain, it will seem that any other knowledge that might be relevant could not be allowed to amount to already knowing something in the domain in question. Knowledge of anything at all in that domain is what we want to explain, and if we simply assume from the outset that the person has already got some of that knowledge we will not be explaining all of it. Any knowledge we do grant to the person will be of use to him only if he can somehow get from that knowledge to some knowledge in the domain in question. Some inference or transition would therefore appear to be needed – for example, some way of going from what he is aware of in perception to knowledge of the facts he claims to know. But any such inference will be a good one, and will lead the person to knowledge, only if it is based on something the person also knows or has some reason to believe. He cannot just be making a guess that he has got good evidence. He has to know or at least have reason to believe something that will help get him from his evidential base to some knowledge in the domain in question. That "something" that he needs to know cannot simply be part of his evidential base, since it has to get him beyond that base. But it cannot go so far beyond that base as to imply something already in the domain in question either, since the knowledge of anything at all in that domain is just what we are trying to explain. So it would seem that on either possibility we cannot explain with the proper generality how the kind of knowledge we want to understand is possible. If the person does know what he needs to know, he has already got some knowledge in the domain in question, and if he does not, he will not be able to get there from his evidential base alone.

This apparent dilemma is a familiar quandary in traditional epistemology. I think it arises from our completely general explanatory goal. We want to explain a certain kind of knowledge, and we feel we must explain it on the basis of another, prior kind of knowledge that does not imply or presuppose any of the knowledge we are trying to explain. Without that, we will not be explaining the knowledge in question in the proper, fully general way. This felt need is what so easily brings into the epistemological project some notion or other of what is usually called "epistemic priority" – one kind of knowledge being prior to another. I believe it has fatal consequences for our understanding of our knowledge. It is often said that traditional epistemology is generated by nothing more than a misguided "quest for certainty," or a fruit-less search for absolutely secure "foundations" for knowledge, and that once we abandon such a will-o'-the-wisp we will no longer be threatened by skep-ticism, or even much interested in it.[2] But that diagnosis seems wrong to me – in fact, completely upside down. What some philosophers see as a poorly motivated demand for "foundations" of knowledge looks to me to be the natural consequence of seeking a certain intellectual goal, a certain kind of understanding of human knowledge in general.

In the philosophical problem of other minds, for example, we pick out observable physical movements or "behavior" and ask how on that basis alone, which is the only basis we have, we can ever know anything about the mind behind the "behavior." Those observable facts of "behavior" are held to be "epistemically prior" to any facts about the mind in the sense that it is possible to know all such facts about others' "behavior" without knowing any-thing about their minds. We insist on that condition for a properly general explanation of our knowledge of other minds. But in doing so we need not suppose that our beliefs about that "behavior" are themselves indubitable or incorrigible "foundations" of anything. Levels of relative epistemic prior-ity are all we need to rely on in pressing the epistemological question in that way.

In the case of our knowledge of the material objects around us we single out epistemically prior "sensations" or "sense data" or "experiences" or what-ever it might be, and then ask how on that basis alone, which is the only basis we have, we can know anything of the objects around us. We take it that knowledge of objects comes to us somehow by means of the senses, but if we thought of sensory knowledge as itself knowledge of material objects around us we would not get an appropriately general explanation of how any knowl-edge of any objects at all is possible by means of the senses. We would be explaining knowledge of some material objects only on the basis of knowl-edge of some others. "Data," "the given," "experiences," and so on, which traditional epistemologists have always trafficked in, therefore look to me much more like inevitable products of the epistemological enterprise than elusive "foundations," the unmotivated quest for which somehow throws us into epistemology in the first place.

But once we accept the idea of one kind of knowledge being prior to another as an essential ingredient in the kind of philosophical understanding we seek, it immediately becomes difficult even to imagine, let alone to find, anything that could satisfy us. How *could* we possibly know anything about the minds of other people on the basis only of truths about their "behavior" if those truths do not imply anything about any minds? If we really are restricted in perception to "experiences" or "sense data" or "stimulations" which give us information that is prior to any knowledge of objects, how *could* we ever know anything about what goes on beyond such prior "data"? It would seem to be possible only if we somehow knew of some connection between what we are restricted to in observation and what is true in the wider domain we are interested in. But when knowing even that there was such a connection would be knowing something about that wider domain after all, not just about what we are restricted to in observation. And then we would be left with no satisfactorily general explanation of our knowledge.

In short, it seems that if we really were in the position the traditional account in terms of epistemic priority describes us as being in, skepticism would be correct. We could not know the things we think we know. But if, in order to resist that conclusion, we no longer see ourselves in that traditional way, we will not have a satisfactorily general explanation of all our knowledge in a certain domain.

Theorists of knowledge who accept the traditional picture of our position in the world obviously do not acknowledge what I see as its skeptical or otherwise unsatisfactory consequences. Some philosophers see their task as that of exhibiting the general structure of our knowledge by making explicit what they think are the "assumptions" or "postulates" or "epistemic principles" that are needed to take us from our "data" or evidence in a particular area to some richer domain of knowledge we want to explain.[3] The fact that certain "postulates" or "principles" can be shown to be precisely what is needed for the knowledge in question is somehow taken to count in their favour. Without those "principles," it is argued, we wouldn't know what we think we know.

However illuminating such "rational reconstructions" of our knowledge might be, they cannot really satisfy us if we want to understand how we actually do know the things we think we know. If it had been shown that there is a certain "postulate" or "principle" which we have to have some reason to accept if we are to know anything about, say, the world around us, we would not thereby have come to understand how we do know anything about the world around us. We would have identified something we need, but its indispensability would not show that we do in fact have good reason to accept it. We would be left with the further question whether we know that that "principle" is true, and if so how. And all the rest of the knowledge we wanted to explain would then be hanging in the balance, since it would have been shown to depend on that "principle." Trying to answer the question of its justification would lead right back into the old dilemma. If the "principle" involved says or implies something richer than anything to be found in the prior evidential base – as it seems it must if it is going to be of any help –

there will be nothing in that base alone that could give us reason to accept it. But if we assume from the outset that we do know or have some reason to accept that "principle," we will be assuming that we already know something that goes beyond our prior evidential base, and that knowledge itself will not have been explained. We would therefore have no completely general explanation of how we get beyond that base to any knowledge of the kind in question.

The threat of a regress in the support for any such "principles" leads naturally to the idea of two distinct sources or types of knowledge. If the "principles" or presuppositions of knowledge could be known independently, not on the basis of the prior evidence, but in some other way, it might seem that the regress could be avoided. This might be said to be what Kant learned from Hume:[1] if all our knowledge is derived from experience, we can never know anything. But Kant did not infer from that conditional proposition the categorical skeptical conclusion he thought Hume drew from it. For Kant the point was that if we do have knowledge from experience we must also have some knowledge that is independent of experience. Only in that way is experiential knowledge possible. We must know some things *a priori* if we know anything at all.

As a way of explaining how we know the things we do, this merely postpones or expands the problem. It avoids the skeptical regress in sensory knowledge of the world by insisting that the basic "principles" or presuppositions needed for such empirical knowledge do not themselves depend on empirical, sensory support. But that says only that those "principles" are *not* known by experience; it does not explain how they are known. Merely being presupposed by our empirical knowledge confers no independent support. It has to be explained how we know anything at all *a priori*, and how in particular we know those very things we need for empirical knowledge. And then the old dilemma presents itself again. If our *a priori* knowledge of those "principles" is derived from something prior to them which serves as their evidential base, it must be shown how the further "principles" needed to take us from that base to the "principles" in question could themselves be supported. If we assume from the outset that we do know some "principles" *a priori*, not all of our *a prior* knowledge in general will have been explained. It would seem that *a priori* knowledge in general could be explained only in terms of something that is not itself *a priori* knowledge. But empirical knowledge cannot explain *a priori* knowledge – and it would be no help here even if it could – so either we must simply accept the unexplained fact that we know things *a priori* or we must try to explain it without appealing to any other knowledge at all.

I do not want to go further into the question of *a priori* knowledge. Not because it is not difficult and important in its own right, but because many theorists of knowledge would now argue that it is irrelevant to the epistemological project of explaining our knowledge of the world around us. They find they can put their finger precisely on the place where the traditional philosophical enterprise turns inevitably towards skepticism. And they hold that that step is wrong, and that without it there is no obstacle to finding a satisfactory account of our epistemic position that avoids any commitment to skepticism. This claim for a new "enlightened" theory of knowledge that does not take that allegedly skeptical step is what I what to question.

I have already sketched the hopeless plight I think the old conception leaves us in. The trouble in that conception is now thought to enter at just the point at which the regress I have described apparently gets started. To get from his "evidence" to any of the knowledge in question the person was said to need some "principle" or assumption that would take him from that "evidence" to that conclusion. But he would also need some reason for accepting that "principle" – he would have to know something else that supports it. And then he would need some reason for accepting that "something else," and it could not be found either in his evidential base or in the "principles" he originally needed to take him beyond that base. It must be found in something else in turn – another "something else" – and so on *ad infinitum*. What is wrong in this, it is now thought, is not the idea that the person cannot find such reasons, or that he can only find them somehow mysteriously *a priori*. What is wrong is the requirement that he himself has to find such reasons, that he has to be able to support his "principles," at all. The new "enlightened" approach to knowledge insists that there is a clear sense in which he does not.

The objection can be put another way. What is wrong with the traditional epistemological project that leads so easily to skepticism, it is said, is that the whole thing assumes that anyone who knows something must know that he knows it. He must himself know that his reasons are good ones, or that his prior "evidence" is adequate to yield knowledge of the kind in question. And then, by that same assumption, he must know that he knows that, and so on. But that assumption, it is argued, is not correct. It is obviously possible for someone to know something without knowing that he knows it. The theory of knowledge asks simply whether and how people knows things. If that can be explained, that is enough. The fact that people sometimes do not know that they know things should not make us deny that they really do know those things – especially if we have a satisfactory theory that explains that knowledge.

Now it certainly seems right to allow that someone can know something even when we recognize that he does not know that he knows it. Think of the simplest ordinary examples. Someone is asked if he knows who won the battle of Hastings, and when it took place, and he tentatively replies "William the Conqueror, 1066." He knew the answer. He had learned it in school, perhaps, and had never forgotten it, but at the time he was asked he did not know whether he had really retained that information. He was not sure about the state of his knowledge, but as for the winner and the date of the battle of Hastings, he knew that all along. He knew more than he thought he did. So whether somebody knows something is one thing; whether he knows that he knows it is something else. That seems to be a fact about our everyday assessments of people's knowledge.

The question is not whether that is a fact, but what significance it has for the prospects of the philosophical theory of knowledge. Obviously it turns on what a satisfactory philosophical account is supposed to do. The goal as I have presented it so far is to take ourselves and our ways of knowing on the one hand, and a certain domain of truths that we want to know about on the other, and to understand how we know any of those truths at all on the basis of prior knowledge that does not amount to already knowing something in the domain we are interested in. The question was what support we could find for the bridge that would be needed to get us from that prior basis to the knowledge in question. The present suggestion amounts in effect to saying that no independent or *a priori* support is needed on the part of the knower. All that is needed is that a certain proposition should be true; the person doesn't have to know that it is true in order to know the thing in question. If he has the appropriate prior knowledge or experience, and there is in fact a truth linking his having that knowledge or experience with his knowing something in the domain in question, then he does in fact know something in that domain, even if he is not aware of the favorable epistemic position he is in.

The truth in question will typically be one expressing the definition of knowledge, or of having reason to believe something. The search for such definitions is what many philosophers regard as the special job of the philosophical theory of knowledge. If knowing something could be defined solely in terms of knowledge or experience in some unproblematic, prior domain, then that definition could be fulfilled even if you didn't know that you knew anything in that domain. You yourself would not have to find a "bridge" from your evidential basis to the knowledge in question. As long as there actually was a "bridge" under your feet, whether you knew of it or not, there would be no threat of a skeptical regress.

In one form, this anti-skeptical strategy has been applied to the problem of induction. Hume had argued that if a long positive correlation observed to hold between two sorts of things in the past is going to give you some reason now to expect a thing of the second sort, given an observed instance of the first, you will also have to have some reason to think that what you have observed in the past gives you some reason to believe something about the future. P. F. Strawson replied that you need no such thing. Having observed a long positive correlation between two sorts of things under widely varied circumstances in the past is just what it is – what it means – to have reason to expect a thing of the second sort, given that a thing of the first sort has just appeared.[5] If that is a necessary truth about reasonable belief it will guarantee that you do in fact have a reasonable belief in the future as long as you have had the requisite experience of the past and present. You do not have to find some additional reason for thinking that what you have observed in the past gives you good reason to believe something about the future.

This has come to be called an "externalist" account of knowledge or reasonable belief. It would explain knowledge in terms of conditions that are available from an "external," third-person point of view, independent of what the knower's own attitude towards the fulfillment of those conditions might be. It is not all smooth sailing. To give us what we need, it has to come up with an account of knowledge or reasonable belief that is actually correct – that distinguishes knowledge from lack of knowledge in the right way. I think the account just given of inductive reasons does not meet that test. As it stands, it does not state a necessary truth about reasons to believe.[6] To come closer to being right, it would have to define the difference between a "law-like" generalization and a merely "accidental" correlation which does not give reason to believe it will continue. That task is by no means trivial, and it faces a "new riddle of induction" all over again.[7] But if we do draw a distinction between having good reasons and not having them it would seem that there must be some account that captures what we do. It is just a matter of finding what it is.

The same goes for definitions of knowledge. One type of view says that knowing that p is equivalent to something like having acquired and retained a true belief that p as a result of the operation of a properly functioning, reliable belief-forming mechanism.[8] That general scheme still leaves many things unexplained or undefined, and it is no trivial task to get it to come out right. But I am not concerned here with the details of "externalist" definitions of knowledge. My reservations about the philosophical theory of knowledge are not just that it is difficult. I have doubts about the satisfactoriness of what you would have even if you had an "externalist" account of knowledge which as far as you could tell matched up completely with those cases in which we think other people know things and those in which we think they do not.

Here we come up against another, and perhaps the most important, dimension of generality I think we seek in the theory of knowledge. We want an account that explains how human knowledge in general is possible, or how anyone can know anything at all in a certain specified domain. The difficulty arises now from the fact that we as human theorists are ourselves part of the subject-matter that we theorists of human knowledge want to understand in a certain way. If we merely study another group and draw conclusions only about them, no such difficulty presents itself. But then our conclusions will not be completely general. They will be known to apply only to those others, and we will be no closer to understanding how our own knowledge is possible. We want to be able to apply what we find out about knowledge to ourselves, and so to explain how our own knowledge is possible.

I have already suggested why I think we cannot get a satisfactory explanation along traditional Cartesian lines. The promise of the new "externalist" strategy is that it would avoid the regress that seems inevitable in that project. A person who knows something does not himself have to know that what he has got in his prior evidential base amounts to knowledge in the domain in question. As long as he in fact satisfies the conditions of knowing something in the domain we are interested in, there is nothing more he has to do in order to know things in that domain. No regress gets started.

The question now is: can we find such a theory satisfactory when we apply it to ourselves? To illustrate what I find difficult here I return to Descartes, as we so often must do in this subject. Not to his skeptical argument in the *First meditation*, but to the answer he gives to it throughout the rest of the *Meditations*. He eventually comes to think that he does know many of the things that seemed to be thrown into doubt by his earlier reflections on dreaming and the evil demon. He does so by proving that God exists and is not a deceiver and that everything in us, including our capacity to perceive and think, comes from God. So whatever we clearly and distinctly perceive to be true is true. God would not have it any other way. By knowing what I know about God I can know that He is not a deceiver and therefore that I do know the things I think I know when I clearly and distinctly perceive them. If I am careful, and keep God and his goodness in mind, I can know many things, and the threat of skepticism is overcome.

Many objections have been made to this answer to Descartes's question about his knowledge. One is the "externalist" complaint that Descartes's whole challenge rests on the assumption that you don't know something unless you know that you know it. Not only do my clear and distinct perceptions need some guarantee, but on Descartes's view I have to know what that guarantee is. That is why he thinks the atheist or the person who denies God in his heart cannot really know those things that we who accept Descartes's proof of God's existence and goodness can know.[9] But according to "externalism" that requirement is wrong; you don't have know that you know in order to know something.

Another and perhaps the most famous objection is that Descartes's proof of the guarantee of his knowledge is no good because it is circular. The knowledge he needs in order to reach the conclusion of God's existence and goodness is available to him only if God's existence and goodness have already been proved. What he calls his clear and distinct perception of God's existence will be knowledge of God's existence only if whatever he clearly and distinctly perceives is true. But that is guaranteed only by God, so he can't know that it is guaranteed unless he already knows that God exists.

Taking these two objections together, we can see that if the first is correct, the second is no objection at all. If Descartes is assuming that knowing requires knowing that you know, and if that assumptions is wrong, then the charge of circularity has no force against his view. If "externalism" were correct, Descartes's inability to prove that God exists and guarantees the truth of our clear and distinct perceptions would be no obstacle to his knowing the truth of whatever he clearly and distinctly perceives. He would not have to know that he knows those things. As long as God did in fact exist and did in fact make sure that his clear and distinct perceptions were true, Descartes would have the knowledge he started out thinking he had, even if God's existence and nature remained eternally unknown to him. The soundness of his proof would not matter. All that would matter for the everyday knowledge Descartes is trying to account for is the truth of its conclusion – God's existence and goodness. If that conclusion is in fact true, his inability to know that it is true would be no argument against his account.

To develop this thought further we can try to imagine what an "enlightened" or "externalist," but still otherwise Cartesian, theory might look like. It would insist that the knowing subject does not have to know the truth of the theory that explains his knowledge in order to have the knowledge that the theory is trying to account for. Otherwise, the theory would retain the full Cartesian story of God and his goodness and his guarantee of the truth of our clear and distinct perceptions. What would be wrong with accepting such an "enlightened" theory? If we are willing to accept the kind of theory that says that knowing that p is having acquired the true belief that p by some reliable belief-forming mechanism, why would we not be equally or even more willing to accept a theory that says that knowing that p is having acquired the true belief that p by clearly and distinctly perceiving it – a method of belief formation that is reliable because God guarantees that whatever is clearly and distinctly perceived is true? It is actually more specific than a completely general form of "externalism" or "reliabilism." It explains *why* the belief-forming mechanism is reliable. What, then, would be wrong with accepting it?

I think most of us simply don't believe it. We think that God does not in fact exist and is not the guarantor of the reliability of our belief-forming mechanisms. So we think that what this theory says about human knowledge is not true. Now that is certainly a defect in a theory, but is it the only thing standing in the way of our accepting it and finding it satisfactory? It seems to me it is not, and perhaps by examining its other defects, beyond its actual truth-value, we can identify a source of dissatisfaction with other "external-ist" theories as well.

We have to admit that if the imagined "externalist" Cartesian theory were true, we would know many of the things we think we know. So skepticism would not be correct. But in the philosophical investigation of knowledge we want more than the falsity of skepticism and more than the mere possession of the knowledge we ordinarily think we've got. We want to understand how we know the things we know, how skepticism turns out not to be true. And even if this "enlightened" Cartesian story were in fact true, if we didn't know that it was, or if we didn't have some reason to believe that it was, we would be no further along towards understanding our knowledge than we would be if the theory were false. So we need some reason to accept a theory of knowledge if we are going to rely on that theory to understand how our knowledge is possible. That is what I think no form of "externalism" can give a satisfactory account of.

Suppose someone had said to Descartes, as they in effect did, "Look, you have no reason to accept any of this story about God and his guarantee of the truth of your clear and distinct perceptions. Of course, if what you say were true you would have the knowledge you think you have, but your whole proof of it is circular. You could justify your explanation of knowledge only if you already knew that what you clearly and distinctly perceive is true." Could an "enlightened" "externalist" Descartes reply: "That's right. I suppose I have to admit that I can give no good reason to accept my explanation. But that doesn't really bother me any more, now that I am an "externalist." Circularity in my proofs is no objection to my theory if "externalism" is correct. I still do believe my theory, after all, and as long as that theory is in fact true – whether I can give any reason to accept it or not – skepticism will be false and I will in fact know the things that I clearly and carefully claim to know."

I take it that that response is inadequate. The "externalist" Descartes I have imagined would not have a satisfactory understanding of his knowledge. It is crucial to what I want to say about "externalism" that we recognize some inadequacy in his position. It is admittedly not easy to specify exactly what the deficiency or the unsatisfactoriness of accepting that position amounts to. I think this much can be said: if the imagined Descartes responded only in that way he would be at best in the position of saying, "If the story that I accept is true, I do know the things I think I know. But I admit that if it is false, and a certain other story is true instead, then I do not." If "externalism" is correct, what he would be saying here is true. His theory, if true, would explain his knowledge. The difficulty is that until he finds some reason to believe his theory rather than some other, he cannot be said to have explained how he knows the things he knows. That is not because he is assuming that a person cannot know something unless he knows that he knows it. He has explicitly abandoned that assumption. He admits that people know things whether they know the truth of his theory or not. The same of course holds for him. And he knows that implication. That is precisely what he is saying: if his theory is true he will know the things he thinks he knows. But he is, in addition, a theorist of knowledge. He wants to understand how he knows the things he thinks he knows. And he cannot satisfy himself on that score unless he can see himself as having some reason to accept the theory that he (and all the rest of us) can recognize would explain his knowledge if it were true. That is not because knowing implies knowing that you know. It is because having an explanation of something in the sense of understanding it is a matter of having good reason to accept something that would be an explanation if it were true.

The question now is whether an "externalist" scientific epistemologist who rejects Descartes's explanation and offers one of his own is in any better position when he comes to apply his theory to his own knowledge than the imagined "externalist" Descartes is in. He begins by asking about all knowledge in a specified domain. A philosophically satisfactory explanation of such knowledge must not explain some of the knowledge in the domain in question by appeal to knowledge of something else already in the domain. But the scientific student of human knowledge must know or have some reason to believe his theory of knowledge if he is going to understand how knowledge is possible. His theory about our belief-forming mechanisms and their reliability is a theory about the interactions between us and the world around us. It is arrived at by studying human beings, finding out how they get the beliefs they do, and investigating the sources of the reliability of those belief-forming mechanisms. Descartes claimed knowledge of God and his goodness, and of the relation between those supernatural facts and our earth-bound belief-forming mechanisms. A more naturalistic epistemologist's gaze does not reach so high. He claims knowledge of nothing more than the familiar natural world in which he thinks everything happens. But he will have an explanation of human knowledge, and so will understand how people know the things they do, only if he knows or has some reason to believe that his scientific story of the goings-on in that world is true.

If his goal was, among other things, to explain our scientific knowledge of the world around us, he will have an explanation of such knowledge only if he can see himself as possessing some knowledge in that domain. In studying other people, that presents no difficulty. It is precisely by knowing what he does about the world that he explains how others know what they do about the world. But if he had started out asking how anyone knows anything at all about the world, he would be no further along towards understanding how any of it is possible if he had not understood how he himself knows what he has to know about the world in order to have any explanation at all. He must understand himself as knowing or having reason to believe that his theory is true.

It might seem that he fulfills that requirement because his theory of knowledge is meant to identify precisely those conditions under which knowledge or good reason to believe something is present. If that theory is correct, and he himself fulfills those conditions in his own scientific investigations of human knowledge, he will in fact know that his theory of knowledge is true, or at least he will have good reason to believe it. He studies others and finds that they often satisfy the conditions his theory says are sufficient for knowing things about the world, and he believes that theory, and he believes that he too satisfies those same conditions in his investigations of those other people. He concludes that he does know how human beings know what they do, and he concludes that he therefore understands how he in particular knows the things he knows about the world. He is one of the human beings that his theory is true of. So the non-Cartesian, scientific "externalist" claims to be in a better position than the imagined "externalist" Descartes because he claims to know by a reliable study of the natural world that his explanation of human knowledge is correct and Descartes's is wrong. In accepting his own explanation he claims to fulfill the conditions his theory asserts to be sufficient for knowing things.

I think this theorist would still be in no better position than the position the imagined "externalist" Descartes is in. If his theory is true, he will in fact know that his explanation is correct. In that sense he could be said to possess an explanation of how human beings know the things they know. In that same sense the imagined "externalist" Descartes would possess an explanation of his knowledge. He accepts something which, if true, would explain his knowledge. But none of this would be any help or consolation to them as epistemologists. The position of the imagined "externalist" Descartes is deficient for the theory of knowledge because he needs some reason to believe that the theory he has devised is true in order to be said to understand how people know the things they think they know. The scientific "externalist" claims he does have reason to believe his explanation of knowledge and so to be in a better position than the imagined "externalist" Descartes. But the way in which he fulfills that condition, even if he does, is only in an "externalist" way, and therefore in the same way that the imagined Descartes fulfills the conditions of knowledge, if he does. *If* the scientific "externalist's" theory is correct about the conditions under which knowledge or reasonable belief is present, and if he does fulfill those conditions in coming to believe his own explanation of knowledge, then he is in fact right in thinking that he has good reason to think that his explanation is correct. But that is to be in the same position with respect to whether he has good reason to think his explanation is correct as the imagined "externalist" Descartes was in at the first level with respect to whether he knows the things he thinks he knows.

It was admitted that if that imagined Descartes's theory were true he would know the things he thinks he knows, but he could not be said to see or to understand himself as possessing such knowledge because he had no reason to think that his theory was true. The scientific "externalist" claims to have good reason to believe that his theory is true. It must be granted that if, in arriving at his theory, he did fulfill the conditions his theory says are sufficient for knowing things about the world, then if that theory is correct, he does in fact know that it is. But still, I want to say, he himself has no reason to think that he does have good reason to think that his theory is correct. He is at best in the position of someone who has good reason to believe his theory if that theory is in fact true, but has no such reason to believe it if some other theory is true instead. He can see what he *would* have good reason to believe if the theory he believes were true, but he cannot see or understand himself as knowing or having good reason to believe what his theory says.

I am aware that describing what I see as the deficiency in this way is not really satisfactory or conclusive. It encourages the "externalist" to re-apply his theory of knowing or having good reason to believe at the next level up, and to claim that he can indeed understand himself to have good reason to believe his theory because he has good reason to believe that he does have good reason to believe his theory. That further belief about his reasons is arrived at in turn by fulfilling what his theory says are the conditions for reasonably believing something. But then he is still in the same position two levels up that we found the imagined "externalist" Descartes to be in at the first level. If the imagined Descartes's claim to self-understanding was inadequate there, any similar claim will be equally inadequate at any higher level of knowing that one knows or having reason to believe that one has reason to believe. That is why our reaction to the original response of the imagined "externalist" Descartes is crucial. Recognition of its inadequacy is essential to recognizing the inadequacy of "externalism" that I have in mind. It is difficult to say precisely what is inadequate about that kind of response, especially in terms that would be acceptable to an "externalist." Perhaps it is best to say that the theorist has to see himself as having good reason to believe his theory in some sense of "having good reason" that cannot be fully captured by an "externalist" account.

So even if it is true that you can know something without knowing that you know it, the philosophical theorist of knowledge cannot simply insist on the point and expect to find acceptance of an "externalist" account of knowledge fully satisfactory. If he could, he would be in the position of someone who says: "I don't know whether I understand human knowledge or not. If what I believe about it is true and my beliefs about it are produced in what my theory says is the right way, I do know how human knowledge comes to be, so in that sense I do understand. But if my beliefs are not true, or not arrived at in that way, I do not. I wonder which it is. I wonder whether I understand human knowledge or not." That is not a satisfactory position to arrive at in one's study of human knowledge – or of anything else.

It might be said that there can be such a thing as unwitting understanding, or understanding you don't know you've got, just as there can be unwitting knowledge, or knowledge you don't know you've got. Such "unwitting understanding," if there is such a thing, is the most that the "externalist" philosophical theorist about human knowledge could be said to have of his own knowledge. But even if there is such a thing, it is not something it makes sense to aspire to, or something to remain content with having reached, if you happen to have reached it. We want witting, not unwitting, understanding. That requires knowing or having some reason to accept the scientific story you believe about how people know the things they know. And in the case of knowledge of the world around us, that would involve already knowing or having some reason to believe something in the domain in question. Not all the knowledge in that domain would thereby be explained.

I do not mean that there is something wrong with our explaining how people know certain things about the world by assuming that they or we know certain other things about it. We do it all the time. It is only within the general epistemological enterprise that that otherwise familiar procedure cannot give us what we want. And when I say that "externalism" cannot give us what we want I do not mean that it possesses some internal defect which prevents it from being true. The difficulty I am pointing to is an unsatisfactoriness involved in *accepting* an "externalist" theory and claiming to understand human knowledge in general in that way. And even that is too broad. It is not that there is any difficulty in understanding other people's knowledge in those terms. It is only with self-understanding that the unsatisfactoriness or loss of complete generality makes itself felt. "Externalism," if it got the conditions of knowledge right, would work fine for other people's knowledge. As a third-person, observational study of human beings and other animals, it would avoid the obstacles to human understanding apparently involved in the first-person Cartesian project. But the question is whether we can take up such an "external" observer's position with respect to ourselves and our knowledge and still gain a satisfactorily general explanation of how we know the things we know. That is where I think the inevitable dissatisfaction comes in.

The demand for completely general understanding of knowledge in a certain domain requires that we see ourselves at the outset as not knowing anything in that domain and then coming to have such knowledge on the basis of some independent and in that sense prior knowledge or experience. And that leads us to seek a standpoint from which we can view ourselves without taking for granted any of that knowledge that we want to understand. But if we could manage to detach ourselves in that way from acceptance of any truths in the domain we are interested in, it seems that the only thing we could discover from that point of view is that we can never know anything in that domain. We could find no way to explain how that prior knowledge alone could yield any richer knowledge lying beyond it. That is the plight the traditional view captures. That is the truth in skepticism. If we think of our knowledge as arranged in completely general levels of epistemic priority in that way, we find that we cannot know what we think we know. Skepticism is the only answer.

But then that seems absurd. We realize that people do know many things in the domains we are interested in. We can even explain how they know such things, whether they know that they do or not. That is what the third-person point of view captures. That is the truth in "externalism." But when we try to explain how we know those things we find we can understand it only by assuming that we have got some knowledge in the domain in question.

And that is not philosophically satisfying. We have lost the prospect of explaining and therefore understanding all of our knowledge with complete generality.

For these and other reasons I think we need to go back and look more carefully into the very sources of the epistemological quest. We need to see how the almost effortlessly natural ways of thinking embodied in that traditional enterprise nevertheless distort or misrepresent our position, if they do. But we should not think that if and when we come to see how the epistemological enterprise is not fully valid, or perhaps not even fully coherent, we will then possess a satisfactory explanation of how human knowledge in general is possible. We will have seen, at best, that we cannot have any such thing. And that too, I believe, will leave us dissatisfied.

Notes

I would like to thank Janet Broughton, Thompson Clarke, Fred Dretske, Alvin Godman, Samuel Guttenplan, and Christopher Peacocke for helpful comments on earlier versions of this paper.

1   R. Descartes, *Meditations on First Philosophy* in *The Philosophical Writings of Descartes*, vol. I, tr. J. Cottingham, R. Stoothoff, D. Murdoch (Cambridge, 1985).
2   This charge has been laid against traditional epistemology at least since Dewey's *The Quest for Certainty* and is by now, I suppose, more or less philosophical orthodoxy. For more recent expressions of it see, for example, Michael Williams, *Groundless Belief* (Oxford, 1977), and Richard Rorty, *Philosophy and the Mirror of Nature* (Princeton, 1979).
3   Perhaps the best example of this, with a list of metaphysical and epistemological "postulates" deemed to be necessary, is B. Russell, *Human Knowledge: Its Scope and Limits* (London, 1948). For a more recent version of the same project concentrating only on "epistemic principles" see the epistemological writings of R. Chisholm, e.g., *Theory of Knowledge* (Englewood Cliffs, N.J., 1977) or *The Foundations of Knowing* (Minneapolis, 1980).
4   See, e.g., I. Kant, *Critique of Pure Reason*, tr. N. Kemp Smith (New York, 1965), B 19–20.
5   P. F. Strawson, *Introduction to Logical Theory* (London, 1952), pp. 256–7.
6   I have made the point in more detail in my *Hume* (London, 1977), pp. 64–6.
7   See N. Goodman, "The New Riddle of Induction," in *Fact, Fiction, and Forecast* (Cambridge, Mass., 1955).
8   What the mechanism is, how its reliability is to be defined, and what other conditions are necessary vary from one "externalist" theory to another. See, e.g., F.

Dretske, *Knowledge and the Flow of Information* (Cambridge, Mass., 1981), or A. Goldman, *Epistemology and Cognition* (Cambridge, Mass., 1986).

9   R. Descartes, "Third Set of Objections with the Author's Replies" and "Author's Replies to the Sixth Set of Objections," in *The Philosophical Writings of Descartes*, vol. I, pp. 137, 289 (Cambridge, 1985).

6

RELIABILISM AND INTELLECTUAL VIRTUE

Ernest Sosa

Externalism and reliabilism go back at least to the writings of Frank Ramsey early in this century.[1] The generic view has been developed in diverse ways by David Armstrong, Fred Dretske, Alvin Goldman, Robert Nozick, and Marshall Swain.[2]

A.   Generic Reliabilism

Generic reliabilism might be put simply as follows:

> S's belief that p at t is justified iff it is the outcome of a process of belief acquisition or retention which is reliable, or leads to a sufficiently high preponderance of true beliefs over false beliefs.

That simple statement of the view is subject to three main problems: the generality problem, the new evil-demon problem, and the metaincoherence problem (to give it a label). Let us consider these in turn.

The generality problem for such reliabilism is that of how to avoid processes which are too specific or too generic. Thus we must avoid a process with only one output ever, or one artificially selected so that if a belief were the output of such a process it would indeed be true; for every true belief is presumably the outcome of some such too-specific processes, so that if such processes are allowed, then every true belief would result from a reliable process and would be justified. But we must also avoid processes which are too generic, such as perception (period), which surely can produce not only justified beliefs but also unjustified ones, even if perception is on the whole a reliable process of belief acquisition for normally circumstanced humans.[3]

The evil-demon problem for reliabilism is not Descartes's problem, of course, but it is a relative. What if twins of ours in another possible world were given mental lives just like ours down to the most minute detail of experience or thought, etc., though they were also totally in error about the nature of their surroundings, and their perceptual and inferential processes of belief acquisition accomplished very little except to sink them more and more deeply and systematically into error? Shall we say that we are justified in our beliefs while our twins are not? They are quite wrong in their beliefs, of course, but it seems somehow very implausible to suppose that they are unjustified.[4]

The meta-incoherence problem is in a sense a mirror image of the new evil-demon problem, for it postulates not a situation where one is internally justified though externally unreliable, but a situation where one is internally unjustified though externally reliable. More specifically, it supposes that a belief (that the President is in New York) which derives from one's (reliable) clairvoyance is yet *not* justified if either (a) one has a lot of ordinary evidence against it, and none in its favor; or (b) one has a lot of evidence against one's possessing such a power of clairvoyance; or (c) one has good reason to believe that such a power could not be possessed (e.g., it might require the transmission of some influence at a speed greater than that of light); or (d) one has no evidence for or against the general possibility of the power, or of one's having it oneself, nor does one even have any evidence either for or against the proposition that one believes as a result of one's power (that the President is in New York).[5]

B.   Goldman's Reliabilisms

How might reliabilism propose to meet the problems specified? We turn first to important work by Goldman, who calls his theory "Historical Reliabilism," and has the following to say about it:

> The theory of justified belief proposed here, then, is an *Historical* or *Genetic* theory. It contrasts with the dominant approach to justified belief, an approach that generates what we may call (borrowing a phrase from Robert Nozick) *Current Time-Slice* theories. A Current Time-Slice theory makes the justificational status of a belief wholly a function of what is true of the cognizer *at the time* of the belief. An Historical theory makes

the justificational status of a belief depend on its prior history. Since my Historical theory emphasizes the reliability of the belief-generating processes, it may be called *Historical Reliabilism*.[6]

The insights of externalism are important, and Goldman has been perceptive and persistent in his attempts to formulate an appropriate and detailed theory that does them justice. His proposals have stimulated criticism, however, among them the three problems already indicated.

Having appreciated those problems, Goldman in his book[7] moves beyond Historical Reliabilism to a view we might call rule reliabilism, and, in the light of further problems,[8] has made further revisions in the more recent "Strong and Weak Justification." The earlier theory, however, had certain features designed to solve the new evil-demon problem, features absent in the revised theory. Therefore, some other solution is now required, and we do now find a new proposal.

Under the revised approach, we now distinguish between two sorts of justification:

A belief is *strongly justified* if and only if it is well formed, in the sense of being formed by means of a process that is truth-conducive in the possible world in which it is produced, or the like.

A belief is *weakly justified* if and only if it is blameless though illformed, in the sense of being produced by an unreliable cognitive process which the believer does not believe to be unreliable, and whose unreliability the believer has no available way of determining.[9]

Notice, however, that it is at best in a *very* weak sense that a subject with a "weakly justified" belief is thereby "blameless." For it is not even precluded that the subject take that belief to be very ill-formed, so long as he is in error about the cognitive process that produces it. That is to say, S might hold B, and believe B to be an output of P, and hold P to be an epistemically unreliable process, while in fact it is not P but the equally unreliable P′ that produces B. In this case S's belief B would be weakly justified, so long as S did not believe P′ to be unreliable, and had no available means of determining its unreliability. But it seems at best extremely strained to hold S epistemically "blameless" with regard to holding B in such circumstances, where S takes B to derive from a process P so unreliable, let us suppose, as to be epistemically vicious.

The following definition may perhaps give us a closer approach to epistemic blamelessness.

A belief is *weakly justified (in the modified sense)* if and only if it is blameless though ill-formed, in the sense of being produced by an unreliable
cognitive process while the believer neither takes it to be thus ill-formed
nor has any available way of determining it to be ill-formed.

With these concepts, the Historical Reliabilist now has at least the beginnings of an answer both for the evil-demon problem and for the meta-
incoherence problem. About the evil demon's victims, those hapless twins of
ours, we can now say that though their beliefs are very ill-formed – and are
no knowledge even if by luck they, some of them, happen to be true – still
there is a sense in which they are justified, as justified as our corresponding
beliefs, which are indistinguishable from theirs so far as concerns only the
"insides" of our respective subjectivities. For we may now see their beliefs to
be weakly justified, in the modified sense defined above.[10]

About the meta-incoherence cases, moreover, we can similarly argue that,
in some of them at least, the unjustified protagonist with the wrong (or
lacking) perspective on his own well-formed (clairvoyant) belief can be seen
to be indeed unjustified, for he can be seen as subjectively unjustified through
lack of an appropriate perspective on his belief: either because he positively
takes the belief to be ill-formed, or because he "ought" to take it to be ill-
formed given his total picture of things, and given the cognitive processes
available to him.

Consider now the following definition:

A belief is *meta-justified* if and only if the believer does place it in appropriate perspective, at least in the minimal sense that the believer neither
takes it to be ill-formed nor has any available way of determining it to
be ill-formed.

Then any belief that is weakly justified (again, sticking to the unmodified
sense) will be meta-justified, but there can be meta-justified beliefs which are
not weakly justified. Moreover, no strongly justified belief will be weakly justified, but a strongly justified belief can be meta-justified. Indeed one would
wish one's beliefs to be not only strongly justified but also meta-justified. And
what one shares with the victim of the evil demon is of course not weak justification. For if, as we suppose, our own beliefs are strongly justified, then our
own beliefs are not weakly justified. What one shares with the evil demon's
victim is rather metajustification. The victim's beliefs and our beliefs are
equally metajustified.

Does such meta-justification – embedded thus in weak justification – enable
answers both for the new evil-demon problem and for the problem of meta-

incoherence? Does the victim of the evil demon share with us meta-justification, unlike the meta-incoherent? The notion of weak justification does seem useful as far as it goes, as is the allied notion of meta-justification, but we need to go a bit deeper,[11] which may be seen as follows.

C. Going Deeper

Beliefs are states of a subject, which need not be occurrent or conscious, but may be retained even by someone asleep or unconscious, and may also be acquired unconsciously and undeliberately, as are acquired our initial beliefs, presumably, whether innate or not, especially if deliberation takes time. Consider now a normal human with an ordinary set of beliefs normally acquired through sensory experience from ordinary interaction with a surrounding physical world. And suppose a victim in whom evil demons (perhaps infinitely many) inplant beliefs in the following way. The demons cast dice, or use some other more complex randomizer, and choose which beliefs to inplant at random and in ignorance of what the other demons are doing. Yet, by amazing coincidence, the victim's total set of beliefs is identical to that of our normal human. Now let's suppose that the victim has a beautifully coherent and comprehensive set of beliefs, complete with an epistemic perspective on his object-level beliefs. We may suppose that the victim has meta-justification for his object-level beliefs (e.g., for his belief that there is a fire before him at the moment), at least in the minimal sense defined above: he does not believe such beliefs to derive from unreliable processes, nor has he any available means of determining that they do. Indeed, we may suppose that he has an even stronger form of meta-justification, as follows:

> S has meta-justification, in the stronger sense, for believing that p iff (a) S has weaker meta-justification for so believing, and (b) S has meta-beliefs which positively attribute his object beliefs in every case to some faculty or virtue for arriving at such beliefs in such circumstances, and further meta-beliefs which explain how such a faculty or virtue was acquired, and how such a faculty or virtue, thus acquired, is bound to be reliable in the circumstances as he views them at the time.

And the victim might even be supposed to have a similar meta-meta-perspective, and a similar meta-meta-meta-perspective, and so on, for many more levels of ascent than any human would normally climb. So everything would be brilliantly in order as far as such meta-reasoning is concerned, meta-reasoning supposed flawlessly coherent and comprehensive. Would it follow that the victim was internally and subjectively justified in every reasonable sense or respect? Not necessarily, or so I will now try to show.

Suppose the victim has much sensory experience, but that all of this experience is wildly at odds with his beliefs. Thus he believes he has a splitting headache, but he has no headache at all; he believes he has a cubical piece of black coal before him, while his visual experience is as if he had a white and round snowball before him. And so on. Surely there is then something internally and subjectively wrong with this victim, something "epistemically blameworthy." This despite his beliefs being weakly justified, in the sense defined by Goldman, and despite his beliefs being meta-justified in the weaker and stronger senses indicated above.

Cartesians and internalists (broadly speaking) should find our victim to be quite conceivable. More naturalistic philosophers may well have their doubts, however, about the possibility of a subject whose "experience" and "beliefs" would be so radically divergent. For these there is a different parable. Take our victim to be a human, and suppose that the demon damages the victim's nervous system in such a way that the physical inputs to the system have to pass randomizing gates before the energy transmitted is transformed into any belief. Is there not something internally wrong with this victim as well, even though his beliefs may be supposed weakly and meta-justified, as above?

It may be replied that the "internal" here is not internal in the right sense. What is internal in the right sense must remain restricted to the subjectivity of the subject, to that which pertains to the subject's psychology; it must not go outside of that, even to the physiological conditions holding in the subject's body; or at least it must not do so under the aspect of the physiological, even if in the end it is the physiological (or something physical anyhow) that "realizes" everything mental and psychological.

Even if we accept that objection, however, a very similar difficulty yet remains for the conception of the blameless as the weakly justified or meta-justified (in either the weaker or the stronger sense). For it may be that the connections among the experiences and beliefs of the victim are purely random, as in the example above. True, in that example the randomness derives from the randomizing behavior of the demons involved. But there is no reason why the randomizing may not be brought inside. Thus, given a set of experiences or beliefs, there may be many alternative further beliefs that might be added by the subject, and there may be no rational mechanism that selects only one to be added. It may be rather that one of the many alternatives pops in at random: thus it is a radically random matter which alternative further belief is added in any specific case. Our evil demon's victim, though damaged internally in that way, so that his inner mental processes are largely random, may still by amazing coincidence acquire a coherent and comprehensive system of beliefs that makes him weakly justified and even meta-justified, in both the weaker and stronger senses indicated above. Yet is there not something still defective in such a victim, something that would preclude our holding him to be indiscernible from us in all internal respects of epistemic relevance?

Consider again the project of defining a notion of weak justification, however, a notion applicable to evil-demon victims in accordance with our intuitions; or that of defining a notion of meta-justification as above, one applicable equally to the victims and to ourselves in our normal beliefs. These projects may well be thought safe from the fact that a victim might be internally defective in ways that go beyond any matter of weak or meta-justification. Fair enough. But then of course we might have introduced a notion of superweak justification, and provided sufficient conditions for it as follows:

> S is superweakly justified in a certain belief if (1) the cognitive process that produces the belief is unreliable, but (2) S has not acquired that belief as a result of a deliberate policy of acquiring false beliefs (a policy adopted perhaps at the behest of a cruel master, or out of a deep need for epistemic self-abasement).

Someone may propose that a similarity between the victim of the evil demon on one side and ourselves on the other is that we all are super-weakly justified in our object-level beliefs in fires and the like. And this is fair and true enough. But it just does not go very far, not far enough. There is much else that is epistemically significant to the comparison between the victim and ourselves, much else that is left out of account by the mere notion of superweak justification. Perhaps part of what is left out is what the notion of weak justification would enable us to capture, and perhaps the notion of meta-justification, especially its stronger variant, would enable us to do even better. Even these stronger notions fall short of what is needed for fuller illumination, however, as I have tried to show above through the victims of randomization, whether demonderived or internally derived. In order to deal with the new evil-demon problem and with the problem of meta-incoherence we need a stronger notion than either that of the weakly justified or that of the metajustified, a stronger notion of the internally or subjectively justified.

D. A Stronger Notion of the "Internally Justified": Intellectual Virtue

Let us define an intellectual virtue or faculty as a competence in virtue of which one would mostly attain the truth and avoid error in a certain field of propositions F, when in certain conditions C. Subject S believes proposition P at time t out of intellectual virtue only if there is a field of propositions F, and there are conditions C, such that: (a) P is in F; (b) S is in C with respect to P; and (c) S would most likely be right if S believed a proposition X in field F when in conditions C with respect to X. Unlike Historical Reliabilism, this view does not require that there be a cognitive process leading to a belief in order for that belief to enjoy the strong justification required for constituting knowledge. Which is all to the good, since requiring such a process makes it hard to explain the justification for that paradigm of knowledge, the Cartesian cogito. There is a truth-conducive "faculty" through which everyone grasps their own existence at the moment of grasping. Indeed, what Descartes noticed about this faculty is its infallible reliability. But this requires that the existence which is grasped at a time t be existence at that very moment t. Grasp of earlier existence, no matter how near to the present, requires not the infallible cogito faculty, but a fallible faculty of memory. If we are to grant the cogito its due measure of justification, and to explain its exceptional epistemic status, we must allow faculties which operate instantaneously in the sense that the outcome belief is about the very moment of believing, and the conditions C are conditions about what obtains at that very moment – where we need place no necessary and general requirements about what went before.

By contrast with Historical Reliabilism, let us now work with intellectual virtues or faculties, defining their presence in a subject S by requiring

that, concerning propositions X in field F, once S were in conditions C with respect to X, S would most likely attain the truth and avoid error.

In fact a faculty or virtue would normally be a fairly stable disposition on the part of a subject *relative to an environment*. Being in conditions C with respect to proposition X would range from just being conscious and entertaining X – as in the case of "I think" or "I am" – to seeing an object O in good light at a favorable angle and distance, and without obstruction, etc. – as in "This before me is white and round." There is no restriction here to processes or to the internal. The conditions C and the field F may have much to do with the environment external to the subject: thus a moment ago we spoke of a C that involved seeing an external object in good light at a certain distance, etc. – all of which involves factors external to the subject.

Normally, we could hope to attain a conception of C and F which at best and at its most explicit will still have to rely heavily on the assumed nature of the subject and the assumed character of the environment. Thus it may appear to you that there is a round and white object before you and you may have reason to think that in conditions C (i.e., for middle-sized objects in daylight, at arm's length) you would likely be right concerning propositions in field F (about their shapes and colors). But of course there are underlying reasons why you would most likely be right about such questions concerning such objects so placed. And these underlying reasons have to do with yourself and your intrinsic properties, largely your eyes and brain and nervous system; and they have to do also with the medium and the environment more generally, and its contents and properties at the time. A fuller, more explicit account of what is involved in having an intellectual virtue or faculty is therefore this:

> Because subject S has a certain inner nature (I) and is placed in a certain environment (E), S would most likely be right on any proposition X in field F relative to which S stood in conditions C. S might be a human; I might involve possession of good eyes and a good nervous system including a brain in good order; E might include the surface of the earth with its relevant properties, within the parameters of variation experienced by humans over the centuries, or anyhow by subject S within his or her lifetime or within a certain more recent stretch of it; F might be a field of propositions specifying the colors or shapes of an object before S up to a certain level of determination and complexity (say greenness and squareness, but not chartreuseness or chiliagonicity); and C might be the conditions of S's seeing such an object in good light at arm's length and without obstructions.

If S believes a proposition X in field F, about the shape of a facing surface before him, and X is false, things might have gone wrong at interestingly different points. Thus the medium might have gone wrong unknown to the subject, and perhaps even unknowably to the subject; or something within the subject might have changed significantly: thus the lenses in the eyes of the subject might have become distorted, or the optic nerve might have become defective in ways important to shape recognition. If what goes wrong lies in the environment, that might prevent the subject from knowing what he believes, ever if his belief were true, but there is a sense in which the subject would remain subjectively justified or anyhow virtuous in so believing. It is this sense of internal virtue that seems most significant for dealing with the new evil-demon argument and with the meta-incoherence objection. Weak justification and meta-justification are just two factors that bear on internal value, but there are others surely, as the earlier examples were designed to show – examples in which the experience/belief relation goes awry, or in which a randomizer gate intervenes. Can something more positive be said in explication of such internal intellectual virtue?

Intellectual virtue is something that resides in a subject, something relative to an environment – though in the limiting case, the environment may be null, as perhaps when one engages in armchair reflection and thus comes to justified belief.

> A subject S's intellectual virtue V relative to an "environment" E may be defined as S's disposition to believe correctly propositions in a field F relative to which S stands in conditions C, in "environment" E.

It bears emphasis first of all that to be in a certain "environment" is *not* just a matter of having a certain spatio-temporal location, but is more a matter of having a complex set of properties, only some of which will be spatial or temporal. Secondly, we are interested of course in non-vacuous virtues, virtues which are not possessed simply because the subject would never be in conditions C relative to the propositions in F, or the like, though there may be no harm in allowing vacuous virtues to stand as trivial, uninteresting special cases.

Notice now that, so defined, for S to have a virtue V relative to an environment E at a time t, S does not have to be *in* E at t (i.e., S does not need to have the properties required). Further, suppose that, while outside environment E and while not in conditions C with respect to a proposition X in F, S still retains the virtue involved, *relative to E*, because the following ECF conditional remains true of S:

> (ECF)   that if in E and in C relative to X in F, then S would most likely be right in his belief or disbelief of X.

If S does so retain that virtue in that way, it can only be due to some components or aspects of S's intrinsic nature I, for it is S's possessing I together with being in E and in C with respect to X in F that fully explains and gives rise to the relevant disposition on the part of S, namely the disposition to believe correctly and avoid error regarding X in F, when so characterized and circumstanced.

We may now distinguish between (a) possession of the virtue (relative to E) in the sense of possession of the disposition, i.e., in the sense that the appropriate complex and general conditional (ECF) indicated above is true of the subject with the virtue, and (b) possession of a certain ground or basis of the virtue, in the sense of possessing an inner nature I from which the truth of the ECF conditional derives in turn. Of course one and the same virtue might have several different alternative possible grounds or bases. Thus the disposition to roll down an incline if free at its top with a certain orientation, in a certain environment (gravity, etc.), may be grounded in the sphericity and rigidity of an object, or alternatively it may be grounded in its cylindricality and rigidity. Either way, the conditional will obtain and the object will have the relevant disposition to roll. Similarly, Earthians and Martians may both be endowed with sight, in the sense of having the ability to tell colors and shapes, etc., though the principles of the operation of Earthian sight may differ widely from the principles that apply to Martians, which would or might presumably derive from a difference in the inner structure of the two species of being.

What now makes a disposition (and the underlying inner structure or nature that grounds it) an intellectual virtue? If we view such a disposition as defined by a C-F pair, then a being might have the disposition to be right with respect to propositions in field F when in conditions C with respect to them, relative to one environment E but not relative to another environment E'. Such virtues, then, i.e., such C-F dispositions, might be virtuous only relative to an environment E and not relative to a different environment E'. And what makes such a disposition a virtue relative to an environment E seems now as obvious as it is that having the truth is an epistemic desideratum, and that being so constituted that one would most likely attain the truth in a certain field in a certain environment, when in certain conditions *vis-à-vis* propositions in that field, is so far as it goes an epistemic desideratum, an intellectual virtue.

What makes a subject intellectually virtuous? What makes her inner nature meritorious? Surely we can't require that a being have all merit and virtue before it can have any. Consider then a subject who has a minimal virtue of responding, thermometer-like, to environing food, and suppose him to have the minimal complexity and sophistication required for having beliefs at all – so that he is not literally just a thermometer or the like. Yet we suppose him further to have no way of relating what he senses, and his sensing of it, to a wider view of things that will explain it all, that will enable him perhaps to make related predictions and exercise related control. No, this ability is a relatively isolated phenomenon to which the subject yields with infant-like, unselfconscious simplicity. Suppose indeed the subject is just an infant or a higher animal. Can we allow that he knows of the presence of food when he has a correct belief to that effect? Well, the subject may of course have reliable belief that there is something edible there, without having a belief as reliable as that of a normal, well-informed adult, with some knowledge of food composition, basic nutrition, basic perception, etc., and who can at least implicitly interrelate these matters for a relatively much more coherent and complete view of the matter and related matters. Edibility can be a fairly complex matter, and how we have perceptual access to that property can also be rather involved, and the more one knows about the various factors whose interrelation yields the perceptible edibility of something before one, presumably the more reliable one's access to that all-important property.

Here then is one proposal on what makes one's belief that-p a result of enough virtue to make one internally justified in that belief. First of all we need to relativize to an assumed environment, which need not be the environment that the believer actually is in. What is required for a subject S to believe that-p out of sufficient virtue relative to environment E is that the proposition that-p be in a field F and that S be in conditions C with respect to that proposition, such that S would not be in C with respect to a proposition in F while in environment E, without S being most likely to believe correctly with regard to that proposition; and further that by comparison with epistemic group G, S is not grossly defective in ability to detect thus the truth in field F; i.e., it cannot be that S would have, by comparison with G:

(a)   only a relatively very low probability of success,
(b)   in a relatively very restricted class F,
(c)   in a very restricted environment E,
(d)   in conditions C that are relatively infrequent,

where all this relativity holds with respect to fellow members of G and to their normal environment and circumstances. (There is of course some variation from context to context as to what the relevant group might be when one engages in discussion of whether or not some subject knows something or is at least justified in believing it. But normally a certain group will stand out, with humanity being the default value.)

E.   Intellectual Virtue Applied

Consider now again the new evil-demon problem and the problem of meta-incoherence. The crucial question in each case seems to be that of the internal justification of the subject, and this in turn seems not a matter of his superweak or weak or meta justification, so much as a matter of the virtue and total internal justification of that subject relative to an assumed group G and environment E, which absent any sign to the contrary one would take to be the group of humans in a normal human environment for the sort of question under consideration. Given these assumptions, the victim of the evil demon is virtuous and internally justified in every relevant respect, and not just in the respects of enjoying superweak, weak, and meta justification; for the victim is supposed to be just like an arbitrarily selected normal human in all cognitively relevant internal respects. Therefore, the internal structure and goings on in the victim must be at least up to par, in respect of how virtuous all of that internal nature makes the victim, relative to a normal one of us in our usual environment for considering whether we have a fire before us or the like. For those inclined towards mentalism or towards some broadly Cartesian view of the self and her mental life, this means at a minimum that the experience-belief mechanisms must not be random, but must rather be systematically truth-conducive, and that the subject must attain some minimum of coherent perspective on her own situation in the relevant environment, and on her modes of reliable access to information about that environment. Consider next those inclined towards naturalism, who hold the person to be either just a physical organism, or some physical part of an organism, or to be anyhow constituted essentially by some such physical entity; for these it would be required that the relevant physical being identical with or constitutive of the subject, in the situation in question, must not be defective in cognitively relevant internal respects; which would mean, among other things, that the subject would acquire beliefs about the colors or shapes of facing surfaces only under appropriate prompting at the relevant surfaces of the relevant visual organs (and not, e.g., through direct manipulation of the brain by some internal randomizing device).[12]

We have appealed to an intuitive distinction between what is intrinsic or internal to a subject or being, and what is extrinsic or external. Now when a subject receives certain inputs and emits as output a certain belief or a certain choice, that belief or choice can be defective either in virtue of an internal factor or in virtue of an external factor (or, of course, both). That is to say, it may be that everything inner, intrinsic, or internal to the subject operates flawlessly and indeed brilliantly, but that something goes awry – with the belief, which turns out to be false, or with the choice, which turns out to be disastrous – because of some factor that, with respect to that subject, is outer, extrinsic, or external.[13]

In terms of that distinction, the victim of the demon may be seen to be internally justified, just as internally justified as we are, whereas the meta-incoherent are internally unjustified, unlike us.

My proposal is that justification is relative to environment. Relative to our actual environment A, our automatic experience-belief mechanisms count as virtues that yield much truth and justification. Of course relative to the demonic environment D such mechanisms are not virtuous and yield neither truth nor justification. It follows that relative to D the demon's victims are not justified, and yet *relative to A their beliefs are justified*. Thus may we fit our surface intuitions about such victims: that they lack knowledge but not justification.

In fact, a fuller account should distinguish between "justification" and "aptness"[11] as follows:

(a) The "justification" of a belief B requires that B have a basis in its inference or coherence relations to other beliefs in the believer's mind – as in the "justification" of a belief derived from deeper principles, and thus "justified," or the "justification" of a belief adopted through cognizance of its according with the subject's principles, including principles as to what beliefs are permissible in the circumstances as viewed by that subject.

(b) The "aptness" of a belief B relative to an environment E requires that B derive from what relative to E is an intellectual virtue, i.e., a way of arriving at belief that yields an appropriate preponderance of truth over error (in the field of propositions in question, in the sort of context involved).

As far as I can see, however, the basic points would remain within the more complex picture as well. And note that "justification" itself would then amount to a sort of inner coherence, something that the demon's victims can obviously have despite their cognitively hostile environment, but also something that will earn them praise relative to that environment only if it is not just an inner drive for greater and greater explanatory comprehensiveness, a drive which leads nowhere but to a more and more complex tissue of falsehoods. If we believe our world not to be such a world, then we can say that, relative to our actual environment A, "justification" as inner coherence earns its honorific status, and is an intellectual virtue, dear to the scientist, the philosopher, and the detective. Relative to the demon's D, therefore, the victim's belief may be inapt and even unjustified – if "justification" is essentially honorific – or if "justified" simply because coherent then, relative to D, that justification may yet have little or no cognitive worth. Even so, relative to our environment A, the beliefs of the demon's victim may still be both apt and valuably justified through their inner coherence.

The epistemology defended in this volume – virtue perspectivism – is distinguished from generic reliabilism in three main respects:

(a)   Virtue perspectivism requires not just any reliable mechanism of belief acquisition for belief that can qualify as knowledge; it requires the belief to derive from an intellectual virtue or faculty (a notion defined more fully in "Intellectual Virtue in Perspective").

(b)   Virtue perspectivism distinguishes between aptness and justification of belief, where a belief is apt if it derives from a faculty or virtue, but is justified only if it fits coherently within the epistemic perspective of the believer – perhaps by being connected to adequate reasons in the mind of the believer in such a way that the believer follows adequate or even impeccable intellectual procedure ("Methodology and Apt Belief"). This distinction is used as one way to deal with the new evil-demon problem. (See "Intellectual Virtue in Perspective", Section D.)

(c)   Virtue perspectivism distinguishes between animal and reflective knowledge. For animal knowledge one needs only belief that is apt and derives from an intellectual virtue or faculty. By contrast, reflective knowledge always requires belief that not only is apt but also has a kind of justification, since it must be belief that fits coherently within the epistemic perspective of the believer (see "Knowledge and Intellectual Virtue", in Ernest Sosa, *Knowledge in Perspective* (Cambridge, Mass.: Cambridge University Press, 1991), 225–44, Section IX). This distinction is used earlier in this chapter to deal with the metaincoherence problem, and it also opens the way to a solution for the generality problem. (See "Intellectual Virtue in Perspective", Section D.)

Notes

1   Frank Ramsey, *The Foundations of Mathematics and Other Logical Essays* (London: Routledge & Kegan Paul, 1931).

2   David Armstrong, *Belief, Truth and Knowledge* (Cambridge University Press, 1973); Fred Dretske, "Conclusive Reasons," *Australasian Journal of Philosophy* 49 (1971): 1–22; Alvin Goldman, "What Is Justified Belief?" in George Pappas, ed., *Justification and Knowledge* (Dordrecht: D Reidel, 1979); Robert Nozick, *Philosophical Explanations* (Cambridge, Mass.: Harvard University Press, 1981), chapter 3; Marshall Swain, *Reasons and Knowledge* (Ithaca, N.Y.: Cornell University Press, 1981).

3   This problem is pointed out by Goldman himself (Goldman, "What Is Justified Belief?", p. 12), and is developed by Richard Feldman in "Reliability and Justification," *The Monist* 68 (1985): 159–74.

4   This problem is presented by Keith Lehrer and Stewart Cohen in "Justification, Truth, and Coherence," *Synthese* 55 (1983): 191–207.

5   This sort of problem is developed by Laurence Bonjour in "Externalist Theories of Empirical Knowledge," in *Midwest Studies in Philosophy, Vol. 5: Studies in Epistemology*, ed. P. French et al. (Minneapolis: University of Minnesota Press, 1980).

6   See Goldman, "What Is Justified Belief?" pp. 13–14.

7   Alvin Goldman, *Epistemology and Cognition* (Cambridge, Mass.: Harvard University Press, 1986); Goldman, "Strong and Weak Justification," in *Philosophical Perspectives, Vol. 2: Epistemology (1988)*: 51–71.

8   Some of these are pointed out in my "Beyond Scepticism, to the Best of our Knowledge," *Mind 97* (1988): 153–88.

9   Goldman, "Strong and Weak Justification," p. 56.

10 I will use the modified sense in what follows because it seems clearly better as an approach to blamelessness; but the substance of the critique to follow would apply also to the unmodified sense of weakly justified belief.

11 Though, actually, it is not really clear how these notions will deal with part (d) of the problem of meta-incoherence: cf. Goldman, *Epistemology and Cognition*, pp. 111–12.

12 As for the generality problem, my own proposed solution appears in "Intellectual Virtue in Perspective", in Ernest Sosa, *Knowledge in Perspective* (Cambridge, Mass.: Cambridge University Press, 1991), 270–93.

13 This sort of distinction between the internal virtue of a subject and his or her (favorable or unfavorable) circumstances is drawn in "How Do You Know?", in Ernest Sosa, *Knowledge in Perspective* (Cambridge, Mass.: Cambridge University Press, 1991), 19–34. There knowledge is relativized to epistemic community, though not in a way that imports any subjectivism or conventionalism, and consequences are drawn for the circumstances within which praise or blame is appropriate (see especially the first part of Section II).

14 For this sort of distinction, see, e.g., "Methodology and Apt Belief," in Ernest Sosa, *Knowledge in Perspective* (Cambridge, Mass.: Cambridge University Press, 1991), 245–56. The more generic distinction between external and internal justification may be found in "The Analysis of 'Knowledge That P'," in *Knowledge in Perspective*, 15–18.

7

WHAT AM I TO BELIEVE?

Richard Foley

The central issue of Descartes's *Meditations* is an intensely personal one. Descartes asks a simple question of himself, one that each of us can also ask of ourselves, "What am I to believe?" One way of construing this question – indeed, the way Descartes himself construed it – is as a methodological one. The immediate aim is not so much to generate a specific list of propositions for me to believe. Rather, I want to formulate for myself some general advice about how to proceed intellectually.

If this is what I want, I am not likely to be content with telling myself that I am to use reliable methods of inquiry. Nor will I be content with telling myself to believe only that which is likely to be true given my evidence. It is not as if such advice is mistaken. It is just unhelpful. I knew all along that it is better for me to use reliable methods rather than unreliable ones, and I also knew that it is better for me to believe that which is likely to be true rather than that which is not. Besides, I cannot simply read off from the world what methods are reliable ones, nor can I read off when something is likely to be true given my evidence. These are just the sorts of things about which I want advice.

An appeal to the prevailing intellectual standards will not provide what I am looking for either. I will not be satisfied with a recommendation that tells me to conduct my inquiries in accordance with the standards of my community, or alternatively in accordance with the standards of those recognized in my community as experts. I will want to know whether these standards are desirable ones. The dominant standards in a community are not always to be trusted and those of the recognized experts are not either.

My question is a more fundamental one and also a more egocentric one. It is not that I think that the task of working out intellectual guidelines is one that is best conducted by myself in solitude. If I do think this, I am being foolish. A task of this sort is better done in full public view, with results being shared. This increases the chances of correction and decreases the chances of self-deception. In the end, however, I must make up my own mind. I must make up my own mind about what is true and who is reliable and what is worth respecting in my intellectual tradition. It is this that prompts the question, what am I to believe? The question is one of how I am to go about making up my own mind.

Here is one way of answering this question: I am to make up my mind by marshalling my intellectual resources in a way that conforms to my own deepest epistemic standards. If I conduct my inquiries in such a way that I would not be critical of the resulting beliefs even if I were to be deeply reflective, then these beliefs are rational for me in an important sense, an egocentric sense. There are various ways of trying to spell out exactly what this amounts to, but for purposes here the details can be left open. The basic idea is that if I am to be egocentrically rational, I must not have internal reasons for retraction, ones whose force I myself would acknowledge were I to be sufficiently reflective.

An answer of this sort has the right egocentric flavor, but as advice it is not very satisfying. It seems misdirected. When I am trying to formulate some intellectual advice for myself, or more generally when I am deliberating about what to believe and how to proceed intellectually, my concern is not with my own standards. The point of my deliberations is not to find out what I think or would think on deep reflection about the reliability of various methods. My concern is with what methods are in fact reliable; it is with the objective realities, not my subjective perceptions.

Be this as it may, the recommendation that I conform to my own standards is an appropriate answer to the egocentric question, "What am I to believe?" More precisely, it is an appropriate answer if the question is interpreted as one about what I am to believe insofar as my ends are epistemic. Even more precisely, it is an appropriate philosophical answer to this question, the one that should be given if the question is pushed to its limit. The reflection prompted by the egocentric question initially has an outward focus. The object of my concern is the world. I wonder whether this or that is true. If pushed hard enough, however, the reflection ultimately curls back upon me. I become concerned with my place in the world, especially my place as an inquirer. I want to know what methods of inquiry are suitable for me insofar as I am trying to determine whether this or that is true. Should I trust the evidence of my senses? Should I use scientific methods? Should I rely on sacred texts? Should I have confidence in my intuitions?

These questions can lead to still others. They can make me wonder about the criteria that I am presupposing in evaluating various methods. Meta-issues thus begin to occupy me. My primary concern is no longer with whether it would be more reliable for me to use this method rather than that one. Nor is it with what each would have me believe. Rather, it is with my criteria for evaluating these various methods and in turn with the criteria for these criteria, and so on. This is the point at which the egocentric question can be appropriately answered by talking about me. What am I to believe? Ultimately, I am to believe that which is licensed by my own deepest epistemic standards. An answer of this sort is the appropriate one for epistemologists. It is the appropriate answer for those whose reflections on the egocentric question take them to this level.

Insofar as nonepistemologists raise the question of what they are to believe, they are principally interested in a different kind of answer. They want an answer that gives them marks of truth and reliability. Epistemologists also want such marks, but once their deliberations reach the meta-level that is characteristic of epistemology, they are forced to admit that regardless of how they marshal their intellectual resources, there are no non–question-begging guarantees that the way that they are marshalling them is reliable. Vulnerability to error cannot be avoided. It is built into us and our methods. However, vulnerability to self-condemnation is not, and it is essentially this that egocentric rationality demands. It demands that we have beliefs that we as truth-seekers would not condemn ourselves for having even if we were to be deeply reflective. This is the post-Cartesian answer to the Cartesian question.

It is also an answer that is bound to be disappointing to anyone who thinks that an essential part of the epistemologist's job is to provide intellectual guidance. Much of the attractiveness of the Cartesian method of doubt is that it purports to do just this. It purports to provide us with a way of proceeding intellectually, and a concrete one at that. The proposed method tends to strike the contemporary reader as overly demanding, but it would nonetheless seem to be to Descartes's credit, indeed part of his greatness, that he at least attempted to provide such guidance. Contemporary epistemology is apt to seem barren by comparison. Concrete intellectual advice has all but disappeared from it. Of course, no one expects epistemologists to provide advice about local intellectual concerns. The specialist is better placed to give us that – the physicist, the mathematician, the meteorologist, whoever the relevant expert happens to be. What we might like from epistemologists, however, is useful advice about the most basic matters of intellectual inquiry, but it is just this that contemporary epistemology fails to provide.

This is to be regretted only if epistemologists are in a privileged position to give such advice, but they are not. They may be in a privileged position to say something about the general conditions of rational belief. Likewise, they may be able to say interesting things about the conditions of knowledge and other related notions. The mistake is to assume that these conditions should provide us with useful guidelines for the most basic matters of intellectual inquiry. They cannot. The conditions will either be misdirected or not fundamental enough or both.

Consider the proposal that at least in one sense, being rational is essentially a matter of using methods that are reliable. Perhaps this is so, but if a proposal of this sort is meant to provide me with intellectual guidance, I must be able to distinguish reliable from unreliable methods. However, this is precisely one of the matters about which I will want advice. It is also a matter about which epistemologists are not in a privileged position to give advice, except indirectly. They may have useful and even surprising things to say about what reliability is, but once these things are said, it will be up to the rest of us to apply what they say. We will have to determine what methods and procedures are in fact reliable. So, no condition of this sort will be able to provide me with fundamental intellectual advice. On the contrary, if such conditions are to help guide inquiry, I must already be able to make the kind of determinations that they themselves imply are fundamental for me to make if I am to be rational. I reliably must be able to pick out which methods are reliable.

The same is true of other proposals. One proposal, for instance, is that I am rational only if I conform to the standards of the acknowledged experts.[1] If I am to use this to guide inquiry, I once again must be able to make determinations of just the sort that are said to be fundamental to my being rational. How am I to determine what the relevant expert standards are? Presumably by conducting an inquiry that itself conforms to the standards of the experts. But which standards are these, I want to know.

Suppose that the proposal is more inwardly looking. In particular, consider the proposal that it is rational in an important sense, an egocentric sense, for me to believe only that which I would not be motivated to retract even on deep reflection. If what I want is advice, this proposal is a non-starter. It is misdirected. Besides, I do not have the time to be deeply reflective about everything that I believe. So, even here I would be confronted with the problem of knowing how to apply the recommendation. How am I to determine whether my practices and my resulting beliefs conform with my own deep epistemic standards, the ones that I would approve of on reflection? Presumably by conforming to those very standards. But what I want to know, and what is often by no means obvious, is how I am to do this, short of being deeply reflective about all of these practices and beliefs?

The only way to avoid problems of this sort is to make the conditions of rationality ones to which we have immediate and unproblematic access. But this has a familiar and unpromising ring to it. Recall Bertrand Russell's epistemology, for example. He claimed that we are directly acquainted with certain truths and that these truths make various other propositions probable for us. If this kind of epistemology is to provide us with fundamental intellectual advice, we must be capable of determining immediately and unproblematically when we are directly acquainted with something and when we are not. Likewise, we must be capable of determining immediately and unproblematically what propositions are made probable by the truths with which we are directly acquainted. Otherwise we will want advice about how to make these kinds of determinations. Russell's epistemology leaves room for the possibility that we do have these capabilities. Being directly acquainted with something is itself the sort of phenomenon with which we can be directly acquainted. Similarly, according to Russell's epistemology, we can be directly acquainted with the truth that one thing makes another thing probable.[2]

An epistemology of direct acquaintance or something closely resembling it is our only alternative if we expect the conditions of rationality to give us useful advice about those matters that the conditions themselves imply are fundamental to our being rational. It is also the kind of epistemology that few are willing to take seriously anymore. But if not, we must give up the idea that epistemology is in the business of giving fundamental intellectual advice. For that matter, we must give up the whole idea that there is such advice to be had. There can be no general recipe for the conduct of our intellectual lives, if for no other reason than that questions can always arise about how to follow the recipe, questions to which the recipe itself can give no useful answer.

By contrast, consider the kind of advice that logic professors sometimes give their students. They sometimes tell them to try to solve difficult proofs from "both ends," working alternatively down from the premises and up from the desired conclusion. This is advice that is often useful for students, but it is also advice that has no pretenses of being about the most fundamental issues of inquiry. It is not even about the most fundamental matters of logical inference. This is no accident. It is useful precisely because it is embedded in a prior intellectual enterprise, one in which certain skills and abilities are taken for granted.

This is an obvious enough point once it is made explicit, but it is nonetheless a point that is easy enough to overlook. It is overlooked, for instance, by those internalists who argue against externalist conditions of rational belief on the grounds that they are unhelpful insofar as we are interested in advice about how to go about improving our belief systems. As a complaint against externalism, this will not do, but not because externalist conditions of rational belief provide us with useful advice. They do not. It is not especially useful to be told that we are to have beliefs that are products of reliable cognitive processes, for example. The problem, rather, is that internalist conditions of rational belief do not provide us with genuinely useful advice either.

Of course, internalists have often thought otherwise. One of Descartes's conceits, for example, was that the method of doubt provides advice to inquirers that is at once both useful and fundamental. By this I do not mean that Descartes intended his method to be used by everyone, even the fishmonger and the butcher. He did not. He intended it to be used only by philosopher-scientists, and he intended that even they use it only for a special purpose. It was not to be used in their everyday lives. It was to be used only for the purpose of conducting secure theoretical inquiry. However, the method was intended to provide advice at the most fundamental level about how to conduct such inquiry.

But, in fact, it fails to do this. It faces the same difficulties as other attempts to give intellectual advice that is both fundamental and useful. Either it presupposes that philosopher-scientists can make determinations of a sort that the recommendation itself says is fundamental or it is misdirected advice or perhaps both. Which of these difficulties Descartes's advice is subject to depends on how we understand it.

Suppose the advice is for philosopher-scientists to believe just those propositions whose truth they cannot doubt when they bring them clearly to mind. Then the advice faces both difficulties. First, it is not fundamental enough. It need not be immediately obvious to philosopher-scientists just what is indubitable for them in this sense and what is not. They thus can have questions about that which the advice says is fundamental to their being rational, and these will be questions that the advice cannot help them answer. Second, the advice is misdirected. It is advice that looks inward rather than outward. Insofar as the goal of philosopher-scientists is to conduct theoretical inquiry in an absolutely secure manner, their interest is to find propositions that cannot be false rather than ones that cannot be doubted. Of course, Descartes thought that there was a linkage between the two. He thought that what cannot be subjectively doubted cannot be objectively false, but there is no reason to think that he was right about this.

Suppose, then, that we interpret Descartes as offering more objective advice. He is telling philosopher-scientists to believe just those propositions that are clear and distinct for them, and he is stipulating from the very beginning that only truths can be genuinely clear and distinct. Then this exacerbates the first difficulty. If philosopher-scientists try to take the advice to heart, the question of whether something really is clear and distinct in this sense becomes one of the fundamental issues about which they will want advice.[3]

So, contrary to his hopes, Descartes did not succeed in providing advice that is both useful and fundamental. More precisely, he did not succeed in providing advice about the conduct of inquiry as opposed to its goals. For despite the above difficulties, we can still view Descartes as making a recommendation about what our intellectual goal should be. He is advising us to make certainty our goal, at least for theoretical purposes. We should try to believe as much as possible without encountering the risk of error. Of course, even this is advice that few of us would be willing to take seriously. The goal is far too demanding. Almost all of us are willing to put up with some risks of error in our theoretical pursuits.

But the important point here is that even if I did have this as my intellectual goal, Descartes has no good, substantive advice for me about how to achieve it. The advice he gives is either misdirected or not fundamental enough. If the advice is to believe what is clear and distinct, where by definition only truths are clear and distinct, it is not fundamental enough. If the advice is to believe what I cannot doubt, it is misdirected. At best, it is a piece of meta-advice. Indeed, when stripped of its spurious guarantees of truth, the advice amounts only to this: insofar as my goal is to believe as much as possible without risk, then from my perspective the way to go about trying to achieve this goal is to believe just that which strikes me as being risk-free and then hope for the best.

This is a sensible enough recommendation but also an altogether safe one. After all, someone can give me this kind of advice even if she has no convictions one way or the other about whether or not I am constituted in such a way that what I find impossible to doubt is in fact true. It is not much different from telling me to do what I think is best about the problem I have confided to her, even when she has no idea whether what I think best really is best.

Of course, if she were presumptuous enough, she could go on to advise me about what I myself deep-down really think is the best way to deal with the problem. Indeed, this would be the counterpart of Descartes's strategy. He first recommends that I believe just those propositions that I cannot doubt, and he then tries to tell me, albeit with a notorious lack of success, which propositions these are. On the other hand, if she is not in this way presumptuous, if she simply tells me to do what I think is best and then leave matters at that, this is not so much genuine advice as a substitute for it. She is not trying to tell me what is best for me. She leaves this to me to figure out for myself.

The recommendation that I have beliefs that I as a truth-seeker would not condemn myself for having, even if I were to be deeply reflective, has a similar status. This recommendation is internalistic in character, since it emphasizes matters of perspective. But insofar as it is conceived as a piece of advice, it is at best meta-advice. If it were interpreted as an attempt to provide me with something more than this – if it were interpreted, for example, as an attempt to provide me with serious, substantive intellectual guidance – it would be clearly inadequate. So, this cannot be the charitable way to interpret it. It must instead be conceived as a different kind of recommendation.

What kind of recommendation? It is a recommendation about the conditions of rational belief – more exactly, the conditions for a certain kind of rational belief, egocentrically rational belief. The goal is to provide a notion of rational belief that is both enlightening and recognizable: enlightening in that it helps us think more clearly about related notions – truth, knowledge, skepticism, dogmatism, and intellectual disagreement, to name a few; and recognizable in that it helps us to understand the ascriptions of rationality that we want to make, both the ones we are inclined to make in our everyday lives and also the ones we are inclined to make when doing epistemology.

This conception takes epistemology, even internalist epistemology, out of the business of giving intellectual advice. The primary epistemological project is to offer an account of the conditions of rational belief, and there is no reason why this project must generate useful advice. Indeed, epistemology is not even the part of philosophy that is most closely tied to the giving of intellectual advice. Studies in logic and probability are more likely to generate useful advice than is epistemology proper. But even here, expectations should not be too high. Nothing extensive in the way of advice will come out of these studies either.

In part, this is so because logic and probability theory do not tell how to react when we discover logical inconsistency and probabilistic incoherence. There will be any number of ways for us to restore consistency or coherency. Similarly, when inconsistency or incoherency threatens, there will be any number of ways for us to avoid them. In neither case does logic or probability theory have anything to tell us about which of these many ways is preferable.[1]

So, there will not be much in the way of concrete positive advice that can come out of either logic or probability theory. In addition, there are limits even to the usefulness of the negative advice they are able to generate. Part of this is because of a familiar problem. Insofar as the advice is always to avoid inconsistency and incoherency, this is often difficult advice to follow. To do so, we need to be able to determine whether or not a set of opinions is inconsistent or incoherent, but the original advice cannot help with this. For help with this problem, we will need new advice – in effect, advice about how to apply the original advice.

Moreover, there is an even more basic limitation on this advice. It is not always good advice. It is not always and everywhere desirable to avoid inconsistency and incoherency. Doing so might make my overall situation worse. It might even make it intellectually worse. If I recognize that my opinions are inconsistent or incoherent, I know that they cannot possibly all be accurate. So, I know that my opinions are less than ideal. But from this it does not immediately follow that it is irrational for me to have these opinions. What is rational for me in such situations depends upon what realistic alternatives I have.[5] In betting situations, it is often rational to adopt a strategy that I know in advance is less than ideal, one in which I am sure to lose at least some of my bets. Moreover, this can be rational even when there are available to me other strategies that hold out at least some possibility of a flawless outcome. These other strategies may be unduly daring or unduly cautious. The same is true of beliefs. Sometimes it is rational for me to have beliefs that I know cannot possibly all be accurate. Indeed, this is the real lesson of the lottery, the preface, and other such paradoxes.[6]

None of this is to say that logic and probability theory do not have a special role to play in intellectual guidance. They obviously do. Logical inconsistency and probabilistic incoherence indicate that my opinions are less than ideal. They thus put me on guard about these opinions. What they do not tell me is how to react to this situation. From the fact that my opinions are less than ideal, it does not automatically follow that I must on pains of irrationality change any of these opinions. And even in those cases where I do have to change something, nothing in logic or probability theory tells me which opinions to change. They give me no concrete advice about this.[7]

Of course, things are different when it is issues of logic and probability theory that are themselves being debated. Similarly, they are different when other specifically philosophical issues are being debated. The relevant philosophical experts will then be in a special position to give me substantive advice. But when it is not philosophical matters that are at issue, advice will have to come from other sources. Fortunately, there is no shortage of such sources. Most are relatively specific in nature. I am confronted with an intellectual problem. So, I go to an expert on the topic in question or consult a reference work or perhaps simply ask a knowledgeable friend.

There are also sources that hold out the hope of more general advice, and it is no accident that among the richest of these are ones in which philosophers have become more and more interested – cognitive science and the history of science. Of course, there are other philosophical motives for interest in these fields. Nevertheless, there is a story to be told here, one whose rough outlines are that as it became increasingly obvious that epistemology could not be expected to give fundamental intellectual advice, philosophers became increasingly interested in empirical disciplines that had human intellectual inquiry as part of their subject matter.

It is not as if these disciplines can be expected to provide the kind of fundamental advice that epistemology fails to provide. If this were their aim, they would encounter all the familiar problems. There would be problems of how to apply the advice, for example. But with these disciplines, unlike epistemology, there is not even a pretense of their being able to provide fundamental advice. This is so not just because we can have questions about the way inquiry is conducted within these disciplines themselves, although this is true enough. It is also because the kind of information that these disciplines are in a position to provide will itself call for interpretation. The fact that scientists have historically used procedures of a certain kind or the fact that we are disposed to make inferences of a certain kind are themselves facts that need to be evaluated before they can provide us with intellectual advice. We will especially want to know whether these procedures and inferences are reliable ones. But to answer this question, we will need to appeal to something more than the history of science and cognitive science.

On the other hand, if what we seek is not advice about the most fundamental matters of inquiry but rather some useful rules of thumb, these disciplines can be of help. At their best, they are able to provide a rich supply of data from which, with persistence and with the help of still other disciplines, we may be able to tease out some useful advice.

Sometimes it may not even take much teasing, especially for negative advice. Recent cognitive science is filled with studies that purport to show recurrent patterns of error in the way that we make inferences. The errors arise, for example, from an insensitivity to sample size or an under-utilization of known prior probabilities in making predictions or an inclination in certain kinds of situations to assign a higher probability to a conjunction than one of its conjuncts.[8] These are data from which we can fashion intellectual advice for ourselves – advice that alerts us about our tendency to make these kinds of errors.

Extracting intellectual advice from the history of science is seldom so straightforward a matter, but it, too, can provide us with useful data. It does so in part because historical examples are less easily manipulable than purely hypothetical ones. This is not to say that dreamed-up examples cannot instruct. They obviously can, and indeed they are often more convenient, since they are more neat than real life examples. They can be designed to our purposes, with extraneous features deleted. But, of course, this is just the danger as well. It is sometimes all too easy to tailor them to suit our purposes. Actual cases in all of their detail are not so malleable.[9]

Suppose, then, that I have looked at the history of science and at the findings of cognitive science and at various other studies that provide data about human inquiry. So, I now have all this data. How am I to go about using the data to generate some rules of thumb for the conduct of inquiry? Sometimes it will be obvious, since sometimes the data will reveal that I have a tendency to make what I myself readily concede to be errors. But matters will not always be so obvious, and besides, I want positive as well negative advice. Is there any general advice to be had about this, the process of using the available data to generate intellectual advice?

Those who have been influenced by contemporary moral theory might advise me to employ something akin to the method of wide reflective equilibrium. The rough idea would be that I am to begin with my initial intuitions about what constitute sound methods of inquiry. Then I am to test these intuitions against all the data and all the cases that strike me as relevant – data from cognitive science about characteristic patterns of inference, cases from the history of science, imaginary cases, and anything else that I take to be relevant. Finally, I am to use my best judgment to resolve any conflicts among these intuitions, data, and cases. Sometimes I will judge that my original intuitions are sound. Other times the data or the cases will convince me to alter the original intuitions, and still other times I will be disposed to alter both by a process of give-and-take.[10]

The problem with this recommendation is the familiar one. It is not so much mistaken as unhelpful. At best, it is meta-advice. Indeed, it is essentially the same meta-advice that is implicit in the notion of egocentric rationality. It tells me essentially this: take into account all the data that I think to be relevant and then reflect on the data, solving conflicts in the way that I judge best. On the other hand, it does not tell me what kinds of data are relevant, nor does it tell me what is the best way to resolve conflicts among the data. It leaves me to muck about on these questions as best I can.

And muck I must, for this is part of the human intellectual predicament. It is not that there is no useful intellectual advice to be had. There obviously is. It is just that philosophy is not in a particularly privileged position to provide it. The kind of intellectual advice that philosophy has been sometimes thought to be in a privileged position to give – viz., general advice about the most fundamental issues of intellectual inquiry – is precisely the kind of advice that cannot be usefully given. Attempts to provide this kind of advice are inevitably misdirected or not sufficiently fundamental.

On the other hand, philosophy in general and epistemology in particular has no special claim on more modest kinds of advice – e.g., specific advice on local intellectual concerns or general rules of thumb about the conduct of inquiry. The relevant expert is better positioned for the former, while the latter is best produced by reflection upon all of the available data. We can potentially use anything to fashion intellectual rules of thumb, from the findings of cognitive science to studies in the history of science to mnemonic devices and other intellectual tricks, even relatively trivial ones, such as carrying nines, for example.

This is a project to which philosophers can make important and diverse contributions. They can help us to appreciate that there are various ends at which inquiry might be aimed, for example. Some of these ends are epistemic in nature, in that they are concerned with the accuracy and comprehensiveness of our belief systems. Others are more pragmatic. Moreover, there are distinctions to be made even among those ends that are epistemic. Some are synchronic (roughly, getting things as right as we can for the moment), while others are diachronic (roughly, getting things right eventually). Such distinctions can be important when we are trying to provide ourselves with intellectual advice, since certain kinds of recommendations – for example, the recommendation that we prefer the simplest of otherwise equal hypotheses – will seem plausible relative to some of these aims and not so plausible relative to others.

There is much else of relevance that philosophers can tell us. They can tell us what it is to have an explanation of something, or what it is to have a merely verbal disagreement as opposed to a substantive one. They can distinguish different sorts of arguments for us, emphasizing that different criteria are appropriate for evaluating these arguments. More generally, they can act as intellectual gadflies, examining and criticizing the developments in other intellectual disciplines. And of course, they can also try to describe the conditions under which inquiry is conducted rationally, only these conditions will not be of a sort that provides us with much useful intellectual guidance.

There are those who will insist that this will not do. They will insist that one of our most important intellectual projects is that of generating sound intellectual advice and that we need guidance about how to conduct this project. There are better and worse ways of doing so, and it is epistemology's special role to instruct us about this. Nothing else is positioned to do so. Science, for example, cannot do so, since what we need is advice that is prior to inquiry rather than the result of inquiry. It is only epistemology that can provide us with this kind of fundamental guidance.

This is a view that sees epistemology as the arbiter of intellectual procedures. The presupposition is that epistemology can be prior to other inquiries and that as such it is capable of providing us with a non–question-begging rationale for using one set of intellectual procedures rather than another. Just the reverse is true. Epistemology begins at a late stage of inquiry. It builds on preexisting inquiry and without that inquiry it would be subjectless. One consequence of this is that there is no alternative to using antecedent opinion and methods in thinking about our intellectual procedures. There is no way of doing epistemology *ex nihilo*, and hence it is no more capable of giving us non–question-begging advice about basic issues of intellectual procedure than is anything else.

There is deeper presupposition that also must be abandoned, the presupposition that it is important for us to have such advice. Descartes and the Enlightenment figures who followed him – Locke, for example – thought that this was important, since they thought that the alternative was intellectual anarchy, and perhaps as a result religious and political anarchy as well. Their assumptions seemed to be that there are countless ways of proceeding intellectually, that we are pretty much free to choose among them as we please, and that there must be a non–question-begging rationale for preferring one of these ways over the others if intellectual chaos is to be avoided. Descartes and Locke saw it as their task, the task of the epistemologist, to provide such a rationale.

If this were an accurate description of our intellectual situation, they might have been right. But in fact, this is not our situation. It is not as if we are each given a menu of basic intellectual procedures and that our task is either to find a non–question-begging way of choosing among these procedures or to face intellectual anarchy. Our problem tends to be the opposite one. By the time we reach the point at which it occurs to us that there might be fundamentally different kinds of intellectual procedures, we are largely shaped intellectually. We come to this point equipped not only with a battery of assumptions about the world but also a battery of intellectual skills and habits. All of our intellectual inquiries are grounded in these resources, and the bulk of our intellectual lives must be conducted using them in largely automatic fashion. We have no choice about this. Fundamental rules for the direction of the mind would do us little good even if we had them. We would not have the time or resources to make proper use of them. Insofar as our goal is intellectual improvement, the emphasis is better placed on the development of skills and habits that we think will help make us more reliable inquirers.

The project of building up such skills and habits lacks the drama of the Cartesian project. It is inevitably a piecemeal project. To engage in it, we must draw upon an enormous number of background assumptions, skills, and habits, ones that for the time being we are content to use rather than reform. Questions can still arise about this background. We may realize that had we

been born with significantly different cognitive equipment or into a significantly different environment, these assumptions, skills, and habits might have
been considerably different. These possibilities are mainly of theoretical interest, however. They are of interest for epistemology. They can be used to
discuss skeptical worries, for instance. On the other hand, they normally will
not be of much interest insofar as our purpose is epistemic improvement.
After all, most of these fundamentally different ways of proceeding will not
be real options for us. It is not as if we are radically free to reconstitute ourselves intellectually in any way that we see fit and that we need some guidance about whether to do so or how to do so.

Of course, we are not entirely without options. We cannot alter our fundamental intellectual procedures by a simple act of will, but by making incre-
mental changes over a long enough period of time, we perhaps could train
ourselves to use procedures that are very different from those that we currently employ. Perhaps there are even ways of bringing about the changes
more immediately. Drugs might do the trick, for instance. There are those
who have recommended peyote or LSD as a way to truth. But even here,
insofar as our worry is intellectual chaos, the search need not be for a
non–question-begging way of deciding which procedures, our present ones
or the drug-induced ones, are the more reliable. It is enough to point out that
from our present undrugged perspective, most of us have no reason to think
that the drugged perspective is the more reliable one. Quite the contrary, from
our current perspective it seems far less reliable. Thus, insofar as our ends are
epistemic, we have no motivation to drug ourselves.

Descartes and Locke notwithstanding, our primary intellectual threat is not
that of chaos, and our primary intellectual need is not for advice about the
most fundamental matters of intellectual outlook. We cannot help but be
largely guided by our intellectual inheritance on these matters. The primary
threat is rather that of intellectual conformity, and our primary need is for
intellectual autonomy. Little in life is more difficult than resisting domination
by one's intellectual environment. It is all too easy for us to be intellectual
lemmings. We do not have the ability to cast off wholesale the effects of our
environment and adopt a radically new intellectual outlook, so this cannot be
the basis of our intellectual autonomy. It is instead based upon our ability to
use our existing opinions and existing methods to examine our opinions and
methods. It resides in our ability to make ourselves into an object of study, to
evaluate and monitor ourselves, and moreover to do so not so much in terms
of the prevailing standards but rather in terms of our own standards. This
ability creates a space for intellectual autonomy.

But it is only a space. Self-monitoring in terms of our own personal standards does not altogether eliminate the threat of intellectual domination. As

Foucault emphasized recently and as Marx had argued earlier, the most effective kind of control is that which is internalized.[11] We accept as our own the very norms by which we are controlled. Be this as it may, our only alternative is to monitor ourselves for this as well, to try as best we can to make ourselves aware of this possibility and thus prevent it. Of course, there is no guarantee that we will be successful. If the domination is thorough enough, leaving no trace of its influence, then no amount of self-monitoring will do much good.

But in this respect, the possibility of complete and utter domination is not much different from the possibility of complete and utter deception. Just as a powerful enough demon could use our own experiences to deceive us thoroughly without our being aware of it, so too a powerful enough dominating force could use our own standards to control us thoroughly without our being aware of it. But neither of these gives us a rationale to be dismissive of our intellectual projects. The possibility of radical error does not mean that knowledge is altogether impossible for us, and the possibility of radical domination does not mean that intellectual autonomy is altogether impossible for us.

Our intellectual standards cannot help but show the effects of our intellectual environment, but they need not be swallowed up by it. My standards can and presumably sometimes do differ from the standards of the people who surround me. When they do, intellectual autonomy as well as egocentric rationality requires that I conform to my standards rather than the prevailing ones.

Notes

1 "[W]hen we judge someone's inference to be normatively inappropriate, we are comparing it to (what we take to be) the applicable principles of inference sanctioned by expert reflective equilibrium" (Stephen Stich, "Could Man be an Irrational Animal?" *Synthese* 64 [1985]: 115–35).

2 Bertrand Russell, *The Problems of Philosophy* (Oxford: Oxford University Press, 1959). See also Richard Fumerton, *Metaphysical and Epistemological Problems of Perception* (Lincoln, Neb.: University of Nebraska Press, 1985), especially 57–8.

3 Roderick Chisholm's epistemology faces analogous problems. Like Descartes, Chisholm thinks that our "purpose in raising [epistemological] questions is to correct and improve our own epistemic situation; . . . we want to do our best to improve our set of beliefs – to replace those that are unjustified by others that are justified and to replace those that have a lesser degree of justification with others that have a greater degree of justification." See Chisholm, *Theory of Knowledge*, 3d edn. (Englewood Cliffs, N.J.: Prentice-Hall, 1989), 1. He takes this

to show that the notion of epistemic justification cannot be explicated in an externalist manner. Instead, the conditions of epistemic justification must be both "*internal* and *immediate* in that one can find out directly, by reflection, what one is justified in believing at any time" (p. 7). However, the conditions that Chisholm himself defends, as expressed in his principles of epistemic justification, are often very complicated. They are difficult enough to understand and even more difficult to apply, especially since many of them make reference to the believer's total evidence and total set of beliefs. Thus, even if I thoroughly understand Chisholm's principles, it is unlikely that I will always be able to determine by reflection on my state of mind whether or not a belief is justified according to them. Moreover, even if this always were at least theoretically possible, it need not always be obvious to me how I am to go about making these determinations. I will not always be able to look inward and simply read off whether Chisholm's conditions are met. So, not just any kind of reflection will do. But if not, I will want to know how to conduct these reflections, and Chisholm's principles do not provide me with any helpful advice about this.

4   Points of this sort have been especially emphasized by Gilbert Harman. See his *Change of View* (Cambridge, Mass.: MIT Press, 1986).

5   Again, see Harman, *Change of View*. Also see Christopher Cherniak, *Minimal Rationality* (Cambridge, Mass.: MIT Press, 1988).

6   Similarly, it can be rational for me to have a degree of confidence in a proposition that cannot possibly be an accurate reflection of its objective probability. Suppose I am presented with a logically complex claim and told by an utterly reliable source that either it or its negation is a tautology. I thus know that its objective probability is either 1 or 0. After much effort, I construct a complicated proof that it is a tautology, but I am unsure of the proof. Moreover, it may be reasonable for me to be unsure. After all, the proof is a complicated one. But if so, it can be rational for me to believe the claim with something less than full confidence.

7   This is one of the reasons why treatises on informal logic and critical reasoning tend to be either unhelpful or theoretically unsatisfying. Insofar as the project is seen to be one of deriving useful advice for our everyday intellectual lives from the rules of logic and the axioms of the probability calculus, there simply is not a lot of useful advice to be had. On the other hand, insofar as the treatise does contain useful rules of thumb, these rules must have extralogical sources. But then, we will want to have information about these sources, information that we are rarely given.

8   See, e.g., Richard Nisbet and Lee Ross, *Human Inference: Strategies and Shortcomings of Social Judgement* (Englewood Cliffs, N.J.: Prentice-Hall, 1980).

9   The detail is important, however. Without it, real cases and real arguments can be manipulated just as easily as hypothetical ones. Witness textbook examples of the so-called 'informal fallacies'. Often enough, the examples are arguments from real sources that have been taken out of context and then uncharitably interpreted as deductive.

10   Compare with Nelson Goodman, *Fact, Fiction and Forecast* (Indianapolis: Bobbs-Merrill, 1965).

11   Karl Marx, *The German Ideology* (London: Lawrence and Wishart, 1938); Michel Foucault, *The History of Sexuality*, trans. R. Hurley (New York: Vintage Books, 1980). See also Gary Gutting's discussion of Foucault's views on these matters in his *Michel Foucault's Archaeology of Scientific Reason* (Cambridge: Cambridge University Press, 1989).

8

EPISTEMIC PERSPECTIVISM

Frederick Schmitt

Epistemic perspectivism is the view that for one important evaluative property, the property of being epistemically justified – justified in the sense required for knowledge – thinking makes it so: a subject's belief is justified in virtue of being sanctioned by the subject's outlook or perspective on justification. In this respect justified belief differs fundamentally from natural properties like being an electron or being red, for which thinking does not make it so. On perspectivism, justified belief is by its nature *perspectival belief* – belief sanctioned by the subject's epistemic perspective, by his or her judgments of justification or of justificatorily relevant properties (or by his or her epistemically guiding cognition). To say that the subject's belief is sanctioned by the perspective is not to say that it satisfies or conforms to some principle that is the content of a judgment of justification, but that it is *judged* to satisfy such a principle. Here are two examples of the view:

(a) *Reliabilist iterativism*: S is justified in believing p just in case S is justified in believing that the belief p is reliable.[1]

This is a version of perspectivism if S's perspective is taken to consist of propositions of the form "The belief p is reliable" that S is justified in believing, and the belief p is taken to be sanctioned by S's perspective when there is a proposition in the perspective corresponding to p. Laurence BonJour is committed to this view by various arguments he gives in *The Structure of Empirical Knowledge* (1985). For convenience, I use the term "reliable" where BonJour uses "likely to be true," which, it is clear, is supposed to be a statistical property of the form: having a feature F such that beliefs with F are generally true. I will refer to reliabilist iterativism as simply "iterativism."

(b)   *Counterfactual reflective perspectivism*: S is justified in believing p just in case S would on reflection believe that the proposition p is reliable.

This too is a version of perspectivism if the perspective is taken to consist of beliefs about reliability one would hold on reflection. Richard Foley (1987) proposes this view. For simplicity, I use the term "reliable" in application to a proposition where Foley says that it is the conclusion of an argument likely to be truth-preserving, with premises of which there is no reason to be suspicious. I will refer to counterfactual reflective perspectivism in what follows as simply "reflective perspectivism." There may be other versions of perspectivism. It is plausible enough to class John Pollock's (1986) view that a justified belief is one that conforms to a norm that guides the subject in cognition as a version of perspectivism. This view emphasizes the dependence of justification on background cognition as (a) and (b) do. However, guidance by a norm does not entail ascribing justification or other epistemically relevant property to the justified belief as (a) and (b) do. It is problematic whether reflective equilibrium theories of justified belief count as versions of perspectivism; they do not have either of the perspectivist features just mentioned. But I will have to set aside these theories to deal with (a) and (b).

It should be evident from these examples that perspectivism enjoys broad acceptance in current epistemology, receiving endorsement from such otherwise rival philosophers as BonJour, Foley, Pollock, and Keith Lehrer (1990). Perspectivism has indeed made such inroads in current epistemology that even staunch reliabilists like Alvin Goldman (1986) and Ernest Sosa (1991) make large concessions to it. Despite its popularity, the motivation for perspectivism has remained obscure. The burden of this paper is to assess possible motivations. My aim in doing so will be to determine whether there is any role for perspectival belief in epistemic evaluation.

What is at issue in judging perspectivism? I shall consider in detail one important issue – whether perspectival belief plays a significant role in epistemic evaluation. But there is a broader and more elusive issue I can only gesture at here. It is clear that perspectivism is supposed to contrast with reliabilism and more generally externalism. Certainly it is intended to be a form of internalism. It is actually a difficult issue whether all versions of perspectivism meet my lower bound on an internalist theory – i.e., entail what I call *mental internalism,* or the supervenience of justification on the subject's mentality. But perspectivism is at any rate distinguished from other theories of justification that do meet this lower bound – versions of coherentism, foundationalism, and accessibility internalism. At stake in the dispute between perspectivists and everyone else is whether we are to conceive of justification as conforming to a law given by ourselves or by nature. The issue between perspectivists and accessibility internalists and everybody else is whether justification is a matter of self-maintenance or maintenance by nature – whether it escapes or falls prey to a certain kind of luck. And the issue between perspectivists (and others) and externalists is whether justification escapes or involves being embedded in one's environment in an intimate way – whether justification is an ecological matter. Despite the importance of these issues, I must pass over them to discuss more fine-grained matters.

1   The Intuitive Case for Iterativism

The intuitive case for iterativism begins with the observation that perspective affects justification in significant ways.

(i) It is uncontroversial that justification is *undermined* by justified *negative* evaluation in the sense that a subject cannot be justified in a belief if he or she justifiedly judges it unreliable. That is, S is justified in believing p only if S is not justified in believing that the belief p is unreliable. Iterativism has a ready explanation for this condition: it follows more or less immediately from the iterativist claim that S is justified in believing p only if S is justified in believing that the belief p is reliable. But of course this requirement of justified *positive* evaluation of the belief p goes much beyond the requirement of the *absence* of a justified negative evaluation that is needed to explain the example. The strength of the case of iterativism here must rest on the lack of alternative nonperspectivist explanations of undermining by justified negative evaluation. Reliabilist explanations of undermining, for example, attempt to explain it by appeal to the requirement that justified beliefs be reliable.[2]

The perspectivist can best head off such explanations by showing that the requirement of reliability is too strong. BonJour has attempted exactly this by appealing to the demon example: subjects can be justified even though their beliefs are unreliable because they are deceived by a demon. But even if we accept BonJour's example and abandon reliability, we still have the option of explaining both the example and undermining by appeal to a nonperspectivist version of coherentism. A suitable version of coherentism might entail that coherence is present in the demon example, while negative evaluation of the belief p is incoherent with the belief p. Admittedly, such a version of coherentism would require a broad conception of coherence subsuming but not entailing perspectival belief. No one has offered such a version. Most versions of coherentism simply define coherence by a list that includes sanctioning by perspective as one (optional) kind of coherence and condemnation by perspective as a kind of incoherence. And that ultimately yields no *explanation* of the phenomena to which BonJour appeals. Nevertheless, BonJour's appeal makes an unwarranted bet that no such version of coherentism can be made out – that any well-motivated version of coherentism must collapse into iterativism. Until BonJour has ruled out the sort of coherentism I have in mind, appeal to undermining and the demon example cannot favor iterativism.

(ii) The other part of the intuitive case for iterativism is the claim that intuitively perspectival belief (as understood by iterativism) *suffices* for justified belief: if S is justified in believing that the belief p is reliable, then plausibly S is justified in believing p. Suppose I must choose between exercising two processes. I believe process A to be reliable, and B to be unreliable. Surely I am justified in the belief that results from A, even if it turns out later that my belief that A is reliable was mistaken. However, it seems rather likely that reliabilism can explain this intuition. For instance, it is plausible that the inference from "A is reliable and yields the belief p" to "p" is itself a (conditionally) reliable inference: in general, when the premise is true, the conclusion tends to be true. If so, reliabilism will entail that the belief p is justified (in a propositional sense) when this inference is available (and epistemically relevant) and the premise that the belief p is reliable is justified. This is so despite the fact that A turns out to be unreliable. In short, according to reliabilism, perspectival belief entails that the belief p is reliable, and thus it suffices for justified belief. Of course, intuitively, if I exercise B, which I take to be unreliable, my belief is not justified, even though B is reliable. But our intuition here may be explained by appeal to the idea that justification is undermined by my justified belief that B is not reliable. And thus reliabilism will explain our intuition here if it explains undermining.

Now, BonJour has attempted to argue that reliabilism does not itself give a sufficient condition of justification, and if this were so, reliabilism could not explain why perspectival belief suffices for justified belief. In particular, he asks us to imagine that clairvoyant belief is (unknown to the subject) reliable, and he claims that such beliefs would not be justified. But whether clairvoyant belief counts as justified on reliabilism depends on whether the clairvoyant process counts as epistemically relevant. If pragmatic considerations like whether evaluators tend to recognize the processes or judge their reliability accurately enter into relevance, then clairvoyant belief will not be justified. The power of BonJour's example to show that reliability is not sufficient for justified belief, and to preempt a reliabilist account of the sufficiency of perspectival belief for justified belief, thus depends on ruling out pragmatic constraints on relevance. And that will be an uphill battle. As things now stand, we have no serious argument that perspectivism alone explains the sufficiency of perspectival belief for justified belief.

In short, it is relatively uncontroversial that perspectival belief is sufficient for justified belief, and that justified belief requires the absence of negative evaluation. But we have no reason to think that an iterativist account is the only one that can explain these facts. And of course we have no intuitive reason to take perspectival belief to be *necessary* for justification. So we have no intuitive case for iterativism here. There is even less of an intuitive case for reflective perspectivism.

I would now like to argue that there is a powerful intuitive case against requiring perspectival belief. To ensure that we cite an example in which justified positive evaluation is absent, it is best to choose an example of perception by a cognitively immature subject, one who lacks the cognitive resources to make or be justified in making positive evaluations. I believe it is obvious enough that we unhesitatingly ascribe justified perceptual beliefs to such subjects. But for those who need proof, let me try to produce a convincing case. What we currently know about cognitive development suggests that there is a period of cognitive development, which can vary in children from three to six, during which we ascribe perceptual beliefs, despite the fact that the subject lacks the concept of reliable belief and is thus unable to be justified in a positive evaluation. To cite just one pertinent experimental result, Willats relates the case of a girl who drew a basketball as a circle, suggesting that her line represents the occluding contour of the ball and the interior of the circle represents the surface of the ball. In short, she drew the basketball to a first approximation as it appears. However, when asked to draw the mold mark on the basketball,

> the child first drew a line *outside* the first circle, saying as she did so "I can't draw it here because it's not inside the ball." Finally she drew a line on top of the first circle, saying "And I can't draw it here because it won't show up. So I can't do it." It is hard to resist the conclusion that for this child the shape enclosed by the circle stood for the whole volume

of the ball, while the circle stood for the surface of the ball, dividing the inside of the ball from the space outside. (p. 90)

The girl is unable to represent the mold mark by drawing it the way it appears. Her explanation about her inability to do this suggests that her drawing does not represent the surface of the ball or its appearance at all, but is a two-dimensional topological diagram representing the space inside and the space outside the surface of the ball. Of course when adults represent the surface of a ball, they draw it as a circle, and it might be thought that the girl was doing the same thing and intended her drawing to resemble the appearance of the ball. But the fact that she could not draw the mold mark across the circle suggests that the girl does not treat the area of the circle as appearing the way the surface of the ball appears. One explanation of why the girl does not do so would be that her artistic resources are restricted to topological representations. But this itself needs explanation. And it is not implausible that the explanation is that she lacks a concept much like our concept of visual appearance. It could be that she is prevented from representing the appearance of the ball because having the concept of appearance is necessary for successful drawing. Perhaps the recognition of appearance is needed to represent things as they appear.[3]

Yet at the same time there is little doubt that we would ascribe justification to the child's perceptual beliefs: she is justified in believing that this is a basketball, that the basketball is round, etc. It seems consistent with our knowledge of children's cognitive development that there is a stage at which we ascribe justification to the child's perceptual beliefs even though she lacks the concept of appearance. At any rate, I do not think that the discovery that children lack the concept of appearance would cause us to withdraw our attribution of justification to their perceptual beliefs. On any plausible view of reliability, however, perceptual beliefs are reliable when they are of certain types, instances of which are frequently true, and these types are defined (at least in part) by perceptual appearances. Thus a subject can have beliefs about the reliability of perceptual beliefs only if she possesses a concept of appearance. In short, it is at least consistent with our knowledge of development that there is a stage at which we ascribe justification to the child's perceptual beliefs even though she lacks the concept of reliability and is thus unable to have, and therefore to be justified in having, beliefs about reliability. Intuitively, a belief can be justified even though the subject is not justified in believing it reliable.

At this point some philosophers – Sosa (1991), for example – have wanted to distinguish between reflective and animal knowledge, ascribe the latter to small children, and deny that such knowledge requires justified belief. But I doubt whether there is any intuitive distinction of this sort: intuitively the child knows and is justified in her perceptual beliefs in the same sense that I know and am justified in mine. Nor is it clear why the dichotomy is between *reflective* and animal knowledge. These are not contradictories (are they even contraries?), and it would need to be argued that all nonanimal knowledge is reflective. Of course reflection and justification for believing that one's belief is justified may well be desirable and required for mature thinkers to be justified. But whether there is such a requirement is not the issue. The issue is the source of the requirement. Does this requirement stem from the nature of justified belief itself, so that it pertains to all justified beliefs, or only from the special endowments of mature subjects under a conception of justified belief that applies more broadly? Perspectivism requires the former, but our intuitions say otherwise. I shall cover obliquely below the related question whether there is a theoretical point to making such a distinction.

2   The Responsibility Argument for Iterativism

I have argued that we are far from having a full intuitive case for iterativism. Nor do I see any real prospect of one. The perspectivist must therefore supply an alternative route to the view by locating a significant epistemic role for perspectival belief. If the perspectivist can locate such a role and argue that justified belief plays just this role, that will be quite enough to establish perspectivism as the correct account of justified belief. What are the prospects for such a case? I would like to devote the rest of this paper to considering the matter in detail.

What is wanted here is an innocuous formal conception of justified belief, one that wears its evaluative significance on its sleeve, but that must nevertheless be characterized by perspectival belief. Perspectivists have in fact attempted to locate such a formal conception and to deduce perspectivism from it.

I would like to begin with the idea, deriving from the work of BonJour, that iterativism can be deduced from a conception of justified belief as *epistemically responsible belief*, or belief that results from epistemically responsible cognition. BonJour's argument is this:

> The distinguishing characteristic of epistemic justification is . . . its essential or internal relation to the cognitive goal of truth. It follows that one's cognitive endeavors are epistemically justified only if and to the

extent that they are aimed at this goal, which means very roughly that one accepts all and only those beliefs which one has good reason to think are true. To accept a belief in the absence of such a reason, however appealing or even mandatory such an acceptance might be from some other standpoint, is to neglect the pursuit of truth; such an acceptance is, one might say, *epistemically irresponsible*. My contention here is that the idea of avoiding such irresponsibility, of being epistemically responsible in one's believings, is the core of the notion of epistemic justification. (1985, p. 8)

It is hard to be sure of the exact order of BonJour's argument, but the following is suggested:

1   *The conception of justified belief as epistemically responsible belief*: S is justified in believing p just in case S is epistemically responsible in believing p.
2   *The conception of epistemically responsible belief as well-motivated belief*: S is epistemically responsible in believing p just in case in believing p, S aims (in the right way) at believing what is true.
3   In believing p, S aims (in the right way) at believing what is true just in case S is justified in believing that the belief p is likely to be true.
4   So S is justified in believing p just in case S is justified in believing that the belief p is likely to be true.

Conclusion 4 is of course just iterativism.

There is a serious preliminary problem with this argument. It is not plausible to suppose, as premise 3 has it, that perspectival belief entails aiming at believing what is true. Merely being justified in believing that the belief p is reliable does not entail that one is motivated in a certain way in believing p. Nor can we get around the problem by replacing the biconditionals in 3 and 4 with forward conditionals and leaving the backward conditional of 4 to the intuitive case (discussed in the last section) that perspectival belief entails justified belief. For on perspectivism, perspectival belief entails justified belief and so will once again entail aiming at true belief. I see no way to amend the argument to restore plausibility. But I am willing for the sake of discussion to pass over this problem and proceed to more central defects in the argument.

Premise 1, the conception of justified belief as epistemically responsible belief, has been endorsed by a number of philosophers, including Roderick Chisholm (1977), Hilary Kornblith (1983), and Lorraine Code (1983), but the idea remains deeply underdeveloped. There is little doubt that the status of epistemically responsible belief plays an important role in the constellation of epistemic conditions. But no one, to my knowledge, has ever carefully argued that justified belief is to be identified with epistemically responsible belief, perhaps in part because no one possesses a detailed enough account of epistemically responsible belief to fund such an argument. I will return to the plausibility of premise 1 below, but I wish to begin with the other premises.

Premises 2 and 3 together entail that epistemically responsible belief is perspectival belief. Unfortunately, this consequence seems to be false. We may adapt William Alston's examples (1989) to make the objection.

Suppose that I accept the doctrine of the Trinity, but I see that it appears logically contradictory. I reject various ways of rendering it logically consistent – e.g., by the device of relative identity. I see I have no plausible premises from which I can infer it by deduction or any other reliable inference. After long deliberation, I reject the view that anyone employs a reliable process of revelation to arrive at the doctrine. I regard this view as incompatible with what we know of human cognitive faculties. I recognize that my acceptance of the doctrine is the result of indoctrination. In short, my acceptance is not sanctioned by my perspective. On the contrary, it seems that I am justified in believing that my acceptance is unreliable. For I am justified in believing that I possess no argument for it that would afford me a reliable inference and no reliable noninferential way of arriving at the belief. One might object that I cannot maintain my acceptance of the doctrine and at the same time be justified in believing that my acceptance is unreliable. For the belief in unreliability here would be incoherent with my acceptance of the doctrine: that acceptance would support the availability of revelation or other reliable ways of arriving at the doctrine. But such incoherence is the human condition. It cannot prevent me from maintaining my acceptance and being justified in believing that my acceptance is unreliable. The most it could entail is that I cannot be justified in believing this and at the same time be justified in accepting the doctrine. That is fine. For purposes of the example, we may take the former alternative.

Let us also suppose, however, that try as I might I cannot shake my acceptance of the doctrine. I make my best effort to resist it, but I fail. Then surely I am epistemically responsible in my acceptance, despite the fact that it is not sanctioned by my perspective. We ought to reject the conclusion that epistemically responsible belief is perspectival belief. (Those who wish to segregate religious beliefs as the proper domain of faith and deny on this ground that they are susceptible to any kind of epistemic evaluation at all may choose another example – political beliefs will do just as well.)

It might be replied that my acceptance of the doctrine is not really epistemically responsible here. To be sure, my cognitive *actions* are epistemically responsible – I try to rid myself of this belief. But my *belief* is not *itself* epistemically responsible. For it does not *result* from my best efforts but rather resists them. So the objection does not succeed in showing that I can be epistemically responsible in my belief without its being perspectival.

I confess my grasp of the notion of epistemically responsible belief is not firm enough to yield intuitions about whether my actions can be epistemically responsible without my belief being so because my belief fails to result from my actions. But I am willing to concede this for the sake of argument. This concession does not, however, save the responsibility argument, for two reasons.

First, if we accept the assumption that epistemically responsible belief entails *resulting* from one's best efforts, then we lose the other direction of the equivalence between epistemically responsible and perspectival belief. We lose the claim that perspectival belief *entails* epistemically responsible belief. For, among other things, there could be perspectival beliefs that do not result from epistemically responsible actions. For example, my perspective might sanction beliefs that result from *automatic* perceptual processes or *innate* beliefs even though these do *not* result from any actions at all. Perhaps it will be replied that a belief counts as epistemically responsible when it *would* result from doing one's best. But counterfactualizing the notion of "resulting from" in the account of epistemically responsible belief, if it works here, will prevent the new account from handling the example of irresistible religious belief, since the latter belief *would* still result from my doing my best even though it does not in fact result, and so it will count as epistemically responsible once again on the counterfactualized account.

Second, let it also be noted that even if my acceptance of the doctrine of the Trinity is not epistemically responsible, it can hardly be said to be *irresponsible* either. Then we can make a different objection to 2 and 3. For presumably if, as the perspectivist equivalence for epistemically responsible belief holds, a belief is responsible when it is sanctioned by my perspective, it will be *irresponsible* when *condemned* by my perspective. But my religious belief is in fact condemned (since I regard it as unreliable). Thus the example undercuts the conclusion that epistemically responsible belief is perspectival belief even if this belief is not responsible.

These observations show that epistemically responsible belief and perspectival belief diverge. The former depends on such factors as whether a belief is irresistible, while the later does not: an irresistible belief must be either epistemically responsible or neither epistemically responsible nor irresponsible. Either way the equivalence between epistemically responsible belief and perspectival belief breaks down. The reason is that epistemically responsible belief depends on whether the subject is doing the best he or she can in believing p, and one can do one's best and still believe an irresistible belief that is condemned. Perspectival belief, on the other hand, does not depend on any such thing because one can have justified beliefs about the reliability and unreliability of beliefs independently of whether they are resistible.

One might take all this to show that it was a tactical error for the perspectivist to tie justified belief to epistemically responsible belief. Epistemically responsible belief does not match up with perpectival belief in the desired way. One might maintain, however, that perspectival belief does match up with belief that aims at true belief, and that this is enough for an argument for perspectivism. But this attempt at an end run around the objection meets similar obstacles. Automatic perceptual beliefs can be perspectival without our aiming at the truth in believing them and without resulting from aiming at the truth. And again counterfactualizing aiming does not get the perspectivist out of the fire. It does not help to say that a belief is perspectival just in case it would result from our aiming if we did aim. For irresistible beliefs can fail to be perspectival even though we would believe them if we were to aim at the truth.[1]

It might be replied that my focus on irresistible belief deprives my objection of breadth, but in fact the objection generalizes to many resistible beliefs as well. Resistible beliefs will be epistemically responsible whenever one does one's best in believing them – i.e., whenever it is epistemically cost-effective not to resist them. Thus, resistible beliefs can be epistemically responsible though unjustified and nonperspectival when it is too much (epistemic) trouble to get rid of them. Indeed, the problem with a perspectivist account is a deep one, a point that has been made in effect by William Alston (1989), but cannot be repeated often enough. The account leaves out one of the chief factors in epistemically responsible belief – the cost-effectiveness of forming (or retracting) the belief. Sanctioning by one's perspective is no doubt a factor here, but it can be overridden by factors that affect cost, like control.

It might be suggested that we view perspectival belief as an *idealization* of epistemically responsible belief in which we abstract from factors such as control. If we did, then my objection to the responsibility argument would no longer apply. But what would be the advantage of measuring beliefs against such an ideal standard? By design, idealized belief does not *amount* to epistemically responsible belief. And we have at least one other ideal standard against which we can measure beliefs – namely, reliability.

Perhaps it will be suggested that perspectival belief is what we aim at directly when our ultimate aim is epistemically responsible belief. Of course we aim at true and reliable belief in aiming at epistemically responsible belief. But it might be suggested that we aim at these things indirectly and at perspectival belief directly.

I agree that justified belief is what we aim at directly when we aim at epistemically responsible belief. But I see no plausibility in the claim that we must aim directly at *perspectival* belief. It is true that one could get epistemically responsible belief by aiming at some goals in addition to true, reliable, and epistemically responsible belief. But the conditions of epistemically responsible belief do not themselves constrain us to aim at any particular such goal. All that is required is aiming at these goals guided by considerations like cost of control. Suppose the subject aims at true, reliable, and epistemically responsible belief, relying of course on beliefs about reliability to do so. Suppose the subject takes factors of cost into account in arriving at the belief p. I do not see why such a subject could not be epistemically responsible in believing p, despite that fact that she does not aim at perspectival belief. Now it might be that the subject should consider the plausibility of her metabeliefs about reliability while en route to the belief p. I do not see this as mandatory for epistemically responsible belief – what if there are no doubts about these metabeliefs, or what if there are doubts but considerations of cost militate against considering them? The negative answer I would expect here suggests that what is required of the metabeliefs about reliability on which the subject relies is that they be themselves epistemically responsible, rather than justified (contrary to what is required by perspectival belief). (That is, a qualified iterativism may be true for epistemically responsible belief, though false for justified belief.) The subject might rely on unjustified metabeliefs about reliability whose reliability it is too costly to check. But even if the subject considers their plausibility, it does not follow that she is *aiming* at perspectival belief. So we do not have a case that epistemically responsible belief entails aiming at perspectival belief.

It should be noted that nothing in this section shows that justified belief and perspectival belief diverge. In all of our examples, the beliefs are either both justified and perspectival, or neither justified nor perspectival. The point of this section has rather been that the tie between justified and perspectival belief is less problematic than that between either of these and epistemically responsible or well-motivated belief. There is no gain in appealing to the more problematic tie to establish the less problematic.

3 The Advisory Argument for Reflective Perspectivism

I would like to turn now to another prominent argument for perspectivism which I shall call the *advisory argument*. This argument hinges on the alleged advisory nature of justified belief and the role of perspectival belief in epistemic advice-taking. The argument is that justified belief is advisable belief; the only proper advice is perspectivist advice; so justified belief is perspectival belief. This argument is suggested by remarks of Richard Foley:

> You need a way to proceed in making sense of the world from your own perspective, a way in which it is appropriate for you to proceed, given your own lights. You cannot simply read off from the world what is true, and neither can you read off what methods or procedures are likely to guarantee true beliefs. So, it is unhelpful for you to be told to believe some claim only if it is true, and it is equally unhelpful for you to be told to use only reliable methods. (Foley 1989, p. 171)

Foley's remarks suggest that what it is helpful for you to be told is to believe what you would on reflection deem reliable. Since justified belief is advisable belief, it is belief you would on reflection deem reliable – and this is perspectival belief, as defined by Foley's reflective perspectivism. Apparently the argument favors reflective perspectivism over iterativism. For it is not helpful to be told to believe what you are *justified* in believing reliable, since you do not yet know which beliefs are justified – it is the point of the advice to tell you. The advisory argument rules out iterativism, and indeed any similarly circular account of justification.

The advisory argument comes in several versions. All share the same first premise and differ in the properties they ascribe to proper advice. It will help in getting started to have a particular version before us:

1   *The advisory conception of justified belief.* Justified belief is advisable belief – belief that *conforms* to proper epistemic advice. Let us say that epistemic advice is *proper* when it is advice that would properly be offered to someone who wishes to believe what is reliable. And let us say that a belief *conforms* to epistemic advice when it satisfies the condition specified by the advice. For example, if the advice is reliabilist advice – i.e., advice to believe what is reliable – then a belief conforms to the advice just in case it is reliable.

If the advice is reflective perspectivist advice, then a belief conforms to it just in case the subject would on reflection deem it reliable.

2   Proper epistemic advice is by its very nature advice that we are always able to take – where "always" means "on any occasion on which we seek to believe what conforms to the advice."

3   The only epistemic advice that we are always able to take is the advice to believe what is sanctioned by our perspective.

4   Hence, justified belief is belief sanctioned by our perspective – i.e., perspectival belief.

This version of the advisory argument focuses (in steps 2 and 3) on the sort of advice we are always *able* to take.

The argument does not explicitly assume any tie between justified belief and responsible belief, as the responsibility argument does. It might be that the questions about advisable belief we will discuss apply also to belief that aims at truth, since in aiming at truth it might be inevitable to take advice (in some sense of "taking advice"). At the same time, as we shall see, advisable belief need not be belief that aims at truth. Points about advisable belief will therefore have more general application, and the advisory conception is not committed to a conception of justified belief as well-motivated belief. For this reason, the advisory conception may be able to avoid entailing the relevance of factors, like cost of control, that do not apply to justified belief. The advisory argument may in this regard be more plausible than the responsibility argument.

In other respects, however, the advisory argument may be less plausible. A first reaction to the question whether perspectivist advice is proper might be incredulity at the question: proper advice for whom and in which circumstances? Surely it depends on whom we are talking about. Perhaps perspectivist advice is proper for people who are good at reflection, but not for others. I sympathize with this reaction, but of course if it is right there is something wrong with the advisory conception of justified belief and perhaps with perspectivism as well. If the advisory conception is good, there must be some account of propriety that varies from subject to subject only to the extent that justification does – presumably, at some level, not at all. If we say that perspectivist advice is proper for people who are good at reflection, "good at" presumably means "able to get true belief from," and it begins to look as if perspectival belief is valuable because it gets us reliable belief – a view inconsistent with perspectivism. I am willing to forgo this reaction here. I shall assume for argument's sake that there is only one kind of proper advice, and that justified belief is advisable belief. There will be enough problems with the other premises of the argument.

The version of the argument we have before us is in fact not very promising. It seems impossible to interpret "able to take advice" in such a way that premises 2 and 3 both come out true. For "able to take advice" can mean either "able to *conform* to advice" or "able to *attempt* to conform to advice." If it means the former, then premise 3 is implausible. For we have the same trouble here as with the responsibility argument: we are not able to conform to perspectivist advice in the case of irresistible beliefs.

Moreover, premise 2 is implausible. Both perspectivist and reliabilist advice are inconsistent with 2. And the premise is indeed implausible on this interpretation. Certainly it is not *generally* true of proper advice that we are always able to conform to it. We are not always, on every occasion on which we seek to do what conforms to the advice, able to conform to the advice given in cookbooks, auto maintenance manuals, pop psychology primers, or "How to Prepare for the SAT." To be sure, proper advice is tuned to some degree to the abilities of those to whom it is directed. But the degree of attunement is a product of two conflicting desiderata: the desideratum of satisfying a goal (such as producing delicious food) and the desideratum of giving advice people are able to conform to. Since not everyone is able to cook delicious food, pitching to common abilities would entail failing entirely to honor the desideratum of producing delicious food. Thus advice must be given that is to some degree *ability-insensitive* – such that some who seek the advice will occasionally be unable to conform to it. Nor can we always translate ability-insensitive advice into ability-sensitive advice by giving advice conditional on having certain abilities. For many human activities worth doing require an indefinitely large number and range of abilities – so large and diverse that one cannot expect to be able to write just those abilities into the advice.

One might try to argue for the requirement that advice be ability-sensitive – i.e., for premise 2 – by appeal to the principle that "ought" implies "can." Epistemic advice specifies at some level what it is *epistemically permissible* to believe. Thus, according to this argument, it is epistemically advisable to believe *p* in case it is epistemically permissible to believe *p*. So you ought epistemically always to withhold the belief *p* in case it is not advisable to believe *p*. But since "ought" implies "can," if you ought to withhold the belief *p*, then you can withhold the belief *p*. So you can always withhold an inadvisable belief. This is supposed to establish premise 2: you are always able to conform to advice.

The trouble with appealing to the principle that 'ought" implies "can" to establish premise 2 is that the same examples that lead us to question the premise also lead us to question whether "ought" implies "can." One ought to remove a soufflé from the oven immediately before serving, one ought to expand one's vocabulary before taking the SAT, and so on, regardless of whether one can. Hence "ought" does not always imply "can." So why should we assume that the *epistemic* "ought" implies "can"? Without the principle that the epistemic "ought" implies "can," we lack a persuasive argument for premise 2.

I have offered these doubts about premises 2 and 3 on the interpretation of "taking advice" as *conforming* to the advice." What happens on the alternative interpretation of "taking advice" as merely "*attempting* to conform to the advice"? (Henceforth I shall interpret taking advice in this way unless otherwise indicated.) I am willing to concede premise 2 on this interpretation. It is plausible enough that there is no point in giving advice to people who are unable even to attempt to conform to it, and consequently it is improper to give such advice in circumstances in which people seek belief or in which it is appropriate for them to seek belief.

However, premise 3 remains implausible. For we can surely always *attempt* to conform to reliabilist advice if we can always attempt to conform to perspectivist advice. This is enough to knock down the version of the advisory argument we have been considering.

It is clear, then, that the proponent of the argument must do one of two things: either retreat to a version of the argument on which proper advice requires that we are able to conform to the advice *in some desirable class of circumstances* in which we are able to conform to perspectivist but not reliabilist advice; or complain that reliabilist advice is improper because of some *defect* other than that we are not always able to conform to the advice. Both of these ways of criticizing reliabilist advice are suggested by the remarks of Foley we quoted earlier (p. 15).

It might be objected – and Foley seems to be making this objection – that reliabilist advice is improper because it is *vacuous* in the way that alethic advice (the advice to believe what is true) is vacuous, or in the way that the stockbroker's advice to buy low and sell high is vacuous: this advice merely tells us to do what we initially sought to do – hold a true belief as to whether p. But the charge of vacuity clearly does not apply to reliabilist advice, since the advice does not merely tell us to do what we initially sought to do. It specifies an action *by which* we can do what we initially sought to do: we can believe what is true by believing what is reliable. Reliabilist advice is not useless because it is vacuous.

A different charge that might be made against reliabilist advice is that it is *incomplete*, rather than vacuous. For the task of believing what is reliable is a nonbasic task, and for a nonbasic task, advice must specify the basic action that we must perform by which we perform the task. Perhaps this is what Foley has in mind when he says that we cannot simply "read off from the world" what is reliable. For the task of believing what is reliable, like that of believing what is true, is nonbasic, and we need further instructions for carrying out this task.

This is true, but there is no reason why reliabilist advice, cannot be supplemented with further instructions. A natural supplement would be this: check the frequency of true beliefs in the output of a relevant process (or set of processes) available on the occasion and believe what would result from the exercise of the process if it is reliable. In taking reliabilist advice, the subject must of course rely on beliefs about frequencies of truths, about the relevance and availability of processes, and about what beliefs these processes would yield when exercised. But reliabilist advice implicitly specifies the various basic actions needed to judge what is reliable and thereby believe what is true.

I suspect that Foley has in mind a rather different and deeper complaint about the incompleteness of reliabilist advice – that it is incomplete in an important way: it fails to be what I shall call *closed*. To be closed, advice must provide the subject with some recommendation, not only about whether to believe p, but also about whether to hold the *advisory beliefs*, the beliefs on which the subject must rely in taking the advice. Closed advice, in other words, builds a recommendation about advisory beliefs into its advice. Of course the reliabilist does offer advice about which advisory beliefs to hold – namely, reliabilist advice. But this advice is not built into the advice about believing p, nor could it be. For any attempt to build it in would touch off a regress of recommendations about advisory beliefs. The subject would have to take the same recommendation about the beliefs on which he or she relies in taking the recommendation about advisory beliefs, and so on. Now, any sort of advice would give rise to an internal regress of recommendations if we were to incorporate into it the *same* advice as a recommendation for advisory beliefs. The complaint against reliabilist advice is therefore not that it gives rise to a regress when this is done, but that it incorporates no alternative recommendation for the advisory beliefs. It sets no standards for the advisory beliefs employed in taking reliabilist advice. In this, it might be alleged, it differs from reflective perspectivist advice, which in effect incorporates a recommendation by asking one to believe what one would on reflection deem reliable. It might be claimed that the advisory beliefs on which we rely in taking this advice are beliefs about reliability that would be the products of such reflection.

However, the apparent superiority here of perspectivist advice is an illusion. Reflective perspectivist advice is not closed any more than reliabilist advice. Far from being closed, it does not incorporate any recommendation at all. In taking the advice, we do not rely on a belief about reliability that would be the product of reflection. Rather, we rely on a belief about whether we would on reflection deem the belief p reliable. The advice does not give us any recommendation as to which beliefs of the latter sort we are to rely on. We *could* arrive at a belief as to whether the belief p is reliable by reflecting or simulating reflection, but the advice does not tell us to do so.[5] Lack of closure is no defect, however, since no advice could be closed (other than, trivially, advice that relies on no beliefs at all). In other words, the regress argument generalizes from showing that we cannot give a recommendation that is the *same* as the advice, as in the case of reliabilist advice, to showing that we cannot give a recommendation for *all* the beliefs on which we rely in taking advice. This is enough to lay the present objection to reliabilist advice to rest.

Let us try one final objection to reliabilist advice, related to the issue of closure: that iterated reliabilist advice-taking is ruled out as *circular*. This does finally promise to distinguish reliabilist from perspectivist advice. For in taking reliabilist advice, one relies on advisory beliefs about the reliability of the belief p. This requires one to judge whether beliefs belonging to a reference class of beliefs suitably related to the belief p are generally true. In particular, one must judge whether a certain process R is reliable, and hence whether the outputs of R are generally true. But to judge the latter, we must rely on output beliefs q for sufficiently many q. Unfortunately, taking reliabilist advice regarding these output beliefs is ruled out, since to take such advice, we must again judge whether R generally yields true beliefs, since the belief q is an output of R. And this is circular. Perspectivist advice, it might be claimed, does not succumb to the same charge, since it does not require relying on the same advisory beliefs at more than one order.

It is not easy to judge whether this objection has any force against reliabilist advice. Certainly it cannot be required of advice that we can take advice about advisory beliefs for any number of orders without circularity. For human beings do not have an infinite fund of beliefs on which to rely in taking advice at successive orders. Advice-taking must either terminate or must go circular at some point. There is no way out of circularity in advice-taking, as there is in a regress of justified belief, where the beliefs in the regress may result from something other than advice-taking. The difference between reliabilist and perspectivist advice is only that reliabilist advice goes circular while perspectivist advice terminates. So if there is to be any objection here, it must be that the circularity in taking reliabilist advice occurs at too early an order.

Why would it be too early? Perhaps the most persuasive line here is that advice-taking is designed to answer doubts, and reliabilist advice cannot do so because the output beliefs on which it relies must be doubted if the belief p is doubted. Perspectivist advice might be said to differ in this regard.

This objection has some force. I concede that when the point of taking advice is to answer a doubt, and that doubt extends to all outputs of R, then relying on those outputs is ruled out. It does not follow, however, that taking reliabilist advice is ruled out. This *would* follow if one *had* to rely on the other outputs of R in taking reliabilist advice. The objection does indeed show that taking reliabilist advice cannot answer doubts when all outputs of R are doubted and one is restricted to outputs of R in answering the doubts.

Despite this, there are three points to make in defense of reliabilist advice. First, these are not the only circumstances in which there are doubts. It is not always true that when a belief p is doubted, so are all the other outputs of R. There are *local* doubts that pertain to some outputs of a process and not others. We might doubt the truth of a proposition – e.g., the belief that this is an elm – and not at the same time doubt the truth of another – the belief that *that* is an elm – even though belief in these propositions would count as outputs of the same process R. Taking reliabilist advice may afford an answer to this doubt, despite the fact that one relies on outputs of R in taking the advice.

Second, when *all* the outputs of R are doubted, these doubts can sometimes be answered by relying on beliefs that are not outputs of R. Reliabilist advice-taking may rely on general and theoretical beliefs (e.g., evolutionary beliefs) about correlations between the reliability of processes and other conditions. Beliefs in such correlations must ultimately rely on output beliefs of some processes, but these need not be output beliefs of the process R. It is true that the plausibility of certain theoretical arguments for the reliability of some processes – e.g., evolutionary arguments for the reliability of inductive inference – has been called into serious question recently by Stephen Stich (1990, chapter 3), but I do not think it can seriously be denied that there are some plausible theoretical arguments for the reliability of some processes on practical grounds. Reliabilist advice-taking may therefore answer doubts in a variety of circumstances in which the outputs of R are all doubted.

Moreover, it seems that perspectivist advice-taking must simulate reliance on general beliefs in reflection if it is to answer local doubts. If a local doubt is to be answered by considering what we would on reflection believe reliable, then presumably our determination of what we would believe cannot rely solely on locally doubted beliefs. It must rely on *general* beliefs. So perspectivist advice-taking is in much the same boat regarding local skepticism as reliabilist advice-taking.

Third, perspectivist advice-taking labors under an analogous limitation. To take advice regarding the belief p, one must rely on the counterfactual psychological belief q: one would on reflection believe that the belief p is reliable. To take advice regarding the belief q, one must rely on the counterfactual psychological belief r: one would on reflection believe that the belief that one would on reflection believe that the belief p is reliable is reliable. It is hard to imagine that one would have a serious doubt about q that did not extend to r as well, since r has a similar subject matter and is more complex than q.

These are all the criticisms of the advisory argument for reflective perspectivism that I have for the moment. There does not seem to be any way to argue from an advisory conception of justified belief to the conclusion that justified belief is perspectival belief. We have seen no ground for denying that we can take reliabilist advice.

At this point, perspectivists may try to retreat to the weaker claim that taking perspectivist advice is in a certain sense indispensable in taking advice, in a way that taking reliabilist advice is not. For in *attempting* to conform to reliabilist advice in the right way, we necessarily *conform* to *perspectivist* advice – we necessarily have a perspectival belief.[6] But if "in the right way" means "with justification," this argument runs into the same problem as the responsibility argument – irresistible religious or political beliefs we are justified in believing to be unreliable. We may attempt to conform to reliabilist advice and fail to believe what we are justified in believing reliable – fail to have a perspectival belief – because our belief resists our efforts.

4   Is Perspectivist Advice Proper?

So far we have considered versions of the advisory argument that try to deduce perspectivism from the *formal* nature of advice. Perhaps we should consider a last and somewhat different version of the argument, one that tries to deduce perspectivism from the substantive nature of advice.

What ought a substantive account of proper advice look like? If the advisory conception of justified belief is to be noncircular, we shall have to avoid defining proper advice in terms of justified belief, since the direction of definition is the reverse under the advisory conception. This does not leave us with very many natural candidates for an account of proper advice. Here is the one that comes immediately to mind: proper advice is advice the taking of which tends to lead to reliable beliefs.

On this account, it is difficult to decide between reliabilist and perspectivist advice. Their effects would be similar. In favor of reliabilist advice is the fact that more subjects are able to attempt to conform to it than to perspectivist advice. For example, more subjects have the concept of reliability than have the concept of reflecting on reliability. It might seem that perspectivist advice easily makes up for this by having a higher tendency to lead to reliable belief on each occasion of advice-taking, since reflecting on reliability is more apt to lead to a correct judgment of reliability than mere belief about reliability. But that depends on how good the subject is at reflection. People often become confused and indecisive as a result of reflection, or simply fail to make progress. It is a commonplace of cognitive psychology that subjects who commit fallacies or reason invalidly, when they are invited to reflect on the validity of their inference in debriefing, tend to develop rationalizations of their methods and tend to entrench their way of reasoning. The perspectivist might deny that this is genuine reflection. Perhaps not, but then the point would be that people often tend to reflect in the wrong way, and so are poor at *attempting* to take perspectivist advice. Either way, perspectivist advice has trouble. Of course, debriefing sessions are one thing and reflection in ordinary life is another. But it would not be surprising if people were even worse at reflecting under the pressures of ordinary life than in debriefing. Finally, reflection on reliability takes considerable effort that might otherwise be diverted to exercising reliable processes. This will reduce the number of reliable beliefs and count against perspectivist advice.

5   The Aretaic Argument for Iterativism

There is one last hope for an argument for perspectivism – by appeal to an *aretaic* conception of justified belief, or more exactly, to a specific aretaic conception. There are many things that matter epistemically besides justified belief – abilities and dispositions to exercise reliable processes, the cognitive mechanisms that underlie such processes, powerful cognitive faculties, and justification-supporting cognitive practices, to name just a few. To have a justified belief does not, on any plausible view of justification, entail having the ability or disposition to acquire justified beliefs; in this sense one can be justified by accident. Yet such abilities and dispositions are of the first importance for successful cognition. Justification-supporting practices rely on an infrastructure of such cognitive abilities and dispositions. These abilities and dispositions are among the epistemic virtues. Clearly, however, epistemic virtues matter in large measure because of their relation to justified belief. This suggests that we might rely on our understanding of epistemic virtues to define justified belief.

An aretaic theory of justified belief is one that understands justified belief in relation to intellectual or epistemic virtues like intelligence, wisdom, perspicacity, care, imaginativeness, etc. One might begin with the observation that epistemic virtues matter because they facilitate or give rise to justified belief, and one might turn this around and say that justified beliefs are beliefs of a sort that *result* from certain epistemic virtues. Alternatively, one might say that a justified belief is one that *manifests* certain epistemic virtues, as behavior that helps others manifests the virtue of benevolence, or determination to complete a task in the face of danger manifests courage. I will focus on the latter manifestation account.

Clearly, different epistemic virtues perform different functions. The beliefs that manifest intelligence or imaginativeness need not be justified. And while wisdom and care are often manifested by justified beliefs, they need not be. We must locate a particular virtue, or a small set of virtues, that are typically manifested by justified beliefs. One proposal is that justified belief is belief of a sort that manifests *epistemic integrity* (alternatively: *epistemic autonomy*). On this account of justified belief, if it turns out that perspectival belief is belief that manifests epistemic integrity, then perspectivism follows.

What is epistemic integrity? *Moral* integrity, in one sense at least, is the practice of sticking to one's moral tenets – acting in accordance with what one believes morally right, even, or especially, in the face of opposition to doing so or of the temptation to do otherwise. A person with moral integrity does not stray from her moral judgments or principles even under threat or bribe; she does not knuckle under and act in a hypocritical or unprincipled way. Such judgments may be judgments of particular cases or of general principle. It seems that moral integrity entails a practice of acting in accordance with the moral judgments one is *justified* in making, and not merely the ones one *actually* makes. Sticking to unjustified judgments does not manifest integrity but pigheadedness. *Epistemic* integrity resembles moral integrity in being a practice of believing what is sanctioned by one's justified epistemic judgments or principles – believing what one is justified in deeming reliable – in the face of the temptation to cut corners (e.g., by wishful thinking or hasty generalization) and in the face of interference that threatens to disrupt the cognitive processes one deems reliable (e.g., interference from self-deception, cognitive biases such as recency, latency, and halo effects, confirmation bias, overconfidence, and the like). Epistemic integrity also entails a disposition to reconsider, defend, or amend one's epistemic judgments under counterevidence.

Now to state the aretaic argument for iterativism:

1   Justified belief is belief of a sort that manifests epistemic integrity.
2   The sort of belief that manifests epistemic intergrity is iterativist belief.
3   Therefore, justified belief is iterativist belief.

Is this a persuasive argument for perspectivism? Here are some problems with the argument.

First, it has force only if some aretaic conception of justified belief is plausible. Yet aretaic conceptions have little plausibility. To be sure, the idea behind an aretaic conception – that there is a significant relation between certain epistemic virtues and justified belief – is correct. But we may explain this relation without endorsing the aretaic conception itself. We need not explain the relation by saying that justified belief is belief of a sort that manifests an epistemic virtue. On the contrary, something entirely different is suggested by the observation that got us started on the aretaic conception, the observation that the practice of justification depends on certain character traits. This observation suggests that certain epistemic virtues tend to facilitate and give rise to justified beliefs. Of course not all epistemic virtues do this. Similarly, it may be that not all justified beliefs manifest certain epistemic virtues, or indeed any epistemic virtues at all.

To see this, reflect that there is nothing natural about defining a *deontic* status like justified belief – epistemically permissible belief – as belief of a sort that manifests exemplary traits or virtues. On any charitable epistemology, even those who lack virtues have scads of justified beliefs, and there is no obvious reason why what is permissible for those who are not virtuous should turn out to be what manifests the traits of those who are virtuous. To be sure, a primary point of ascribing virtues is to get people to do good deeds by emulating the deeds of the virtuous. But this no more entails that the only permissible beliefs are those of a sort that manifest virtues – that justified beliefs are always beliefs of a sort that manifest virtues – than the fact that a chief point of ascribing benevolence is to get people to do morally good deeds by emulation entails that the only permissible actions are morally good deeds. A primary point of evaluating permissible beliefs is surely to create a broad space in which people have approved beliefs even when they lack virtues. This space may be necessary to encourage people to make progress toward those virtues. People are bound to stumble in trying to emulate virtuous beliefs;

these are very hard won (unlike reliable beliefs, which do not need the corresponding protection of a status of perspectival belief). More importantly, a space of permissible beliefs may be necessary if people are to maintain and use desirable beliefs though they lack virtues and indeed fail to emulate them. After all, most people fall short of most virtues, and at a certain point stop trying to emulate them. That is why less than exemplary (not very perspicacious, wise, or careful) beliefs can be justified. These are justified beliefs that do not manifest any epistemic virtues.

Of course the heroic proponent of the aretaic conception could respond by insisting that justified but less than exemplary beliefs, though they do not themselves manifest epistemic virtues, are nevertheless beliefs *of a sort* than manifest epistemic virtues. But once this "sort" has been stretched to include beliefs that do not manifest epistemic virtues, the need for an account of what a sort is becomes pressing. It will not do to say that a sort includes just those beliefs sufficiently similar overall to manifestations of epistemic virtues. It is doubtful that a justified but not very perspicacious or careful perceptual belief must be overall more similar to a perceptual belief that manifests perspicacity and care than an unjustified, perspicacious but careless belief. The latter two are, after all, similar in perspicacity. If the relevant sort of belief is to be defined by similarity to beliefs that manifest epistemic virtues, the similarity must be in some particular respect. For example, the justified belief that does not manifest virtue might be similar to the manifesting belief in respect to reliability, coherence, or whatever. The trouble is that once the relevant respect is identified, we can simply define justified belief directly in terms of that respect – in terms of reliability or coherence – and forget about manifesting virtue. Identifying the respect is equivalent to identifying the property that all justified beliefs have in common. In this case, the explanatory work in the apparently aretaic definition of justification is being done by the identified property, and the account of justified belief is, in its explanations of our intuitions about justified beliefs, nonaretaic. For these reasons, an aretaic conception of justified belief seems unpromising.

Even granting the plausibility of an aretaic conception, we may ask: why *this* aretaic conception? Why should *epistemic integrity* be chosen as the virtue justified beliefs must manifest, rather than some combination of perspicacity, care, etc. – virtues that are not always manifested by (or only by) perspectival belief? Certainly if, as I have suggested, certain epistemic virtues facilitate or give rise to justified belief, we would be hard pressed to pick out one among these deserving of the central position in an account of justification accorded to epistemic integrity by the present account. To assume that justified belief is belief that manifests epistemic integrity is to give conformity to one's perspective an importance in cognition that would need as much argument as identifying justified belief directly with perspectival belief.

A final objection to the aretaic argument is that its assumption that perspectival belief is belief of a sort that manifests epistemic integrity is doubtful at best. On one view of manifestation, the beliefs that manifest a virtue are those that result (in an appropriate way) from the virtue. On another view, they are those that somehow represent all of the qualities involved in the virtue – in the case of epistemic integrity, such qualities as a disposition to seek and maintain justified beliefs about reliability. On neither view of manifestation do perspectival beliefs always manifest epistemic integrity.[7]

I have canvassed arguments for perspectivism by appeal to formal conceptions of justified belief – responsibility, advisory, and aretaic conceptions – conceptions that seemed, at least initially, relatively innocuous, yet perhaps rich enough to yield perspectivism. Perspectival belief, whether defined by iterativism or reflective perspectivism, does not fit any of these conceptions. Our lead question was whether there is any role for a status of perspectival belief in epistemic evaluation. The answer suggested by our survey is "None." Of course I have expressed doubts about whether any of these conceptions describes justified belief. Nevertheless, I am inclined to regard epistemically responsible belief as a significant epistemic status distinct from justified belief. But my conclusion is not merely that perspectival belief is not justified belief, but that it is not epistemically responsible, advisable, or virtuous belief either. There is no role for a status of perspectival belief. No doubt BonJour is right that it is (usually) good to be justified in believing that one's belief is reliable. And Foley is right that it is (often) good to believe what results or would result from reflection on reliability. But perhaps this is because for many subjects, one's belief tends to be reliable or coherent just when one is justified in believing that one's belief is reliable, or when one reflects on reliability. The attraction of perspectival belief may trace to its association with another kind of belief – perhaps reliable belief, perhaps coherent belief – that is more intimately related to justified belief.

Notes

I would like to thank Alvin Goldman and participants at the Cincinnati Philosophy Colloquium, March 1992, for helpful comments.

1　A belief is reliable just in case it belongs to a specified class of beliefs most of which are true. Usually, the specified class is held to be the class of beliefs formed by a specified process that forms the belief in question.

2　See Schmitt 1992 for extensive discussion of reliabilist accounts of undermining, as well as responses to the demon example.

3　For an interesting discussion of the significance of this case for the theory of perceptual attitudes, see Morton 1987.

4　It is worth noting that the example of irresistible belief also casts doubt on premise 1, the claim that justified belief is epistemically responsible belief. My irresistible religious belief is unjustified though epistemically responsible.

5　Of course reflective advice could say: reflect as to whether the belief p is reliable. Then it would avoid reliance on any advisory beliefs and thus vacuously be closed. But this reflective advice does not entail perspectivism under the advisory conception of justified belief. Rather it entails that a belief is justified just in case it results from reflection. That is not a perspectivist theory. The perspectivist cannot gain closure by retreating to the advice to reflect.

6　This argument differs from the earlier advisory argument in supporting reliabilist iterativism rather than counterfactual reflective perspectivism.

7　Similar objections may be made to versions of the aretaic argument that substitute epistemic conscientiousness or autonomy for epistemic integrity.

References

Alston, William. 1989. *Epistemic Justification: Essays in the Theory of Knowledge*. Ithaca: Cornell University Press.

BonJour, Laurence. 1985. *The Structure of Empirical Knowledge*. Cambridge, MA: Harvard University Press.

Chisholm, Roderick. 1977. *Theory of Knowledge*. 2nd edn. Englewood Cliffs: Prentice-Hall.

Code, Lorraine. 1983. *Epistemic Responsibility*. Hanover: University of New England Press.

Foley, Richard. 1987. *The Theory of Epistemic Rationality*. Cambridge, MA: Harvard University Press.

Foley, Richard. 1989. "Reply to Alston, Feldman and Swain." *Philosophy and Phenomenological Research* 50: 169–88.

Freeman, N. and M. Cox, eds. 1985. *Visual Order*. Cambridge: Cambridge University Press.

Goldman, Alvin. 1986. *Epistemology and Cognition*. Cambridge, MA: Harvard University Press.

Kornblith, Hilary. 1983. "Justified Belief and Epistemically Responsible Action." *Philosophical Review* 92: 33–48.

Lehrer, Keith. 1990. *Theory of Knowledge*. Boulder: Westview Press.

Morton, Adam. 1987. "The Explanatory Depth of Propositional Attitudes: Perceptual Development as a Test Case". In Russell 1987: 67–80.

Pollock, John. 1986. *Contemporary Theories of Knowledge*. Totowa: Rowman and Littlefield.

Russell, J., ed. 1987. *A Philosophical Perspective of Developmental Psychology*. Oxford: Basil Blackwell.

Schmitt, Frederick. 1992. *Knowledge and Belief*. London: Routledge.

Sosa, Ernest. 1991. *Knowledge in Perspective*. Cambridge: Cambridge University Press.

Stich, Stephen. 1990. *The Fragmentation of Reason*. Cambridge, MA: MIT Press.

Willats, J. 1985. "Drawing Systems Revisited: The Role of Denotation Systems in Children's Figurative Drawings." In Freeman and Cox 1985: 78–100.

9

INTERNALISM EXPOSED

Alvin Goldman

In recent decades, epistemology has witnessed the development and growth of externalist theories of knowledge and justification.[1] Critics of externalism have focused a bright spotlight on this approach and judged it unsuitable for realizing the true and original goals of epistemology. Their own favored approach, internalism, is defended as a preferable approach to the traditional concept of epistemic justification.[2] I shall turn the spotlight toward internalism and its most prominent rationale, revealing fundamental problems at the core of internalism and challenging the viability of its most popular rationale. Although particular internalist theories such as (internalist) foundationalism and coherentism will occasionally be discussed, those specific theories are not my primary concern. The principal concern is rather the general architecture of internalism, and the attempt to justify this architecture by appeal to a certain conception of what justification consists in.

I Deontology, Access, and Internalism

I begin with a certain rationale for internalism that has widespread support. It can be reconstructed in three steps:

(1) The *guidance-deontological* (GD) *conception of justification* is posited.
(2) A certain constraint on the determiners of justification is derived from the GD conception, that is, the constraint that all justification determiners must be *accessible to*, or *knowable by*, the epistemic agent.

(3)   The accessibility or knowability constraint is taken to imply that only internal conditions qualify as legitimate determiners of justification. So justification must be a purely internal affair.[3]

What motivates or underlies this rationale for internalism? Historically, one central aim of epistemology is to guide or direct our intellectual conduct, an aim expressed in René Descartes's title, "Rules for the Direction of the Mind."[1] Among contemporary writers, John Pollock expresses the idea this way:

> I have taken the fundamental problem of epistemology to be that of deciding what to believe. Epistemic justification, as I use the term, is concerned with this problem. Considerations of epistemic justification guide us in determining what to believe. We might call this the "belief-guiding" or "reason-guiding" sense of 'justification' (*Contemporary Theories of Knowledge*, p. 10).

The guidance conception of justification is commonly paired with the deontological conception of justification. John Locke[5] wrote of a person's "duty as a rational creature" (*ibid.*, p. 413), and the theme of epistemic duty or responsibility has been echoed by many contemporary epistemologists, including Laurence BonJour (*The Structure of Empirical Knowledge*), Roderick Chisholm (*Theory of Knowledge*), Carl Ginet, Paul Moser, Matthias Steup, Richard Feldman, and Hilary Kornblith.[6] Chisholm defines cousins of the concept of justification in terms of the relation "more reasonable than", and he re-expresses the relation "p is more reasonable than q for S at t" by saying: "S is so situated at t that his intellectual *requirement*, his *responsibility* as an intellectual being, is better fulfilled by p than by q."[7] Similarly, Feldman says that one's epistemic duty is to "believe what is supported or justified by one's evidence and to avoid believing what is not supported by one's evidence" (*op. cit.*, p. 254).

The guidance and deontological conceptions of justification are intimately related, because the deontological conception, at least when paired with the guidance conception, considers it a person's epistemic duty to guide his doxastic attitudes by his evidence, or by whatever factors determine the justificational status of a proposition at a given time. Epistemic deontologists commonly maintain that being justified in believing a proposition p consists in being (intellectually) required or permitted to believe p; and being unjustified in believing p consists in not being permitted, or being forbidden, to believe p. When a person is unjustified in believing a proposition, it is his duty not to believe it.

It is possible to separate the deontological conception from the guidance idea. In ethical theory, a distinction has been drawn between accounts of moral duty that aim to specify what makes actions right and accounts of moral duty that aim to provide practical decision procedures for what to do.[8] If an account simply aims at the first desideratum, it need not aspire to be usable as a decision guide. Similarly, accounts of epistemic duty need not necessarily be intended as decision guides. When the deontological conception is used as a rationale for epistemic internalism of the sort I am sketching, however, it does incorporate the guidance conception. Only if the guidance conception is incorporated can the argument proceed along the intended lines to the accessibility constraint, and from there to internalism. This is why I shall henceforth speak of the GD conception of justification.

I turn now to the second step of the argument for internalism. Following William Alston,[9] I shall use the term *justifiers* for facts or states of affairs that determine the justificational status of a belief, or the epistemic status a proposition has for an epistemic agent. In other words, justifiers determine whether or not a proposition is justified for an epistemic agent at a given time. It seems to follow naturally from the GD conception of justification that a certain constraint must be placed on the sorts of facts or states of affairs that qualify as justifiers. If a person is going to avoid violating his epistemic duty, he must know, or be able to find out, what his duty requires. By *know*, in this context, I mean only: have an *accurate*, or *true*, belief. I do not mean: have a *justified* true belief (or whatever else is entailed by the richer concept of knowledge). Admittedly, it might be possible to avoid violating one's duties by chance, without knowing (having true beliefs about) what one's duties are. As a practical matter, however, it is not feasible to conform to duty on a regular and consistent basis without knowing what items of conduct constitute those duties. Thus, if you are going to choose your beliefs and abstentions from belief in accordance with your justificational requirements, the facts that make you justified or unjustified in believing a certain proposition at a given time must be facts that you are capable of knowing, at that time, to hold or not to hold. There is an intimate connection, then, between the GD conception of justification and the requirement that justifiers must be accessible to, or knowable by, the agent at the time of belief. If you cannot accurately ascertain your epistemic duty at a given time, how can you be expected to execute that duty, and how can you reasonably be held responsible for executing that duty?[10]

The *knowability constraint on justifiers* which flows from the GD conception may be formulated as follows:

KJ: The only facts that qualify as justifiers of an agent's believing p at
       time t are facts that the agent can readily know, at t, to obtain or not
       to obtain.

How can an agent readily know whether candidate justifiers obtain or do not
obtain? Presumably, the agent must have a way of determining, for any candidate class of justifiers, whether or not they obtain. Such a way of knowing
must be reliable, that is, it must generate beliefs about the presence or absence
of justifiers that are usually (invariably?) correct. Otherwise, the agent
will often be mistaken about what his epistemic duty requires. The way of
knowing must also be "powerful," in the sense that when justifiers obtain it is
likely (certain?) that the agent will believe that they obtain; at least he will
believe this if he reflects on the matter or otherwise inquires into it.[11] As we
shall soon see, internalists typically impose additional restrictions on how justifiers may be known. But the minimal, generic version of KJ simply requires
justifiers to be the sorts of facts that agents have *some* way of knowing. In other
words, justification-conferring facts must be the sorts of facts whose presence
or absence is "accessible" to agents.[12]
    Given the KJ constraint on justifiers, it becomes fairly obvious why inter-
nalism about justification is so attractive. Whereas external facts are facts that
a cognitive agent might not be in a position to know about, internal facts are
presumably the sorts of conditions that a cognitive agent can readily determine. So internal facts seem to be the right sorts of candidates for justifiers.
This consideration leads to the third step of our rationale for internalism.
Only internal facts qualify as justifiers because they are the only ones that
satisfy the KJ constraint; at least so internalists suppose.
    One possible way to criticize this rationale for internalism is to challenge
the GD conception directly. This could be done, for example, by arguing that
the GD conception of justification presupposes the dubious thesis of doxastic voluntarism, the thesis that doxastic attitudes can be "guided" by deliberate choices or acts of will. This criticism is developed by Alston,[13] and I have
sympathy with many of his points. But the voluntarism argument against the
GD conception is disputed by Feldman ("Epistemic Obligations") and John
Heil,[14] among others. Feldman, for example, argues that epistemic deontolo-
gism is not wedded to the assumption of doxastic voluntarism. Many obligations remain in force, he points out, even when an agent lacks the ability to
discharge them. A person is still legally obligated to repay a debt even when
his financial situation makes him unable to repay it. Perhaps epistemic obligations have analogous properties.[15] Since the complex topic of doxastic voluntarism would require article-length treatment in its own right, I set this issue
aside and confine my attention to other issues. Although I do not accept the

GD conception of justification, I take it as given for purposes of the present discussion and explore where it leads. In any case, what is ultimately crucial for internalism is the accessibility requirement that the GD conception hopes to rationalize. Even if the GD conception fails to provide a good rationale, internalism would be viable if some other rationale could be provided for a suitable accessibility requirement.

II Direct Knowability and Strong Internalism

The initial KJ constraint was formulated in terms of knowability plain and simple, but proponents of internalism often add the further qualification that determinants of justification must be *directly* knowable by the cognitive agent. Ginet, for example, writes as follows:

> Every one of every set of facts about S's position that minimally suffices to make S, at a given time, justified in being confident that p must be *directly recognizable* to S at that time (*Knowledge, Perception, and Memory*, p. 34).

Similarly, Chisholm writes:

> [T]he concept of epistemic justification is . . . internal and immediate in that one can *find out directly*, by reflection, what one is justified in believing at any time.[16]

Thus, Ginet and Chisholm do not endorse just the minimal KJ constraint as earlier formulated, but a more restrictive version, which might be written as follows:

KJ$_{dir}$: The only facts that qualify as justifiers of an agent's believing *p* at time *t* are facts that the agent can readily know *directly*, at *t*, to obtain or not to obtain.

An initial problem arising from KJ$_{dir}$ is this: What warrants the imposition of KJ$_{dir}$ as opposed to the looser constraint, KJ? KJ was derived from the GD conception on the grounds that one cannot reasonably be expected to comply with epistemic duties unless one knows what those duties are. How does such an argument warrant the further conclusion that *direct* knowledge of justification must be available? Even indirect knowledge (whatever that is) would enable an agent to comply with his epistemic duties. So the second step of the argument for internalism cannot properly be revised to feature KJ$_{dir}$ in place of KJ. Proponents of KJ$_{dir}$ might reply that direct forms of knowledge are more powerful than indirect knowledge, but this reply is unconvincing. The power requirement was already built into the original version of KJ, and it is unclear how directness adds anything of significance on that score. Whether KJ$_{dir}$ can be derived from GD is a serious problem, because the argument for internalism rests on something like the directness qualification. I shall say more about this later; for now I set this point aside in order to explore where KJ$_{dir}$ leads.

What modes of knowledge count as direct? At least one form of direct knowledge is introspection. A reason for thinking that introspection is what Chisholm means by direct knowledge is that he restricts all determiners of justification to conscious states:

> A consequence of our "internalistic" theory of knowledge is that, if one is subject to an epistemic requirement at any time, then this requirement is imposed by the *conscious state* in which one happens to find oneself at that time (ibid., pp. 59–60).

Since he restricts justifiers to conscious states, it is plausible to assume that direct knowledge, for Chisholm, means introspective knowledge, and knowledge by "reflection" coincides with knowledge by introspection.[17] At least in the case of Chisholm, then, KJ$_{dir}$ might be replaced by:

> KJ$_{int}$: The only facts that qualify as justifiers of an agent's believing *p* at time *t* are facts that the agent can readily know *by introspection*, at *t*, to obtain or not to obtain.

Now, the only facts that an agent can know by introspection are facts concerning what conscious states he is (or is not) currently in, so these are the only sorts of facts that qualify as justifiers under KJ$_{int}$. This form of internalism may be called *strong internalism*:

> SI: Only facts concerning what conscious states an agent is in at time *t* are justifiers of the agent's beliefs at *t*.

Strong internalism, however, is an unacceptable approach to justification, for it has serious, skepticism-breeding, consequences. This is demonstrated by the *problem of stored beliefs*. At any given time, the vast majority of one's beliefs are stored in memory rather than occurrent or active. Beliefs about personal data (for example, one's social security number), about world history, about geography, or about the institutional affiliations of one's professional colleagues, are almost all stored rather than occurrent at a given moment. Furthermore, for almost any of these beliefs, one's conscious state at the time includes nothing that justifies it. No perceptual experience, no conscious memory event, and no premises consciously entertained at the selected moment will be justificationally sufficient for such a belief. According to strong internalism, then, none of these beliefs is justified at that moment. Strong internalism threatens a drastic diminution in the stock of beliefs ordinarily deemed justified, and hence in the stock of knowledge, assuming that justification is necessary for knowledge. This is a major count against this type of theory.

Feldman anticipates this problem because his own account of having evidence also implies that only consciously entertained factors have evidential force ("Epistemic Obligations," pp. 98–9). Feldman tries to meet the threat by distinguishing between occurrent and dispositional senses of epistemic terms. (He actually discusses knowledge rather than justification, but I shall address the issue in terms of justification because that is the target of our investigation.) Feldman is not simply restating the familiar point that "belief" has occurrent and dispositional senses. He is proposing that the term "justified" is ambiguous between an occurrent and a dispositional sense. Feldman apparently claims that in the case of stored beliefs, people at most have dispositional justification, not occurrent justification.

There are two problems with this proposal. First, if having a disposition to generate conscious evidential states qualifies as a justifier of a belief, why would this not extend from memorial to perceptual dispositions? Suppose a train passenger awakes from a nap but has not yet opened his eyes. Is he justified in believing propositions about the details of the neighboring landscape? Surely not. Yet he is *disposed*, merely by opening his eyes, to generate conscious evidential states that would occurrently justify such beliefs. So the dispositional approach is far too permissive to yield an acceptable sense of "justified."[18] Second, can an internalist, especially a strong internalist, live with the idea that certain dispositions count as justifiers? Having or not having a disposition (of the requisite type) is not the sort of fact or condition that can be known by introspection. Thus, the proposal to supplement the occurrent sense of "justified" with a dispositional sense of "justified" is simply the abandonment of strong internalism.

III   Indirect Knowability and Weak Internalism

The obvious solution to the problem of stored beliefs is to relax the KJ constraint: allow justifiers to be merely indirectly knowable. This yields:

KJ$_{ind}$:   The only facts that qualify as justifiers of an agent's believing p at time t are facts that the agent can readily know at t, either directly or indirectly, to obtain or not to obtain.

The danger here is that indirect knowledge might let in too much from an internalist perspective. How are externalist forms of knowledge – for example, perceptual knowledge – to be excluded? Clearly, internalism must propose specific forms of knowledge that conform with its spirit. It is fairly clear how internalism should deal with the problem of stored beliefs: simply allow knowledge of justifiers to include memory retrieval. Stored evidence beliefs can qualify as justifiers because the agent can know that they obtain by the compound route of first retrieving them from memory and then introspecting their conscious contents. This yields the following variant of the KJ constraint:

KJ$_{int+ret}$:   The only facts that qualify as justifiers of an agent's believing p at time t are facts that the agent can readily know, at t, to obtain or not to obtain, *by introspection and/or memory retrieval*.

This KJ constraint allows for a more viable form of internalism than strong internalism. We may call it *weak internalism*, and initially articulate it through the following principle:

WI: Only facts concerning what conscious and/or stored mental states an agent is in at time t are justifiers of the agent's beliefs at t.

WI will certify the justification of many stored beliefs, because agents often have other stored beliefs that evidentially support them. A person who believes that Washington, D.C. is the capital of the United States may have a stored belief to the effect that a map of the U.S. he recently consulted showed Washington as the capital. The latter stored belief is what justifies the former one. So weak internalism is not plagued with the problem of stored justified beliefs. Weak internalism seems to be a legitimate form of internalism because even stored beliefs qualify, intuitively, as internal states.

Although weak internalism is better than strong internalism, it too faces severe problems. First is the *problem of forgotten evidence*.[19] Many justified beliefs are ones for which an agent once had adequate evidence that she subsequently forgot. At the time of epistemic appraisal, she no longer possesses adequate evidence that is retrievable from memory. Last year, Sally read a story about the health benefits of broccoli in the "Science" section of the *New York Times*.

She then justifiably formed a belief in broccoli's beneficial effects. She still retains this belief but no longer recalls her original evidential source (and has never encountered either corroborating or undermining sources). Nonetheless, her broccoli belief is still justified, and, if true, qualifies as a case of knowledge. Presumably, this is because her past acquisition of the belief was epistemically proper. But past acquisition is irrelevant by the lights of internalism (including weak internalism), because only her current mental states are justifiers relevant to her current belief. All past events are "external" and therefore irrelevant according to internalism.

It might be replied that Sally does currently possess evidence in support of her broccoli belief. One of her background beliefs, we may suppose, is that most of what she remembers was learned in an epistemically proper manner. So does she not, after all, now have grounds for the target belief? Admittedly, she has *some* evidence, but is this evidence sufficient for justification? Surely not. In a variant case, suppose that Sally still has the same background belief – namely, that most of what she remembers was learned in an epistemically proper manner – but she in fact acquired her broccoli belief from the *National Inquirer* rather than the *New York Times*. So her broccoli belief was never acquired, or corroborated, in an epistemically sound manner. Then even with the indicated current background belief, Sally cannot be credited with justifiably believing that broccoli is healthful. Her past acquisition is still relevant, and decisive. At least it is relevant so long as we are considering the "epistemizing" sense of justification, in which justification carries a true belief a good distance toward knowledge. Sally's belief in the healthfulness of broccoli is not justified in that sense, for surely she does not know that broccoli is healthful given that the *National Inquirer* was her sole source of information.

The category of forgotten evidence is a problem for weak internalism because, like the problem of stored beliefs facing strong internalism, it threatens skeptical outcomes. A large sector of what is ordinarily counted as knowledge are beliefs for which people have forgotten their original evidence.

In reply to the problem of forgotten evidence, Steup[20] offers the following solution. An additional requirement for memorial states to justify a belief that *p*, says Steup, is that the agent have adequate evidence for believing the following counterfactual: "If she had encountered *p* in a questionable source, she would not have formed the belief that *p*." Steup's suggestion is that in the *National Inquirer* variant, Sally fails to have adequate evidence for this counterfactual, and that is why her broccoli belief is not justified. My response to this proposal is twofold. First, the proposed requirement is too strong to impose on memorially justified belief. It is quite difficult to get adequate evidence for the indicated counterfactual. Second, the proposed requirement seems too weak as well. Sally might have adequate evidence for the counter-factual but still be unjustified in holding her broccoli belief. She might have adequate evidence for the counterfactual without its being true; but if it is not true and the rest of the story is as I told it, her broccoli belief is not justified. So Steup's internalist-style solution does not work.

A second problem confronting weak internalism is what I call the *problem of concurrent retrieval*. Principle WI says that *only* conscious and stored mental states are justifiers, but it does not say that *all* sets or conjunctions of such states qualify as justifiers.[21] Presumably, which sets of such states qualify is a matter to be decided by reference to $KJ_{int+ret}$. If a certain set of stored beliefs can all be concurrently retrieved at time t and concurrently introspected, then they would pass the test of $KJ_{int+ret}$, and could qualify as justifiers under the principle of indirect knowability. But if they cannot all be concurrently retrieved and introspected at t, they would fail the test. Now it is clear that the totality of an agent's stored credal corpus at a time cannot be concurrently retrieved from memory. So that set of stored beliefs does not qualify as a justifier for purposes of weak internalism. Unfortunately, this sort of belief set is precisely what certain types of internalist theories require by way of a justifier. Consider holistic coherentism, which says that a proposition p is justified for person S at time t if and only if p coheres with S's entire corpus of beliefs at t (including, of course, the stored beliefs). A cognitive agent could ascertain, at t, whether p coheres with her entire corpus only by con-currently retrieving all of her stored beliefs. But such concurrent retrieval is psychologically impossible.[22] Thus, the critically relevant justificational fact under holistic coherentism does not meet even the indirect knowability con-straint, much less the direct knowability constraint. Here is a clash, then, between a standard internalist theory of justification and the knowability rationale under scrutiny. Either that rationale is indefensible, or a familiar type of internalism must be abandoned at the outset. Nor is the problem confined to coherentism. Internalist foundationalism might also require concurrent retrieval of more basic (or low-level) beliefs than it is psychologically feasible to retrieve.

IV   Logical and Probabilistic Relations

As these last examples remind us, every traditional form of internalism involves some appeal to logical relations, probabilistic relations, or their ilk. Foundationalism requires that nonbasically justified beliefs stand in suitable logical or probabilistic relations to basic beliefs; coherentism requires that one's system of beliefs be logically consistent, probabilistically coherent, or the like. None of these logical or probabilistic relations is itself a mental state, either a conscious state or a stored state. So these relations do not qualify as justifiers according to either SI or WI. The point may be illustrated more concretely within a foundationalist perspective. Suppose that Jones possesses a set of basic beliefs at t whose contents logically or probabilistically support proposition p. This property of Jones's basic beliefs – the property of supporting proposition p – is not a justifier under WI, for the property itself is neither a conscious nor a stored mental state. Nor is the possession of this property by these mental states another mental state. So WI has no way of authorizing or permitting Jones to believe p. Unless WI is liberalized, no non-basic belief will be justified, which would again threaten a serious form of skepticism.

Can this problem be remedied by simply adding the proviso that all properties of conscious or stored mental states also qualify as justifiers?[23] This proviso is unacceptably permissive for internalism. One property of many conscious and stored mental states is the property of *being caused by a reliable process*, yet surely internalism cannot admit this archetypically externalist type of property into the class of justifiers. How should the class of properties be restricted? An obvious suggestion is to include only formal properties of mental states, that is, logical and mathematical properties of their contents. But should *all* formal properties be admitted? This approach would fly in the face of the knowability or accessibility constraint, which is the guiding theme of internalism. Only formal properties that are knowable by the agent at the time of doxastic decision should be countenanced as legitimate justifiers under internalism. Such properties, however, cannot be detected by introspection and/or memory retrieval. So some knowing operations suitable for formal properties must be added, yielding a liberalized version of the KJ constraint.

How should a liberalized KJ constraint be designed? The natural move is to add some selected computational operations or algorithms, procedures that would enable an agent to ascertain whether a targeted proposition p has appropriate logical or probabilistic relations to the contents of other belief states he is in. Precisely which computational operations are admissible? Again, problems arise. The first is the *problem of the doxastic decision interval*.

The traditional idea behind internalism is that an agent is justified in believing p at *time t* if the evidential beliefs (and perhaps other, nondoxastic states) possessed *at t* have an appropriate logical or probabilistic relation to p. In short, justification is conferred simultaneously with evidence possession. Feldman makes this explicit: "For any person S and proposition p and time t, S epistemically ought to believe p at t if and only if p is supported by the evidence S has at t" ("Epistemic Obligations," p. 254). Once the knowability constraint is introduced, however, simultaneous justification looks problematic. If justification is contingent on the agent's ability to know what justifiers obtain, the agent should not be permitted to believe a proposition p at t unless she can know by t whether the relevant justifiers obtain. Since it necessarily takes some time to compute logical or probabilistic relations, the simultaneity model of justification needs to be revised so that an agent's mental states at t justify her in believing only p at $t + \varepsilon$, for some suitable ε. The value of ε cannot be too large, of course, lest the agent's mental states change so as to affect the justificational status of p. But ε must be large enough to allow the agent time to determine the relevant formal relations.

These two conditions – (1) avoid mental change, but (2) allow enough time to compute formal relations – may well be jointly unsatisfiable, which would pose a severe problem for internalism. Mental states, including perceptual states that generate new evidence, change very rapidly and they could easily change before required computations could be executed. On the other hand, although mental states do change rapidly, the agent's belief system might not be epistemically required to reflect or respond to each change until interval ε has elapsed. Some doxastic decision interval, then, might be feasible.

Is there a short enough decision interval during which justificationally pertinent formal properties can be computed? Coherentism says that S is justified in believing proposition p only if p coheres with the rest of S's belief system held at the time. Assume that coherence implies logical consistency. Then coherentism requires that the logical consistency or inconsistency of any proposition p with S's belief system must qualify as a justifier. But how quickly can consistency or inconsistency be ascertained by mental computation? As Christopher Cherniak[21] points out, determination of even tautological consistency is a computationally complex task in the general case. Using the truth-table method to check for the consistency of a belief system with 138 independent atomic propositions, even an ideal computer working at "top speed" (checking each row of a truth table in the time it takes a light ray to traverse the diameter of a proton) would take twenty billion years, the estimated time from the "big-bang" dawn of the universe to the present. Presumably, twenty billion years is not an acceptable doxastic decision interval!

Any reasonable interval, then, is too constraining for garden-variety coherentism. The knowability constraint again clashes with one of the stock brands of internalism.[25] Dyed-in-the-wool internalists might be prepared to live with this result. "So much the worse for traditional coherentism," they might say, "we can live with its demise." But this does not get internalism entirely off the hook. There threaten to be many logical and probabilistic facts that do not qualify as justifiers because they require too long a doxastic interval to compute. Furthermore, it is unclear what is a principled basis for deciding what is too long. This quandary confronting internalism has apparently escaped its proponents' attention.

A second problem for logical and probabilistic justifiers is the *availability problem*. Suppose that a particular set of *computational operations* – call it COMP – is provisionally selected for inclusion alongside introspection and memory retrieval. COMP might include, for example, a restricted (and hence noneffective) use of the truth-table method, restricted so as to keep its use within the chosen doxastic decision interval.[26] This yields a new version of the KJ constraint:

KJ$_{int+ret+COMP}$: The only facts that qualify as justifiers of an agent's believing p at time t are facts that the agent can readily know within a suitable doxastic decision interval *via introspection, memory retrieval, and/or COMP.*

Now, the KJ constraint is presumably intended to apply not only to the cleverest or best-trained epistemic agents but to all epistemic agents, including the most naive and uneducated persons on the street. After all, the point of the knowability constraint is that justifiers should be facts within the purview of every epistemic agent. Under the GD conception, compliance with epistemic duty or responsibility is not intended to be the private preserve of the logical or mathematical elite. It is something that ought to be attained – and should therefore be attainable – by any human agent. The truth-table method, however, does not seem to be in the intellectual repertoire of naive agents, so it is illegitimate to include COMP operations within a KJ constraint. Unlike introspection and memory retrieval, it is not available to all cognitive agents.

It may be replied that computational operations of the contemplated sort would be within the *capacity* of normal human agents. No super-human computational powers are required. Computing power, however, is not the issue. A relevant sequence of operations must also be *available* in the agent's intellectual repertoire; that is, she must know which operations are appropriate to obtain an answer to the relevant (formal) question.[27] Since truth-table methods and other such algorithms are probably not in the repertoire of ordinary cognitive agents, they cannot properly be included in a KJ constraint.

A third problem concerns the proper methodology that should be used in selecting a KJ constraint that incorporates computational operations. As we see from the first two problems, a KJ constraint that conforms to the spirit of the GD rationale must reflect the basic cognitive skills or repertoires of actual human beings. What these basic repertoires consist in, however, cannot be determined a priori. It can only be determined with the help of empirical science. This fact fundamentally undermines the methodological posture of internalism, a subject to which I shall return in section VII.

Until now, I have assumed a *universal* accessibility constraint, one that holds for all cognitive agents. But perhaps potential justifiers for one agent need not be potential justifiers for another. Justifiers might be allowed to vary from agent to agent, depending on what is knowable by the particular agent. If two agents have different logical or probabilistic skills, then some properties that do not qualify as justifiers for one might yet qualify as justifiers for the other. Indeed, the constraint $KJ_{int+ret+COMP}$ might be read in precisely this agent-relativized way. The subscripts may be interpreted as indicating knowledge routes that are available *to the agent in question*, not necessarily to all agents.

If KJ constraints are agent relativized as a function of differences in knowledge skills, this means that two people in precisely the same evidential state (in terms of perceptual situation, background beliefs, and so on) might have different epistemic entitlements. But if the two agents are to comply with their respective epistemic duties, each must *know* which knowledge skills she has. This simply parallels the second step of the internalist's original three-step argument. If one's epistemic duties or entitlements depend on one's knowledge skills (for example, on one's computational skills), then compliance with one's duties requires knowledge of which skills one possesses. There are two problems with this approach. First, it is unlikely that many people — especially ordinary people on the street – have this sort of knowledge, and this again threatens large-scale skepticism. Second, what is now required to be known by the agent is something about the *truth-getting* power of her cognitive skills – that is, the power of her skills in detecting justifiers. This seems to be precisely the sort of *external* property that internalists regard as anathema. How can they accept this solution while remaining faithful to the spirit of internalism?[28]

V Epistemic Principles

When the KJ constraint speaks of justifiers, it is not clear exactly what these comprehend. Specifically, do justifiers include epistemic principles themselves? I believe that principles should be included, because epistemic principles are among the items that determine whether or not an agent is justified in believing a proposition, which is just how "justifiers" was defined. Furthermore, true epistemic principles are items an agent must know if she is going to determine her epistemic duties correctly. Knowledge of her current states of mind and their properties will not instruct her about her epistemic duties and entitlements unless she also knows true epistemic principles.

How are epistemic principles to be known, according to internalism? Chisholm[29] says that central epistemic principles are normative supervenience principles, which (when true) are necessarily true. Since they are necessary truths, they can be known a priori – in particular, they can be known "by reflection."

> The internalist assumes that, merely by reflecting upon his own conscious state, he can formulate a set of epistemic principles that will enable him to find out, with respect to any possible belief he has, whether he is justified in having that belief.[30]

This passage is ambiguous as to whether (correct) epistemic principles are accessible on reflection just to epistemologists, or accessible to naive epistemic agents as well. The latter, however, must be required by internalism, because justifiers are supposed to be determinable by all epistemic agents.

Are ordinary or naive agents really capable of formulating and recognizing correct epistemic principles? This seems highly dubious. Even many career-long epistemologists have failed to articulate and appreciate correct epistemic principles. Since different epistemologists offer disparate and mutually conflicting candidates for epistemic principles, at most a fraction of these epistemologists can be right. Perhaps none of the principles thus far tendered by epistemologists is correct! In light of this shaky and possibly dismal record by professional epistemologists, how can we expect ordinary people, who are entirely ignorant of epistemology and its multiple pitfalls, to succeed at this task?[31] Nor is it plausible that they should succeed at this task purely "by reflection" on their conscious states, since among the matters epistemic principles must resolve is what computational skills are within the competence of ordinary cognizers. I do not see how this can be answered a priori, "by reflection."

A crippling problem emerges for internalism. If epistemic principles are not knowable by all naive agents, no such principles can qualify as justifiers under the KJ constraint. If no epistemic principles so qualify, no proposition can be justifiably believed by any agent. Wholesale skepticism follows.

VI The Core Dilemma for the Three-Step Argument

I raise doubts here about whether there is any cogent inferential route from the GD conception to internalism via an acceptable KJ constraint. Here is the core dilemma. The minimal, unvarnished version of the KJ constraint does not rationalize internalism. That simple constraint merely says that justifiers must be readily knowable, and some readily knowable facts might be external rather than internal. If *all* routes to knowledge of justifiers are allowed, then knowledge by perception must be allowed. If knowledge by perception is allowed, then facts of an external sort could qualify for the status of justifiers. Of course, no epistemologist claims that purely external facts should serve as justifiers. But partly external facts are nominated by externalists for the rank of justifiers. Consider properties of the form: being a reliable perceptual indicator of a certain environmental fact. This sort of property is at least partly external because reliability involves truth, and truth (on the usual assumption) is external. Now suppose that a certain auditory perceptual state has the property of being a reliable indicator of the presence of a mourning dove in one's environment. Might the possession of this reliable indicatorship property qualify as a justifier on the grounds that it is indeed readily knowable? If every route to knowledge is legitimate, I do not see how this possibility can be excluded. After all, one could use past perceptions of mourning doves and their songs to determine that the designated auditory state is a reliable indicator of a mourning dove's presence. So if unrestricted knowledge is allowed, the (partly) external fact in question might be perfectly knowable. Thus, the unvarnished version of the KJ constraint does not exclude external facts from the ranks of the justifiers.

The simple version of the KJ constraint, then, does not support internalism. Tacit recognition of this is what undoubtedly leads internalists to favor a "direct" knowability constraint. Unfortunately, this extra rider is not rationalized by the GD conception. The GD conception at best implies that cognitive agents must know what justifiers are present or absent. No particular *types* of knowledge, or *paths* to knowledge, are intimated. So the GD conception cannot rationalize a restrictive version of the KJ constraint that unambiguously yields internalism.

Let me put the point another way. The GD conception implies that justifiers must be readily knowable, but are internal facts always *more readily* knowable than external facts? As discussed earlier, probabilistic relations presumably qualify as internal, but they do not seem to be readily knowable by human beings. An entire tradition of psychological research on "biases and heuristics" suggests that naive agents commonly commit probabilistic fallacies, such as the "conjunction fallacy," and use formally incorrect judgmental heuristics, such as the representativeness heuristic and the anchoring-and-adjustment heuristic.[32] If this is right, people's abilities at detecting probabilistic relationships are actually rather weak. People's perceptual capacities to detect external facts seem, by contrast, far superior. The unqualified version of the KJ constraint, therefore, holds little promise for restricting all justifiers to internal conditions in preference to external conditions, as internalism requires.[33]

VII The Methodology of Epistemology: Empirical or A Priori?

Internalism standardly incorporates the doctrine that epistemology is a purely a priori or armchair enterprise rather than one that needs help from empirical science. Chisholm puts the point this way:

> The epistemic principles that [the epistemologist] formulates are principles that one may come upon and apply merely by sitting in one's armchair, so to speak, and without calling for any outside assistance. In a word, one need only consider one's own state of mind.[34]

Previous sections already raised doubts about the merits of apriorism in epistemology, even in the context of the theoretical architecture presented here. I now want to challenge the viability of apriorism in greater depth.

Assume that, despite my earlier reservations, an internalist restriction on justifiers has somehow been derived, one that allows only conscious states and certain of their nonexternal properties to serve as justifiers. How should the epistemologist identify particular conscious states and properties as justifiers for specific propositions (or types of propositions)? In other words, how should specific epistemic principles be crafted? Should the task be executed purely a priori, or can scientific psychology help?

For concreteness, consider justifiers for memory beliefs. Suppose an adult consciously remembers seeing, as a teenager, a certain matinee idol. This ostensible memory could have arisen from imagination, since he frequently fantasized about this matinee idol and imagined seeing her in person. What clues are present in the current memory impression by which he can tell whether or not the recollection is veridical? This is precisely the kind of issue which internalist epistemic principles should address. If there are no differ-

ences in features of memory states that stem from perceptions of real occur-
rences versus features of states that stem from mere imagination, does this not
raise a specter of skepticism over the domain of memory? If there are no
indications by which to distinguish veridical from nonveridical memory
impressions, can we be justified in trusting our memory impressions? Skepticism aside, epistemologists should surely be interested in identifying the features of conscious memory impressions by which people are made more or
less justified (or prima facie justified) in believing things about the past.

Epistemologists have said very little on this subject. Their discussions tend
to be exhausted by characterizations of memory impressions as "vivid" or
"nonvivid." There is, I suspect, a straightforward reason for the paucity
of detail. It is extremely difficult, using purely armchair methods, to dissect
the microfeatures of memory experiences so as to identify telltale differences
between trustworthy and questionable memories. On the other hand,
empirical methods have produced some interesting findings, which might
properly be infused into epistemic principles in a way entirely congenial to
internalism. Important research in this area has been done by Marcia Johnson
and her colleagues.[35] I shall illustrate my points by brief reference to their
research.

Johnson calls the subject of some of her research *reality monitoring*. She tries
to characterize the detectable differences between (conscious) memory traces
derived from veridical perception of events versus memory traces generated
by mere imaginations of events.[36] Johnson and Raye ("Reality Monitoring")
propose four dimensions along which memory cues will typically differ
depending on whether their origin was perceptual or imaginative. As compared with memories that originate from imagination, memories originating
from perception tend to have (1) more perceptual information (for example,
color and sound), (2) more contextual information about time and place, and
(3) more meaningful detail. When a memory trace is rich along these three
dimensions, this is evidence of its having originated through perception.
Memories originating from imagination or thought, by contrast, tend to be
rich on another dimension: they contain more information about the cognitive operations involved in the original thinkings or imaginings (for example,
effortful attention, image creation, or search). Perception is more automatic
than imagination, so a memory trace that originates from perception will tend
to lack attributes concerning effortful operations. Johnson and Raye therefore
suggest that differences in average value along these types of dimensions can
form the basis for deciding whether the origin of a memory is perceptual or
nonperceptual. A memory with a great deal of visual and spatial detail, and
without records of intentional constructive and organizational processes,
should be judged to have been perceptually derived.[37]

Epistemologists would be well-advised to borrow these sorts of ideas and incorporate them into their epistemic principles. A person is (prima facie) justified in believing in the real occurrence of an ostensibly recalled event if the memory trace is strong on the first three dimensions and weak on the fourth dimension. Conversely, an agent is unjustified in believing in the real occurrence of the recalled event if the memory trace is strong on the fourth dimension but weak on the first three dimensions. All of these dimensions, of course, concern features of conscious experience. For this reason, internalist epistemologists should be happy to incorporate these kinds of features into their epistemic principles.

Let me distinguish two categories of epistemologically significant facts about memory experience which empirical psychology might provide. First, as we have seen, it might identify types of representational materials which are generally available in people's memory experiences. Second, it might indicate which of these representational materials are either reliable or counter-reliable indicators of the veridicality of the ostensibly recalled events. Is the reliability of a memory cue a legitimate issue from an internalist perspective? It might be thought not, since reliability is usually classed as an external property. But epistemologists might use reliability considerations to decide which memory characteristics should be featured in epistemic principles. They need not insert reliability per se into the principles. There is nothing in our present formulation of internalism, at any rate, which bars the latter approach. Any KJ constraint provides only a necessary condition for being a justifier; it leaves open the possibility that additional necessary conditions, such as reliable indication, must also be met. Indeed, many internalists do use reliability as a (partial) basis for their choice of justifiers. BonJour (*The Structure of Empirical Knowledge*, p. 7) says that the basic role of justification is that of a *means* to truth, and he defends coherence as a justifier on the ground that a coherent system of beliefs is likely to correspond to reality. This point need not be settled definitively, however. There are already adequate grounds for claiming that internalism cannot be optimally pursued without help from empirical psychology, whether or not reliability is a relevant consideration.

VIII Conclusion

Let us review the parade of problems infecting internalism which we have witnessed, though not all in their order of presentation. (1) The argument from the GD conception of justification to internalism does not work. Internalism can be derived only from a suitably qualified version of the KJ constraint because the unqualified version threatens to allow external facts to count as justifiers. No suitably qualified version of the KJ constraint is derivable from the GD conception. (2) A variety of qualified KJ constraints are possible, each leading to a different version of internalism. None of these versions is intuitively acceptable. Strong internalism, which restricts justifiers to conscious states, is stuck with the problem of stored beliefs. Weak internalism, which allows stored as well as conscious beliefs to count as justifiers, faces the problem of forgotten evidence and the problem of concurrent retrieval. (3) The question of how logical and probabilistic facts are to be included in the class of justifiers is plagued by puzzles, especially the puzzle of the doxastic decision interval and the issue of availability. (4) Epistemic principles must be among the class of justifiers, but such principles fail internalism's knowability requirement. (5) The favored methodology of internalism – the armchair method – cannot be sustained even if we grant the assumption that justifiers must be conscious states.

Internalism is rife with problems. Are they all traceable to the GD rationale? Could internalism be salvaged by switching to a different rationale? A different rationale might help, but most of the problems raised here arise from the knowability constraint. It is unclear exactly which knowability constraint should be associated with internalism, and all of the available candidates generate problematic theories. So I see no hope for internalism; it does not survive the glare of the spotlight.

Notes

An earlier version of this paper was presented in Pittsburgh, at the Central Division meeting of the American Philosophical Association, April 25, 1997. My commentator on that occasion was Matthias Steup, and I am much indebted to him for valuable correspondence on this topic. I am also grateful to Tim Bayne and Holly Smith for very useful suggestions.

1   Prominent statements of externalism include D. M. Armstrong, *Belief, Truth and Knowledge* (New York: Cambridge, 1973); Fred Dretske, *Knowledge and the Flow of Information* (Cambridge: MIT, 1981); Robert Nozick, *Philosophical Explanations* (Cambridge: Harvard, 1981); my *Epistemology and Cognition* (Cambridge: Harvard, 1986); and Alvin Plantinga, *Warrant and Proper Function* (New York: Oxford, 1993).

2   Major statements of internalism include Roderick Chisholm, *Theory of Knowledge* (Englewood Cliffs, NJ: Prentice-Hall, 1966, 1st edition; 1977, 2nd edition; 1989, 3rd edition); Laurence BonJour, *The Structure of Empirical Knowledge* (Cambridge:

Harvard, 1985); John Pollock, *Contemporary Theories of Knowledge* (Totowa, NJ: Rowman and Littlefield, 1986); Richard Foley, *The Theory of Epistemic Rationality* (Cambridge: Harvard, 1987); and Keith Lehrer, *Theory of Knowledge* (Boulder: Westview, 1990). In addition to relatively pure versions of externalism and internalism, there are also mixtures of the two approaches, as found in William Alston, *Epistemic Justification* (Ithaca: Cornell, 1989); Ernest Sosa, *Knowledge in Perspective* (New York: Cambridge, 1991); and Robert Audi, *The Structure of Justification* (New York: Cambridge, 1993).

3 Plantinga also traces internalism to the deontological conception: "If we go back to the source of the internalist tradition, . . . we can see that internalism arises out of deontology; a deontological conception of warrant . . . leads directly to internalism" (Platinga, *Warrant and Proper Function*, pp. 24–25). Alston proposes a slightly different rationale for internalism, although his rationale also proceeds via the knowability constraint (Alston, *Epistemic Justification*, p. 236). He suggests that the concept of justification derives from the interpersonal practice of criticizing one another's beliefs and asking for their credentials. A person can appropriately respond to other people's demands for credentials only if he knows what those credentials are. So it is quite understandable, says Alston, that justifiers must meet the requirement of being accessible to the agent. Clearly, this is one way to derive the accessibility constraint without appeal to the deontological conception. But Alston is the only one I know of who advances this ground for the accessibility constraint. In any case, most of the problems I shall identify pertain to the accessibility constraint itself, which Alston's rationale shares with the deontological rationale.

4 *Philosophical Works of Descartes, Volume I*, Elizabeth Haldane and G. R. T. Ross, trans. (New York: Dover, 1955).

5 *An Essay Concerning Human Understanding, Volume II*, A. C. Fraser, ed. (New York: Dover, 1955).

6 Ginet, *Knowledge, Perception, and Memory* (Dordrecht: Reidel, 1975); Moser, *Empirical Justification* (Dordrecht: Reidel, 1985); Steup, "The Deontic Conception of Epistemic Justification," *Philosophical Studies*, LIII (1988): 65–84; Feldman, "Epistemic Obligations," in J. Tomberlin, ed., *Philosophical Perspectives*, Volume II (Atascadero, CA: Ridgeview, 1988), pp. 235–56; and Kornblith, "Justified Belief and Epistemically Responsible Action," *Philosophical Review*, XCII (1983): 33–48.

7 *Theory of Knowledge*, 2nd edition, p. 14 (emphasis added).

8 For example, R. Eugene Bales distinguishes between two possible aims of act-utilitarianism: as a specifier of a right-making characteristic or as a decision-making procedure. See "Act-utilitarianism: Account of Right-making Characteristics or Decision-making Procedure," *American Philosophical Quarterly*, VIII (1971): 257–65. He defends utilitarianism against certain critics by saying that it does not *have* to perform the latter function.

9 "Internalism and Externalism in Epistemology," reprinted in Alston, *Epistemic Justification*, pp. 185–226, here p. 189.

10   Some internalists explicitly reject externalism on the grounds that it cannot be
      used as a decision guide. For example, Pollock says: "[I]t is in principle impossi-
      ble for us to actually employ externalist norms. I take this to be a conclusive refu-
      tation of belief externalism" (*Contemporary Theories of Knowledge*, p. 134). He would
      not subscribe to the full argument for internalism I am discussing, however,
      because it is committed to the "intellectualist model" of epistemology, which he
      disparages.

11   For the distinction between reliability and power (phrased slightly differently), see
      Goldman, *Epistemology and Cognition*, chapter 6.

12   Jack Lyons points out that to comply with one's epistemic duty it suffices to know
      that one has (undefeated) justifiers for proposition *p*; one does not have to know
      which justifiers these are. So the argument is not entitled to conclude that knowl-
      edge of particular justifiers is required by epistemic duty. Practically speaking,
      however, it is difficult to see how a cognitive agent could know that relevant jus-
      tifiers exist without knowing which particular ones exist. So I shall pass over this
      objection to the internalist line of argument.

13   "The Deontological Conception of Justification," reprinted in Alston, *Epistemic
      Justification*, pp. 115–52.

14   "Doxastic Agency," *Philosophical Studies*, XL (1983): 355–64.

15   Feldman's response, however, undercuts the step from the GD conception of jus-
      tification to the knowability constraint. If epistemic duty does not require that
      the agent be *able* to discharge this duty, there is no longer a rationale for the
      knowability constraint. A different line of response to the voluntarism worry is
      taken by Lehrer, who suggests that epistemological analysis should focus not no
      belief but on *acceptance*, where acceptance is some sort of action that is subject
      to the will – "A Self-Profile," in R. Bogdan, ed., *Keith Lehrer* (Dordrecht: Reidel,
      1981), pp. 3–104.

16   *Theory of Knowledge*, 3rd edition, p. 7; emphasis added and original emphasis
      deleted.

17   Other epistemologists who restrict justifiers to conscious states or discuss access
      in terms of introspection include Moser, p. 174; Feldman, "Having Evidence,"
      in D. Austin, ed., *Philosophical Analysis* (Dordrecht: Kluwer, 1988), pp. 83–104;
      and Audi, "Causalist Internalism," *American Philosophical Quarterly*, XXVI, 4 (1989):
      309–20.

18   Feldman might reply that there is an important distinction between memorial
      and perceptual dispositions; but it is not clear on what basis a principled dis-
      tinction can be drawn.

19   This sort of problem is discussed by Gilbert Harman, *Change in View* (Cambridge:
      MIT, 1986); Thomas Senor, "Internalist Foundationalism and the Justification of
      Memory Belief," *Synthese*, XCIV (1993): 453–76; and Audi, "Memorial Justifica-
      tion," *Philosophical Topics*, XXIII (1995): 31–45.

20   His proposal was part of his commentary (see acknowledgment note above).

21   Obviously, one would need to reject the principle that the knowability of fact
      A and the knowability of fact *B* entail the knowability of the conjunctive fact,
      A & B.

22 The "doxastic presumption" invoked by BonJour (*The Structure of Empirical Knowledge*, pp. 101–6) seems to assume that this is possible, but this is simply an undefended assumption. Pollock (*Contemporary Theories of Knowledge*, p. 136) also raises the problem identified here, though in slightly different terms.

23 More precisely, the contemplated proviso should say that the possession of any property by a mental state (or set of mental states) qualifies as a justifier. This reading will be understood wherever the text talks loosely of "properties."

24 "Computational Complexity and the Universal Acceptance of Logic," *The Journal of Philosophy*, LXXXI, 12 (December 1984): 739–58.

25 This computational difficulty for coherentism is identified by Kornblith, "The Unattainability of Coherence," in J. Bender, ed., *The Current State of the Coherence Theory* (Dordrecht: Kluwer, 1989), pp. 207–14.

26 Because of the contemplated restriction, there will be many questions about formal facts to which COMP cannot deliver answers. Thus, formal facts that might otherwise qualify as justifiers will not so qualify under the version of the KJ constraint that incorporates COMP.

27 Propositional (or "declarative") knowledge of the appropriate sequence of operations is, perhaps, an unduly restrictive requirement. It would suffice for the agent to have "procedural" skills of the right sort. But even such skills will be lacking in naive cognitive agents.

28 It might be argued that internalism's spirit leads to a similar requirement even for universal versions of a KJ constraint, not just for agent-relativized versions. Perhaps so; but so much the worse for the general form of internalism.

29 "The Status of Epistemic Principles," *Noûs*, XXIV (1990): 209–15.

30 *Theory of Knowledge*, 3rd edition, p. 76; emphasis omitted.

31 A similar worry is expressed by Alston in "Internalism and Externalism in Epistemology," pp. 221–2.

32 See Amos Tversky and Daniel Kahneman, "Judgment under Uncertainty: Heuristics and Biases," in Kahneman, P. Slovic, and Tversky, eds., *Judgment under Uncertainty* (New York: Cambridge, 1982), pp. 3–20; and Tversky and Kahneman, "Extensional versus Intuitive Reasoning: The Conjunction Fallacy in Probability Judgment," *Psychological Review*, XCI (1983): 293–315.

33 It is not really clear, moreover, why logical or probabilistic facts intuitively count as "internal" facts. They certainly are not internal in the same sense in which mental states are internal. This is an additional problem about the contours of internalism.

34 *Theory of Knowledge*, 3rd edition, p. 76.

35 See Johnson and Carol Raye, "Reality Monitoring," *Psychological Review*, LXXXVIII (1981): 67–85; and Johnson, Mary Foley, Aurora Suengas, and Raye, "Phenomenal Characteristics of Memories for Perceived and Imagined Autobiographical Events," *Journal of Experimental Psychology: General*, CXVII (1988): 371–6.

36 Memory errors are not confined, of course, to confusions of actual with imagined events. There are also errors that arise from confusing, or blending, two actual events. But this research of Johnson's focuses on the actual/nonactual (or perceived versus imagined) problem.

37 They also recognize that people can compare a target memory with memories of contextually related events to assess the target's veridicality. This kind of "coherence" factor is a stock-in-trade of epistemology, however, and hence not a good example of the distinctive contributions psychology can make to this subject. I therefore pass over it.

10

INTERNALISM DEFENDED

Earl Conee and Richard Feldman

Internalism in epistemology has been getting bad press lately. Externalism is ascendent, partly because insurmountable problems for internalism are supposed to have been identified.[1] We oppose this trend. In our view the purported problems pose no serious threat, and a convincing argument for internalism is untouched by the recent criticism.

Our main goal here is to refute objections to internalism. We begin by offering what we think is the best way to understand the distinction between internalism and externalism. We then present a new argument for internalism. We proceed to consider and reject defenses of internalism based on the premise that epistemic justification is a deontological concept. This frees internalism from what we regard as suspect deontological underpinnings. Finally we reply to what we take to be the most significant objections to internalism.

In our view the primary strength of internalism consists in the merits of a specific internalist theory, evidentialism, which holds that epistemic justification is entirely a matter of internal evidential factors. We shall not concentrate on evidentialism here, however, beyond making an occasional positive observation about it. We respond to the objections largely on behalf of internalism in general. It is a resourceful perspective that makes room for a variety of reasonable responses to the objections.

I. What is Internalism?

Internalism and externalism are views about which states, events, and conditions can contribute to epistemic justification – the sort of justification that, in sufficient strength, is a necessary condition for knowledge. Use of the terms "internalist" and "externalist" to classify theories of justification is a recent development, and the terms are routinely applied to theories that predate their use. Thus, many proponents of theories of justification have not classified their views as internalist or externalist. The recent literature is therefore the best source of information about the nature of the distinction. Here are a few examples of how internalism has been identified. Laurence BonJour writes:

> The most generally accepted account . . . is that a theory of justification is *internalist* if and only if it requires that all of the factors needed for a belief to be epistemically justified for a given person be *cognitively accessible* to that person, internal to his cognitive perspective.[2]

Robert Audi writes:

> Some examples suggest that justification is grounded entirely in what is internal to the mind, in a sense implying that it is accessible to introspection or reflection by the subject – a view we might call *internalism about justification*.[3]

Alvin Plantinga writes:

> The basic thrust of internalism in epistemology, therefore, is that the properties that confer warrant upon a belief are properties to which the believer has some special sort of epistemic access.[1]

Matthias Steup characterizes internalism as follows:

> What makes an account of justification internalist is that it imposes a certain condition on those factors that determine whether a belief is justified. Such factors – let's call them "J-factors" – can be beliefs, experiences, or epistemic standards. The condition in question requires J-factors to be *internal to the subject's mind* or, to put it differently, *accessible on reflection*.[5]

John Pollock writes that:

> Internalism in epistemology is the view that only internal states of the
> cognizer can be relevant in determining which of the cognizer's beliefs
> are justified.[6]

Finally, Ernest Sosa characterizes one version of internalism this way:

> Justification requires only really proper thought on the part of the
> subject: if a believer has obtained and sustains his belief through wholly
> appropriate thought, then the believer is justified in so believing – where
> the appropriateness of the thought is a matter purely internal to the
> mind of the subject, and not dependent on what lies beyond.[7]

We find two distinct but closely related characterizations of internalism in
passages such as these. One characterization uses a notion of access. What
we shall call "accessibilism" holds that the epistemic justification of a person's
belief is determined by things to which the person has some special sort of
access. BonJour calls this access a "suitable awareness."[8] Audi says that the
access is through "introspection or reflection." Others say that the access must
be "direct."[9]

The quotations from Steup, Pollock, and Sosa suggest a somewhat different account. They suggest that internalism is the view that a person's beliefs
are justified only by things that are internal to the person's mental life. We
shall call this version of internalism "mentalism."[10] A mentalist theory may
assert that justification is determined entirely by occurrent mental factors, or
by dispositional ones as well. As long as the things that are said to contribute
to justification are in the person's mind, the view qualifies as a version of
mentalism.

We think it likely that philosophers have not separated mentalism from
accessibilism because they have tacitly assumed that the extensions of the two
do not differ in any significant way. They have assumed that the special kind
of access on which many internalist theories rely can reach only mental items,
and perhaps all mental items, or at least all that might be counted as playing
a role in justification.

We think that simplicity and clarity are best served by understanding internalism as mentalism. "Internalism" is a recent technical term. It has been
introduced to refer to a variety of theories in epistemology that share some
vaguely defined salient feature. Any definition of the term is to some extent
stipulative. Mentalism codifies one standard way in which the word has been
used.

Somewhat more precisely, internalism as we characterize it is committed to the following two theses. The first asserts the strong supervenience of epistemic justification on the mental:

S   The justificatory status of a person's doxastic attitudes strongly supervenes on the person's occurrent and dispositional mental states, events, and conditions.

The second thesis spells out a principal implication of S:

M   If any two possible individuals are exactly alike mentally, then they are alike justificationally, e.g., the same beliefs are justified for them to the same extent.[11]

(M) implies that mental duplicates in different possible worlds have the same attitudes justified for them. This cross world comparison follows from the strong supervenience condition in (S).[12] Externalists characteristically hold that differences in justification can result from contingent non-mental differences, such as differing causal connections or reliability. Theories that appeal to such factors clearly deny (S) and (M). Thus, our way of spelling out the internalism/externalism distinction properly classifies characteristically externalist views.

(M) implies that mental duplicates in two different possible worlds have the same beliefs justified for them. The significance of this can be illustrated by considering a view William Alston has defended. Alston held that for a belief to be justified the believer must have internal grounds that make the belief "objectively probable."[13] If actual frequencies of association, or something else external to the mind and contingent, can make Alston's objective probability vary while the internal grounds remain the same, then his theory is a kind of externalism by our standards. But if it is necessary that the same grounds make the same beliefs objectively probable, then Alston's theory conforms to M and qualifies as a version of internalism. This seems exactly right: it is internalism if and only if contingent factors external to the mind cannot make an epistemic difference.

One advantage of our way of understanding the distinction between internalism and externalism in epistemology is that it closely parallels the counterpart distinctions in the philosophy of mind and ethics.[14] In the philosophy of mind case, the main idea is to distinguish the view that the contents of attitudes depend entirely on things within a person's own cognitive apparatus from the view that there are factors external to the person that help to determine attitudinal content. Mind internalism is naturally rendered as a super-venience thesis. Roughly, the thesis is that a person's mental content supervenes on the person's "purely internal" states, conditions, and events. The relevant supervenience base cannot be specified as "the mental," as we have done for epistemic internalism, since a person's mental states, events, and conditions are trivially sufficient for the person's attitudes with their specific contents. But the root idea is the same. The mind internalist is trying to exclude such plainly external factors as the environmental causal origins of the person's attitudes and their social milieu. Likewise, the epistemic internalist is principally opposed to the existence of any justification determining role for plainly external factors such as the general accuracy of the mechanism that produces a given belief or the belief's environmental origin. Mentalism bears this out.

What internalism in epistemology and philosophy of mind have in common is that being in some condition which is of philosophical interest – being epistemically justified in certain attitudes, or having attitudes with certain contents – is settled by what goes on inside of cognitive beings. The condition of interest is in this sense an "internal" matter, thus justifying the use of the term. Mentalism obviously captures this feature of internalism. Accessibilism captures it only when conjoined with the further thesis that what is relevantly accessible is always internal to something, presumably, the mind.[15]

Internalism in ethics is analogous, but significantly different. It is roughly the view that accepting a moral obligation to act in a certain way entails being motivated to act in that way.[16] This cannot be understood as a supervenience thesis concerning what is inside a person. Being motivated is an internal state on all accounts. Rather, ethical internalism holds that the motivation is "inside" of something much less extensive, namely, the accepting of a moral obligation. The pertinent supervenience thesis is consequently about a much narrower supervenience base. The thesis is roughly the claim that any individuals under any possible circumstances who accept that they have a moral obligation to act in a certain way have some motivation to act in that way.

One modest asset of viewing internalism as mentalism is that it renders readily intelligible the nominal connection of epistemic internalism to mind internalism and ethical internalism. A much stronger consideration in favor of mentalism itself is that it turns out to be entirely defensible, as we shall try to show.

It is worth noting the methodological neutrality of the internalism/externalism distinction as we interpret it. With internalism understood as mentalism, there is no direct connection between internalism and any view about *a priori* knowledge. In particular, internalism does not imply that epistemic principles are *a priori*.[17] This same methodological independence goes the other way as well. Externalists hold that some justificatory differences have an extramental basis. This does not imply that we must discover empirically which extramental factors make that difference.

II. A Defense of Internalism

Our argument for internalism focuses on pairs of examples that we take to be representative. Either in one member of the pair someone has a justified belief in a proposition while someone else's belief in that proposition is not justified, or one person's belief is better justified than the other's.[18] We contend that these contrasts are best explained by supposing that internal differences make the epistemic difference. Here are the examples.

Example 1   Bob and Ray are sitting in an air-conditioned hotel lobby reading yesterday's newspaper. Each has read that it will be very warm today and, on that basis, each believes that it is very warm today. Then Bob goes outside and feels the heat. They both continue to believe that it is very warm today. But at this point Bob's belief is better justified.
Comment: Bob's justification for the belief was enhanced by his experience of feeling the heat, and thus undergoing a mental change which so to speak "internalized" the actual temperature. Ray had just the forecast to rely on.

Example 2   After going out and feeling very warm, Bob goes back in and tells Ray of the feeling. Here are two versions of relevant details:
2a)   Bob is in fact a pillar of integrity, but Ray has no reason to think so. As far as Ray can tell, it is just as likely that Bob is trying to deceive him as that Bob is telling the truth.
2b)   Bob is a pillar of integrity, and Ray has observed and recalls many examples of Bob's honesty and none of dishonesty.
In example (2b) Ray's belief that it is very warm becomes more strongly justified after he hears from Bob. In example (2a) hearing from Bob does affect the strength of Ray's justification for his belief.
Comment: Bob's honesty, something out of Ray's ken in (2a), has become "internalized" by Ray in (2b). Bob's integrity made no justificatory difference to Ray's belief until it was suitably brought into Ray's mind.

Example 3   A novice bird watcher and an expert are together looking for birds. They both get a good look at a bird in a nearby tree. (In order to avoid irrelevant complexities, we can assume that their visual presentations are exactly alike.) Upon seeing the bird, the expert immediately knows that it is a woodpecker. The expert has fully reasonable beliefs about what woodpeckers look like. The novice has no good reason to believe that it is a woodpecker and is not justified in believing that it is.

Comment: The epistemic difference between novice and expert arises from something that differentiates the two internally. The expert knows the look of a woodpecker. The novice would gain the same justification as the expert if the novice came to share the expert's internal condition concerning the look of woodpeckers.

Example 4   A logic TA and a beginning logic student are looking over a homework assignment. One question displays a sentence that they both know to express a truth and asks whether certain other sentences are true as well. The TA can easily tell through simple reflection that some of the other sentences express logical consequences of the original sentence and thus she is justified in believing that they are true as well. The student is clueless.

Comment: Again there is an internal difference between the two. The difference is that the TA has justification for her beliefs to the effect that certain propositions validly follow from the original one. She is expert enough to "see" that the conclusions follow without performing any computations. This case differs from example 3 in that here the mental difference concerns cognizance of necessary truths of logic whereas in example 3 the expert was cognizant of contingent facts about visual characteristics of woodpeckers. But just as in example 3, relevant internal differences make the difference. The beginning student could come to share the epistemic state of the TA by coming to share the TA's familiarity with the logical consequence relation.

Example 5   Initially Smith has excellent reasons to believe that Jones, who works in his office, owns a Ford. Smith deduces that someone in the office owns a Ford. The latter belief is true, but the former is false. Smith's reasons derive from Jones pretending to own a Ford. Someone else in the office, unknown to Smith, does own a Ford. The fact that Jones is merely simulating Ford ownership keeps Smith from knowing that someone in his office is a Ford owner, but it does not prevent Smith from being justified or diminish his justification. At a later time Smith gains ample reason to believe that Jones is pretending. At that point Smith is not justified in believing either that Jones owns a Ford or that someone in his office owns a Ford.

Comment: Again the epistemic change occurs when a suitable external fact – this time, the fact that what Smith has seen is Jones pretending to own a Ford – is brought into Smith's mind. The difference between Smith being justified in believing that Smith owns a Ford (and that someone in the office owns a Ford) in the one case and not in the other is an internal change in Smith.

Example 6   Hilary is a brain in a vat who has been abducted recently from a fully embodied life in an ordinary environment. He is being stimulated so that it seems to him as though his normal life has continued. Hilary believes that he ate oatmeal for breakfast yesterday. His memorial basis for his breakfast belief is artificial. It has been induced by his envatters. Here are two versions of relevant details.
6a)   Hilary's recollection is very faint and lacking in detail. The meal seems incongruous to him in that it strikes him as a distasteful breakfast and he has no idea why he would have eaten it.
6b)   Hilary's recollection seems to him to be an ordinary vivid memory of a typical breakfast for him.
Comment: Although in both (6a) and (6b) Hilary's breakfast belief is false and its basis is abnormal, the belief is not well justified in (6a) and it is well justified in (6b). Hilary in (6a) differs internally from Hilary in (6b). His mental states in (6b) include better evidence for the belief in (6b) than he has in (6a).

In the first five of these examples the location of a relevant item of information – in the mind of a subject or outside of it – makes the epistemic difference. In the sixth example, a purely internal difference is decisive. It is reasonable to generalize from these examples to the conclusion that every variety of change that brings about or enhances justification either internalizes an external fact or makes a purely internal difference. It appears that there is no need to appeal to anything extramental to explain any justificatory difference. These considerations argue for the general internalist thesis that these epistemic differences have an entirely mental origin. In each case, the mental difference is a difference in the evidence that the person has. Variations in its presence or strength correspond to the differences in justification. Evidentialism thus provides the best explanation of the epistemic status of beliefs in these pairs.

We have no proof that there is no exception to the pattern exhibited by our examples. The argument does not establish that internalism or evidentialism is true. It does support these views. Further support will emerge from successful replies to objections. We shall soon turn to those objections and replies.

III. Internalism and Deontology

According to deontological conceptions of epistemic justification, one has a justified belief in a proposition when one deserves praise (or does not deserve blame) for having the belief or when it is one's duty or obligation to believe that proposition (or believing it violates no duty or obligation). Alvin Goldman, Alvin Plantinga, William Alston, and other leading critics of internalism have thought that the central argument for internalism relies on the premise that epistemic justification is a deontological concept. Plantinga speaks for many of these critics when he writes, "It is really this deontological feature of the classical conception of justification that leads to the internalist result."[19] We deny that internalism depends on a deontological conception of justification. In describing and assessing the beliefs in the examples of section II, we did not say anything about what the individuals had a duty or obligation to believe, what they were permitted to believe, or what they might be praised or blamed for believing. There might be deontological truths of these sorts. What we are rejecting are arguments for internalism based on the idea that epistemic concepts are to be analyzed in these deontological terms. In this section we will briefly address three versions of such arguments.[20]

Goldman criticizes an argument that is supposed to establish internalism partly on the basis of a premise asserting the deontological nature of justification.[21] The argument he discusses goes approximately as follows:

> Justification is a matter of not violating any epistemic duties. One can have duties only if the facts that make it the case that one has these duties are facts that one can know. Therefore these facts must be internal facts, since one might not be in a position to know external facts. Thus, the justifiers[22] – roughly, the facts that make a belief justified – must be internal facts.

It is difficult to find much to recommend in this argument. One can know external facts. So, as Goldman points out, the premise that duties depend upon what one can know does not rule out the possibility that they can depend on external facts.[23] Furthermore, since on all accounts knowledge depends on external factors such as the truth of the known proposition, people internally

alike can know different things. The assumption that one's duties depend
upon what one knows does not imply that people who are internally
alike must have the same duties. This leaves open the possibility that different things are justified for people who are internally alike. Thus, we agree
with Goldman that no good argument for internalism can be found among
these considerations.

It might be thought that these problems can be avoided by framing the
argument in terms of justification, avoiding reference to knowledge. The new
argument begins with the assumption that one has a duty to do something if
and only if one is justified in believing that one has the duty. With the added
premise the beliefs in the same duties are justified for those who are internally
alike, it follows that those who are internally alike have the same duties.
Making use of the deontological assumption that justification is a matter of
not violating any epistemic duties, it can be inferred that the same beliefs are
justified for those who are internally alike.

The premise in this argument asserting that beliefs in the same duties are
justified for those who are internally alike needs some defense. Why would
beliefs specifically about duties always be justified on purely internal grounds?
In the absence of a special reason, this assumption seems acceptable only as
an implication of the full generality that people internally alike are justified
in believing the same things. So as it stands this argument depends for its
cogency on the characteristic internalist claim that people internally alike have
the same justified beliefs. The argument therefore relies on internalism rather
than establishing it.

A third and final deontological argument for internalism focuses on
blame.[24] It might be assumed that epistemic justification is a matter of blameless belief, and that people who are internally alike are alike in what they can
be blamed for. So, people who are internally alike will have the same blameless beliefs, and thus the same justified beliefs.

This argument's initial assumption is clearly incorrect. Blameless belief is
not always justified. Someone who innocently holds a belief as a result of
external manipulation or psychological compulsion would be blameless in
holding this belief.[25] Nevertheless, if the belief is induced directly and the
person has good reason to deny the belief and no reason to believe it, then it
is clearly not a justified belief.[26] Also, justified beliefs are not always blameless. Someone who, for barely adequate epistemic reasons, accepts that a
friend has been malicious is epistemically justified in that belief. But such a
person may be blameworthy for having insufficient trust in the friend.

We agree with the critics that there is no cogent argument for internalism
that relies on deontological premises. However, the failure of these arguments
shows no weakness in internalism. The internalist position is independently

well supported. In our view the case for internalism rests primarily on the strengths of its best versions, and as we say, our favorite candidate is evidentialism. These strengths include its explanatory capacities, such as its capacity to account for the epistemic differences in the pairs of examples discussed in section II, and its resistance to objections.

IV. Objections and Replies

The objections that we shall consider fall into two broad and overlapping categories. One sensible general description of internalist theories is that they say that a belief B is justified just in case there is some combination of internal states – typically featuring an experience or another justified belief – that is suitably related to B. Objections of the first sort focus on the existence internal states that are supposed to justify beliefs, arguing that there are some justified beliefs for which there are no internal justifying states. Objections in the second group focus on the connections between candidate internal justifiers and the beliefs they are supposed to justify, arguing that internalists inevitably run into insurmountable difficulties when they attempt to say anything definite about the nature or status of the connections.

While some internalist theories may have trouble dealing with some of these objections, there are several internalist approaches that can deal adequately with all of them. We concentrate primarily on two approaches, one that limits justifying states to currently conscious mental states and one that also includes as potential justifiers whatever is retained in memory. Since theories of each sort surmount all of the objections, the internalist approach is in no danger of a general refutation.

A. Are there enough internal justifiers?

A1. Impulsional evidence
Alvin Plantinga's objection focuses on evidentialist versions of internalism.[27] But the same sort of objection seems equally applicable against any initially plausible internalist view. Plantinga asserts that there are three views evidentialists can hold concerning what constitutes evidence, and he argues that each view renders evidentialism unsatisfactory. The three possibilities are: (1) evidence consists only of other beliefs (all evidence is propositional); (2) evidence consists only of beliefs and sensory states (all evidence is propositional or sensory); (3) evidence can also include the sense of conviction or confidence that accompanies beliefs (all evidence is propositional, sensory, or impulsional).

Plantinga uses knowledge of simple arithmetical facts to defend his objection. He asserts that we do not believe that $2 + 1 = 3$ on the basis of propositional or sensory evidence. So, if evidentialists adopt alternatives (1) or (2), their theory implies that this belief is not justified. Yet, of course, we do know that $2 + 1 = 3$. Plantinga claims that there is a "felt attractiveness" about the content of that belief, and he says $2 + 1 = 5$ "feels wrong, weird, absurd, eminently rejectable."[28] He calls the "felt attractiveness" an "impulse" and classifies it as "impulsional evidence." So internalists might take Plantinga's third alternative and claim that this impulsional evidence is the internal factor that justifies simple mathematical beliefs.

Plantinga argues that there is a problem with this account. He claims that necessarily all beliefs would have similar justification: "You have impulsional evidence for p just in virtue of believing p . . . It isn't even possible that you believe p but lack impulsional evidence for it: how could it be that you believe p although it does not seem to you to be true?"[29] He infers that on this view of evidence, the internalist justification condition for knowledge that consists in having evidence is implied by the belief condition. If Plantinga is right about this, then evidentialists who take alternative (3) are stuck with the unacceptable conclusion that all actual beliefs are justified. The other initially plausible internalist views, for instance, those that appeal to epistemic responsibility as the key to a belief's justification, seem equally susceptible to this sort of objection. The "felt attractiveness" seems equally to render believing the epistemically responsible alternative to take. So, again, all beliefs would be justified.[30]

Plantinga's objection is multiply faulty, however. First, even if he were right in claiming that the evidence for beliefs like $2 + 1 = 3$ is impulsional, he would be mistaken in thinking that all beliefs have any similar sort of evidential support. There are several internal states to distinguish here. Perhaps we feel attracted to the proposition that $2 + 1 = 3$ and we feel impelled to believe it. Not everything we believe feels attractive in this way or any other. For instance, some known propositions are believed reluctantly, on the basis of reasons, in spite of their seeming distinctly unattractive and implausible. Some beliefs result from fears. They need not seem in any way attractive. Correspondingly, the denials of things we believe do not always feel "weird" or 'absurd," even if we think that they are false. There may be a 'sense of obviousness" that accompanies belief in some propositions. This sense may contribute to their evidential support. But quite plainly not all believed propositions share that feature, or anything that resembles it. So it is not true that there is "impulsional evidence" for every believed proposition.

Furthermore, even if there were impulsional evidence for each belief, it would not follow that each belief satisfies any plausible evidential version of

the justification condition for knowledge. The existence of a bit of supporting evidence is clearly not enough. A plausible evidential condition for
knowledge requires something more, such as strong evidence on balance, or
at least evidence undefeated by other evidence. An impulse to believe would
not always qualify as strong evidence on balance, or undefeated evidence.
Moreover, even if there were some impulsional evidence for all beliefs, it
would not follow that all beliefs are justified to any degree. In some cases anything like impulsional evidence is decisively outweighed by competing evidence. Therefore, the existence of impulsional evidence for all beliefs would
not render redundant a plausible evidential condition on knowledge and
would not saddle internalists with the unacceptable result that all beliefs are
justified.

Finally, even with regard to the simplest of mathematical beliefs, impulsional evidence of the sort Plantinga mentions is not our only evidence. We
have evidence about our success in dealing with simple arithmetical matters
and knowledge of the acceptance that is enjoyed by our assertions about these
matters. So, we have these additional reasons to think that our spontaneous
judgments about simple mathematical matters are correct. Furthermore, we
know that we learned these sorts of things as children and we have not had
our more recent assertions about them contradicted by others. If we had been
making mistakes about these kinds of things, it is very likely that problems
would have arisen and we would have been corrected. Moreover, at least
according to some plausible views, we have a kind of *a priori* insight that
enables us to grasp simple mathematical propositions. This insight provides
us with some evidence for the truth of simple mathematical truths. Much of
this evidence is retained in memory; some of it is conscious whenever such
propositions are consciously apprehended. So there seems to be plenty of
additional evidence, whether or not justifiers are restricted to conscious states.
Indeed, the suggestion that our only evidential bases for simple arithmetical
beliefs are impulses to believe is extremely implausible.

Thus, Plantinga's objection makes no real trouble for evidentialism. Any
other reasonable internalist view clearly has similar responses available to the
counterpart objections. Our epistemic responsibilities, for instance, can be
credibly held to stem in part from the discerned practical and social rein-
forcement of our mathematical beliefs, rather than from just our impulses
with regard to them.

A2.   *Stored beliefs*
Alvin Goldman argues that internal states cannot account for the justification
of stored beliefs.[31] The problem is this. At any given moment almost nothing
of what we know is consciously considered. We know personal facts, facts that

constitute common knowledge, facts in our areas of expertise, and so on. Since we know all these things, we believe them. These are stored beliefs, not occurrent beliefs. Since we know them, they are justified beliefs. But on what internalist basis can these beliefs be justified? As Goldman says, "No perceptual experience, no conscious memory event, and no premises consciously entertained at the selected moment will be justificationally sufficient for such a belief."[32] Internalists are stuck with the unacceptable result that these beliefs are not justified, unless something internal that justifies them can be found.

In formulating this objection Goldman assumes two propositions, either of which internalists can sensibly reject. On the one hand, he assumes that virtually all justified beliefs are stored beliefs. On the other hand, he assumes that internalists must find something conscious to serve as their justification. But internalists have good reason to reject this conjunction of propositions. One alternative is to argue that, in the most central sense, almost all justified beliefs are occurrent and very few stored beliefs are justified. The second option is to argue that other non-occurrent internal states can contribute to the justification of non-occurrent beliefs.

The first response relies on the idea that there are occurrent and dispositional senses of "justified," just as there are occurrent and dispositional senses of "belief." In the most fundamental sense of "justified" a belief can be justified for a person only by the person's current evidence, and one's current evidence is all conscious. In this sense, non-occurrent beliefs are typically not justified. However, in the same way that there are stored beliefs, one can have "stored justifications" for these beliefs. That is, one can have in memory reasons that justify the belief.[33] Beliefs like this are dispositionally justified.[34] Thus, although stored beliefs are seldom justified in the most fundamental sense, they are often dispositionally justified.

Goldman objects to a proposal along these lines that one of us made previously.[35] He takes the general idea behind the proposal to be that a disposition to generate a conscious evidential state counts as a justifier. He then raises the following objection:

> Suppose a train passenger awakes from a nap but has not yet opened his eyes. Is he justified in believing propositions about the details of the neighboring landscape? Surely not. Yet he is *disposed*, merely by opening his eyes, to generate conscious mental states that would occurrently justify such beliefs.[36]

The idea behind the current proposal is not what Goldman criticizes here. It is not that any conscious mental state that one is disposed to be in counts as evidence. The idea is that some non-occurrent states that one is already in, such as non-occurrent memories of perceptual experiences, are stored evidence. Presently having this stored evidence justifies dispositionally some non-occurrent beliefs that one already has. The train passenger does not have the evidence that he would receive were he to open his eyes. The dispositional state that he is in, his disposition to see the landscape by opening his eyes, is not stored evidence for propositions about the landscape. It is a potential to acquire evidence, and that is crucially different.

The second solution to the problem of stored beliefs does not invoke a distinction between occurrent and dispositional justification. Internalists can plausibly claim that if we have numerous ordinary justified beliefs that we are not consciously considering, then there is no reason to exclude from what justifies these beliefs further stored beliefs or other memories. These stored justifications are internalist by the standard of (M) and they are plausibly regarded as evidence that the person has.[37]

The description presented here of the second internalist approach leaves open important questions about which stored internal states can justify beliefs and what relation those stored states must have to a belief to justify it. No doubt these are difficult questions. Versions of internalism will differ concerning which stored states they count as justifiers.[38] But there is no reason to think that internalism lacks the resources to provide satisfactory answers to these questions. There is a difficulty here only if people internally alike can nevertheless differ with respect to which stored states are justifiers. We see no reason to admit such a possibility.

However, one might think that external factors having to do with the actual source of a memory belief can affect its justification. In fact, Goldman himself describes something similar to our second internalist approach and claims that it fails for just this reason.[39] We turn next to this objection.

A3. Forgotten evidence
Several authors have raised objections involving forgotten evidence.[40] We will focus on an example Goldman provides:

> Last year Sally read about the health benefits of broccoli in a *New York Times* science-section story. She then justifiably formed a belief in broccoli's beneficial effects. She still retains this belief but no longer recalls her original evidential source (and has never encountered either corroborating or undermining sources). Nonetheless, her broccoli belief is still justified, and, if true, qualifies as a case of knowledge.[41]

This example illustrates something that must be conceded to be common. We now know things for which we have forgotten our original evidence. The problem for internalism arises most clearly if we assume that Sally's original evidence is irretrievably lost and not part of any stored justification that Sally might have. In other words, let us assume that Sally is occurrently entertaining her justified belief about broccoli and that the facts about the original source of the belief are not part of any internalist justification of it. Externalists might argue that the contingent merits of the external source of this belief account for its justification. How can internalists explain why this belief is currently justified?

One internalist answer to this question is that Sally's justification consists in conscious qualities of the recollection, such as its vivacity and her associated feeling of confidence. We see no fatal flaw in this response. It will be most attractive to internalists who hold that only what is conscious can justify a belief. We note that not all memory beliefs are justified according to this theory. Some memory beliefs are accompanied by a sense of uncertainty and a lack of confidence. Other memory beliefs are accompanied by a recognition of competing evidence. This competing evidence can render vivacious memory beliefs unjustified. There are plausible results, so this restrictive version of internalism does have the resources to deal with forgotten evidence.

Another defensible answer is available to internalists who think that not all evidence is conscious. If Sally is a normal contemporary adult, she is likely to have quite of a bit of readily retrievable evidence supporting her belief about broccoli. The healthfulness of vegetables is widely reported and widely discussed. Furthermore, her belief about broccoli is probably not undermined by any background beliefs she is likely to have. Finally, she, like most people, probably has supporting evidence consisting in stored beliefs about the general reliability and accuracy of memory. She knows that she is generally right about this sort of thing. So Sally would have justification for her broccoli belief, though it is not her original evidence. If Sally lacks any supporting background information and also lacks any reason to trust her memory, then we doubt that her belief about the broccoli really is justified.

Goldman considers and rejects this second response on the basis of a new version of the example about Sally. The new example resembles one that Ernest Sosa presents involving a generally reasonable person who believes a conclusion as a result of a "tissue of fallacies" which, however, has now been forgotten.[12] Sosa thinks this origin renders the belief unjustified, no matter what the person now thinks about the source of her belief or her general capacities. The crucial feature of Goldman's revised example is also that a belief originally came from a disreputable source. Sally has the same belief about broccoli and the same background beliefs about the reliability of her relevant capacities. But now it is part of the story that Sally obtained the belief about broccoli from an article in the *National Inquirer*, a source Goldman assumes to be unreliable. Goldman claims that

> Sally cannot be credited with justifiably believing that broccoli is healthful. Her past acquisition is still relevant, and decisive. At least it is relevant so long as we are considering the "epistemizing" sense of justification, in which justification carries a true belief a good distance toward knowledge. Sally's belief in the healthfulness of broccoli is not justified in that sense, for surely she does not know that broccoli is healthful given that the *National Inquirer* was her sole source of information.[13]

We agree that Sally does not know that broccoli is healthful under these conditions. We also agree that facts about her acquisition of the belief determine this result. However, it does not follow that Sally's belief is not justified. The "epistemizing" sense of justification is said by Goldman to be a sense according which a belief that is justified is one that has been carried "a good distance toward knowledge." This fits with our initial characterization of epistemic justification as the sort that is necessary for knowledge. But from the fact that Sally's belief falls short of knowledge, it does not follow that it has not been carried a good distance toward knowledge. Thus, an initial weakness in this objection is that its concluding inference is invalid.

A second fault is that the alleged unjustified belief is actually a Gettier case. We endorse the following rule of thumb for classifying examples of true beliefs that are not knowledge:

> RT   If a true belief is accidentally correct, in spite of its being quite reasonably believed, then the example is a Gettier case.

RT helps to show that the second version of the example about Sally is a Gettier case. Sally believes that broccoli is healthful. She believes (presumably justifiably) that she learned this from a reliable source. She is wrong about her source but, coincidentally, right about broccoli. This fits exactly the pattern of Gettier cases, and RT classifies it as such. It is a quite reasonable belief on Sally's part which, in light of its unreliable source, is just accidentally correct. It is a justified true belief that is not knowledge. Similar remarks apply to Sosa's example.

Our view has an implication that may initially seem odd. When Sally first came to believe that broccoli is healthful, the belief was unjustified because Sally had reason to distrust her source. Yet we seem to be saying that simply because she has forgotten about that bad source, the belief has become justified. We are not quite saying that. As we see it, when she forgets about the source she has lost a defeater of a justification for her broccoli belief. Assuming that Sally knows herself normally to be judicious about her sources, all beliefs she retains thereby have considerable internal support. Whatever beliefs she retains are justified by this, unless they are defeated. A belief is defeated in any case in which she has indications that impeach what it is reasonable for her to take to be the source of her belief. But when she no longer possesses any such indication, as in the present Sally case, the otherwise generally good credentials of her memorial beliefs support the belief and are undefeated.

Some confirmation of our analysis comes from comparing the case as described to a case in which Sally does remember the unreliability of her source but retains the belief anyway. It is clear that there would be something far less reasonable about her belief in that situation. This suggests that forgetting the source does make the belief better justified.

Further confirmation emerges from contrasting the example with yet another variation. Suppose Sally believes both that broccoli is healthful and that peas are healthful. Suppose that her source for the former is still the *National Inquirer* but her source for the latter belief is the reliable *New York Times*. Again she has forgotten her sources, but she correctly and reasonably believes that she virtually always gets beliefs like these from trustworthy sources. Goldman's objection requires differentiating these two beliefs in an unacceptable way. It counts the former belief as unjustified, on the basis of the unreliability of its forgotten source. Yet from Sally's present perspective, the two propositions are on a par. It would be completely unreasonable for her to give up one belief but not the other. The best thing to say is that both are justified, but the broccoli belief does not count as knowledge because it is a Gettier case.

We conclude that internalism does not have any difficulty finding adequate justification in cases of forgotten evidence.

A4. *Concurrent retrieval*

Another problem that Goldman poses for internalism is the problem of concurrent retrieval.[11] The problem purports to affect only those internalist views that are versions of holistic coherentism. Holistic coherentism says that a belief is justified only if it coheres with one's whole corpus of beliefs, including stored beliefs. This leads to a problem for the coherentist who also accepts the deontologically defended claim that one can always find out whether a belief is justified. Ascertaining whether one belief coheres with the rest by bringing them all consciously to mind at once is well beyond the capacities of any person.

This is a problem only when holistic coherentism is conjoined with the deontologically defended thesis just mentioned. A holistic coherentist need not accept a deontological conception of epistemic justification, and can simply deny that epistemic status is something that one always can find out. The holist can also respond to Goldman's objection by denying that finding out epistemic status so as to comply with any relevant duty requires the simultaneous retrieval of all that the status depends on. It might be held to be sufficient for complying with a duty to find out whether a belief, B1, coheres with one's other beliefs simply to form a true belief, B2, that B1 coheres, as long as B2 itself coheres with the rest of one's beliefs.

In any case, problems peculiar to holistic coherentism cast no doubt on internalism generally. There are, however, related questions concerning the accessibility of stored beliefs that might be raised for other internalist theories, including evidentialism. Here is one of them. Suppose that someone has a conscious belief that is supported by some currently conscious evidence. Suppose further that the person also has large number of stored beliefs whose conjunction implies the falsity of the conscious belief. This conjunction is too complex for the person to entertain. Under these circumstances, what is the epistemic status of the current belief and can internalism properly account for that status?

This case does not jeopardize internalism. Consider first internalists who say that stored beliefs are among the mental items relevant to justification. Suppose beliefs that are contradicted by some huge conjunction of stored beliefs are not justified. These internalists can easily explain this result. They can hold that any conjunction of the stored beliefs can serve as a defeater of the justification of current beliefs, regardless of whether the individual can consciously consider the conjunction. If, on the other hand, beliefs such as those under consideration here are justified, internalists who hold that stored beliefs affect justification can also explain this result. They can say that justification supervenes on a restricted class of stored mental items. Perhaps items that are too complex to be retrieved are excluded. In that case, an unbelievably complex conjunction of stored beliefs would not be a defeater. Perhaps only combinations of stored beliefs whose negative relevance to the belief in question has been, or could readily be, noticed or appreciated count as defeaters. Perhaps, as accessibilists hold, only mental items that are in one way or another accessible can be defeaters.

Consider next internalist who hold that only currently accessed evidence is relevant to the epistemic status of occurrently believed propositions. Suppose that the beliefs under discussion are justified. These internalists can easily explain this result, since it is stipulated in the example that the currently accessed evidence does support the belief. The potentially defeating combinations of beliefs that are not accessed would not undermine justification. Internalists who limit sources of justification to what is conscious could not accept the view that these beliefs are not justified. They must instead argue that any appearance of defeat by a combination of merely stored beliefs is illusory. Since it is far from clear that there is any such defeat, the position of such internalists is not untenable.

Some of these approaches seem to us to be more promising than others. For present purposes it is not necessary to defend any particular view. We are arguing here for the explanatory power and credibility of internalist theorists. The devil may lurk in the details, for all that we have shown. But in the absence of any good reason to think that internalists must make *ad hoc* or indefensible claims about stored beliefs, there is no reason to think that there is a general problem here.

B.   *Links and connections*

We turn next to a set of objections concerning the connections between perceptual experiences or other justified beliefs and the beliefs they are supposed to justify. There are difficult questions about exactly how these states manage to justify the beliefs they support. These are problems of detail, and internalists have reasonable choices concerning how to work out the details. As we shall show by responding to several related objections, there are no unresolvable problems here.

B1.   *The need for higher order beliefs*
William Alston has argued that the considerations that support internalism equally support the imposition of what he calls a "higher order requirement" on justification. The idea is that if the argument that leads to the conclusion that only internal factors can serve as justifiers is sound, then there is also a sound argument to the conclusion that for a belief to be justified the believer must be able to tell which factors justify the belief. Alston writes:

> Suppose that the sorts of things that can count as justifiers are always accessible to me, but that it is not accessible to me which items of these sorts count as justifications for which beliefs. I have access to the justifiers but not to their justificatory efficacy. This will take away my ability to do what I am said to have an obligation to do just as surely as the lack of access to the justifiers themselves. To illustrate, let's suppose that experiences can function as justifiers, and that they are accessible to us. I can always tell what sensory experiences I am having at a given moment. Even so, if I am unable to tell what belief about the current

physical environment is justified by a given sensory experience, I am thereby unable to regulate my perceptual beliefs according as they possess or lack experiential justification.[15]

Alston goes on to argue that this higher level requirement is one that few of us are able to satisfy, and he rejects the requirement partly for this reason. Since the argument for the higher order requirement is clearly unsound, Alston concludes that the original argument for internalism is unsound as well.

The argument Alston considers relies on a deontological conception of justification according to which justification is a matter of conforming to duties one must be in a position to know about. As we have noted, internalists are free to reject that conception. They need not defend an identification of justification with duty fulfillment. They need not defend anything that makes having justified beliefs depend on having some way to know what justifies what. To cite our favorite instance, evidentialists hold that the possession of the right evidence by itself secures the justification of the corresponding beliefs. The justification supervenes on the internal possession of appropriate evidence. Neither epistemic evaluations nor duties need enter in at all.

It might be thought that evidentialism should be formulated in ways that require for justification not only supporting evidence but also knowledge of higher level principles about the justificatory efficacy of this evidence. Some internalists do seem to impose such a requirement.[16] We agree with Alston that any such theory is implausible, implying that few people have justified beliefs. However, we see no reason to think that evidentialists must endorse any higher order requirement. Having evidence can make for justification on its own.

The appearance that justifying relations pose a problem for internalism arises partly from formulating the debate between internalists and externalists as a debate over whether all "justifiers" are internal. Indeed, that is exactly how some epistemologists do formulate the debate. For example, Goldman takes to internalists to require that all "justifiers" must be in some suitable way accessible.[17] This way of formulating the issue is problematic. Suppose that a person who believes q on the basis of believing p has a justified belief in q. We might then say, as a first approximation, that the justifiers for q are (i) the belief that p together with its justification, and (ii) the fact that p supports q. The fact in (ii) is not itself an internal state, and so it might be thought that internalists are faced with the difficult task of finding some internal representation of this state to serve as a justifier.[18]

There is a sense in which p's support for q is a "justifier." It is part of an explanation of the fact that the person's belief in q is justified. But this does not imply that internalists are committed to the view that there must be some internal representation of this fact. It may be that a person's being in the state described by (i) is sufficient for the belief that q to be justified. If so, then all individuals mentally alike in that they share that state are justified in believing q. The fact in (ii) may help to account for the justification without the person making any mental use of that fact.

General beliefs that relate evidence to a conclusion sometimes do make a justificatory difference. This occurs in some of the examples in our argument for internalism. But the sort of connecting information that the examples suggest to be necessary is non-epistemic information that justified believers typically have. The logic TA, for example, had justification for beliefs about implication relations that the student lacked. The expert bird watcher had justification for beliefs about what woodpeckers look like. This might take the form of various generalizations, e.g., any bird that looks like that is a woodpecker, any bird with that sort of bill is a woodpecker, etc.[19] The student and the novice bird watcher lacked these justifications. It would be a mistake, however, to argue from these cases to any universal "higher order requirement," especially to a higher order requirement to have epistemic information about what justifies what.

A fully developed internalist theory must state whether linking information of the sort possessed by the logic TA and the expert bird watcher is required in the case of simpler connections. Suppose that a person has a justified belief in some proposition, p. Suppose further that q is an extremely simple and intuitively obvious (to us) logical consequence of p. For the person to be justified in believing q, must he have additional evidence, analogous to the TA's additional evidence, for the proposition that q follows from p?

One possible view is that the answer is "No." According to this view, there are certain elementary logical connections that are necessarily reflected in epistemic connections. The best candidates for this relation include cases where one proposition is a conjunction of which the other is a conjunct. The general idea is that some propositions, p and q, have a primitive or basic epistemic connection. If p and q have this connection, then, necessarily, if a person has a justified belief in p, then the person is also justified in believing q. Perhaps it is part of understanding p that one grasps the connection between p and q. There is, then, no need for additional information about the link between p and q that a person who is justified in believing p might lack. By the test of the supervenience thesis asserted by M, internalists can accept this answer.

Internalists can also hold that the answer to the question above is "Yes." In this case, there is something resembling a higher order requirement. However, it is not any implausible requirement that one have information about justification. It is merely a requirement that one have evidence that

there is a supporting connection – for instance, the logical consequence relation – between what is ordinarily regarded as one's evidence and what it is
evidence for. This evidence can come from direct insight or from any other
source. This is evidence that people normally have in a variety normal
situations.[50]

A similar question arises concerning perceptual beliefs about the qualities
of the objects one is perceiving. We said above that the expert bird watcher
has background information about the look of woodpeckers that justified the
belief that he saw a woodpecker. The novice lacked that information. The
new question concerns simpler qualities such as redness. Must a person with
a clear view of a red object have evidence about the look of red things in
order to be justified in believing that there is something red before him or
is the mere experience of redness (in the absence of defeaters) sufficient for
justification?

Again, it is not crucial to answer this question here. What is important for
present purposes is that internalists have plausible options. If an experience
of the phenomenal quality corresponding to redness automatically justifies
the proposition (absent any defeater), then people internally alike in that they
share the experience will be justified in believing the same external world
proposition. If information about the look of red objects is required, then
people internally alike in that they share this information as well as the experience of red will have the same external world proposition justified. There
is a problem for internalism here only if there is some reason to think that
internal differences are inadequate to account for some difference in justification. We see no threat of that.

B2. *Computational operations*

Goldman poses another objection similar to the one just considered. This
objection concentrates on the justifying relations themselves, rather than any
epistemic fact about the relations. He uses foundationalist versions of internalism to illustrate the point.[51] Foundationalists identify a limited class of basic
justified propositions, usually propositions very closely linked to experiences.
To avoid skeptical consequences, foundationalists typically assert that the rest
of our justified beliefs are justified by being in appropriate relations to the
basics. Candidates usually involve formal relations of logic and probability,
among others. Goldman points out that the existence of a formal relation
between propositions is not an internal state. He infers that foundationalists
who are internalists cannot simply declare that beliefs that are suitably formally related to basics are thereby justified. Such a declaration would yield
an unsatisfactory theory anyway, since many unjustified propositions are
related to basics by formal relations such as implication.[52] Yet some non-

basic beliefs must be justified somehow, or there will be grave skeptical implications.[53]

Goldman considers ways in which internalists might try to solve this problem. The one that he calls "the natural move" proposes that a belief is justified if and only if the fact that it has "appropriate logical or probabilistic relations" to the basics can be ascertained by performing "selected computational operations."[54] Goldman contends that serious problems exist for this way of avoiding skeptical implications. He claims that there is no satisfactory way to identify the admissible computational operations.

There is, however, no need for internalists to identify admissible computational operations. Goldman may be thinking that the relations of basics to further beliefs are justifiers and that all justifiers must be somehow internalized. As we discussed above, this is not the case. What must be internal are sufficient conditions for justification, not facts about their sufficiency. The root internalist idea is that the mental states one is in determine what one is justified in believing. As noted in the previous section, it may be that some ultra-simple logical consequences of justified beliefs are automatically justified, perhaps by the understanding required to have the entailing beliefs. If that is the case, then these simple logical consequences of the basics are justified no matter what additional information about logical consequences one has. Internalism as characterized by M allows this. If, on the other hand, even simple logical consequences are justified only after the implications have been noticed, accepted, or understood, then internalists are in a position to say that only consequences meeting this further mental condition are justified. It is immaterial whether the satisfaction of this further condition results from computation, direct insight, testimonial evidence, or etc.

B3. *Justification of introspective beliefs*

Ernest Sosa raises a problem about how experiences justify introspective beliefs:

> Some experiences in a certain sense "directly fit" some introspective beliefs. But not all experiences directly fit the introspective beliefs that describe them correctly. Thus my belief that at the centre of my visual field there lies a white triangle against a black background would so fit the corresponding experience. But my belief that my visual field contains a 23-sided white figure against a black background would *not* fit that experience.[55]

The question, then, is this: Why does having a suitable experience of a triangle justify the introspective belief that one is having that experience, while no experience of a 23-sided figure justifies for us the belief that one is having that experience?

Internalism has the resources to explain why the two experiences have different epistemic consequences. We can best explain the relevant internal features through consideration of some hypothetical person who does have the ability to identify 23-sided figures in his visual field and contrasting this person with ordinary people who lack that ability. According to one internalist option, someone who has the ability has an experience qualitatively different from those who lack that ability. We will call the quality that underlies the ability "recognition." It can plausibly be held that recognition makes a justificatory difference. When our visual field contains a triangle that contrasts clearly with its surroundings, we recognize it as such. We do not similarly recognize 23-sided figures. the recognition is not a true belief linking the experience to a belief about its content.[56] It is, instead, a feature of experience itself. This experiential feature is what makes it true that triangles optimally viewed are generally seen as triangles, while 23-sided figures, even when optimally viewed, are not generally seen as being 23-sided. It is this aspect of the experience that provides evidential support for the corresponding belief. For most of us, this sort of feature is present when we experience clearly discriminable triangles and not present when we experience 23-sided figures. But a person who did have that remarkable ability would have an experience unlike ours.

Rather than appealing to any qualitative difference in experience, internalists can appeal instead to background information. Ordinary people have learned that the property of being a 3-sided image is associated with a certain sort of visual appearance. They have not learned which sorts of visual appearances are associated with being a 23-sided image. On this view, only by learning some such association could a person have justification from experience for making these sorts of classifications of images. Internalists can plausibly appeal to this sort of background information as the internal difference that accounts for differences in justification in these cases. As in the cases considered in section B1, the information here is not epistemic information about what justifies what, information people typically lack. It is simply information about properties that are associated with experiences of certain types.

We conclude that Sosa is right to say that some but not all experiences lead to justification of introspective beliefs that correctly describe them. But internal differences, either in the experiences themselves or in background information, are available to account for the difference between those that do lead to justification and those that do not.

VII. Conclusion

We have defended internalism not just to praise it, but to move the debate beyond it. No genuine problem for this category of theories has been identified. We have seen that even versions of internalism that depend on only conscious elements have not been refuted. Various less restrictive views about what determines justification have emerged entirely unscathed as well. But on any account of internalism, including the one we recommend, internalism is nothing more than a broad doctrine about the location of the determining factors for epistemic justification. Having argued that internalist views stand in no jeopardy of being generally refuted, we recommend that epistemological attention focus on more specific accounts that are more informative.

Notes

An earlier version of this paper was presented at The Creighton Club, where William Alston commented, and to the University of Rochester philosophy department. We are grateful to Alston and to both audiences for their comments.

1   For a summary of the current state of epistemology that illustrates this sort of view, see Philip Kitcher, "The Naturalists Return," *The Philosophical Review* 101 (1992): 53–114.

2   Laurence BonJour, "Externalism/Internalism," in Jonathan Dancy and Ernest Sosa, eds., *A Companion to Epistemology* (Oxford: Blackwell Publishers, 1992), p. 132.

3   Robert Audi, *Epistemology: A Contemporary Introduction to the Theory of Knowledge* (New York: Routledge, 1998), pp. 233–4. Emphasis in the original.

4   Alvin Plantinga, *Warrant: The Current Debate* (Oxford: Oxford University Press, 1993), p. 6. A very similar formulation appears in William Harper, "Paper Mache Problems in Epistemology: A Defense of Strong Internalism," *Synthese* 116 (1998): 27–49. See p. 28.

5   Matthias Steup, *An Introduction to Contemporary Epistemology* (Upper Saddle River, NJ: Prentice Hall, 1996), p. 84. Emphasis in the original.

6   John Pollock, "At the Interface of Philosophy and AI," in John Greco and Ernest Sosa, eds., *The Blackwell Guide to Epistemology* (Malden, MA: Blackewll, 1999) pp. 383–414. The quotation is from p. 394.

7   Ernest Sosa, "Skepticism and the Internal/External Divide," *The Blackwell Guide to Epistemology*, pp. 145–57. The quotation is from p. 147. Sosa goes on to describe another version of internalism that highlights accessibility.

8   Laurence BonJour, "The Dialectic of Foundationalism and Coherentism," *The Blackwell Guide to Epistemology*, pp. 117–42. The quotation is from p. 118.

9   William Alston, "Internalism and Externalism in Epistemology," reprinted in William Alston, *Epistemic Justification: Essays in the Theory of Knowledge* (Ithaca: Cornell University Press, 1989), pp. 185–226. See p. 186. Also reprinted in this volume.

10 Steup describes internalism as both mentalism and accessibilism in the passage quoted. Pollock does not make explicit that the internal states to which he refers must be mental states. However, it is reasonable to assume that this is what he has in mind.

11 It has become standard to distinguish between an existing belief (or other attitude) being justified and a person being justified in believing (or having another attitude toward) a proposition whether or not the person actually believes it (or has that attitude). We shall use phrases such as "justified belief" to refer to beliefs that are justified and we shall say of a person that he or she is justified in believing a proposition when we mean to say that the latter relation obtains. This distinction will not play a significant role in the discussion that follows. As stated, (S) and (M) are about the justification of existing attitudes. They could easily be reformulated to state internalist constraints on the conditions under which a person is justified in having a particular attitude.

12 Whether (M) implies (S) depends upon details of the supervenience relation which we will not discuss here.

13 William Alston, "An Internalist Externalism," in *Epistemic Justification: Essays in the Theory of Knowledge*, pp. 227–45. See esp. p. 232.

14 Not all philosophers who make this sort of comparison seek an account of internalism with this advantage. James Pryor takes internalism to be accessibilism, notes that internalism in the philosophy of mind is a supervenience thesis, and concludes that the two kinds of internalism are dissimilar. See "Highlights of Recent Epistemology," forthcoming, *British Journal for the Philosophy of Science*.

15 In "Skepticism and the Internal/External Divide," Sosa considers and rejects an argument that has mentalism as a premise and accessibilism as its conclusion. See pp. 146–8.

16 See David Brink, *Moral Realism and the Foundations of Ethics* (Cambridge, 1989), pp. 37–50 for details and references.

17 Some internalists do believe that epistemology is entirely an *a priori*, or at least an armchair, matter. See most notably Roderick Chisholm, *Theory of Knowledge*, 3rd edition (Englewood Cliffs, NJ: Prentice Hall, 1989), pp. 76–7.

18 Some of the examples contrast what one person is justified in believing with what another person is justified in believing.

19 Platinga, *Warrant: The Current Debate*, p. 15.

20 We suspect that deontological arguments for internalism are more the work of internalism's critics than its supporters. However, one can find defenses of versions of the arguments below in Carl Ginet's *Knowledge, Perception, and Memory* (Dordrecht: D. Reidel, 1975), pp. 36–7 and in Mathias Steup's "A Defense of Internalism," in Louis Pojman, ed., *The Theory of Knowledge: Classical and Contemporary Readings*, 2nd edition (Belmont, CA: Wadsworth, 1999), pp. 373–84. See esp. pp. 375–6.

21 Alvin Goldman, "Internalism Exposed," the *Journal of Philosophy* 96 (1999): 271–93. See section I. Also published in this volume.

22 Though it does not affect our assessment of this argument, the term "justifiers" can make trouble. We discuss the potential problem in section IV.A.

23 Goldman, "Internalism Exposed," p. 288.

24 In some passages Plantinga seems to have an argument like this in mind. See Platinga, *Warrant: The Current Debate*, chapter 1, section IV.

25 We also doubt that people are to be blamed for their beliefs in more routine cases of unjustified belief. This depends in large part upon whether blame applies only in cases of voluntary action and whether belief is voluntary in such cases. It may be that ordinary unjustified beliefs are often results of processes that are irresistible, at least in the short term, and consequently the resulting beliefs are not blameworthy.

26 The assumption that people internally alike are to be blamed for the same things is also questionable. Two people could end up in the same internal state as a result of different factors. One might have gotten there through negligence, such as not pursuing important leads concerning some significant proposition. Some internalists would say that the negligent one might deserve blame for the resulting belief. We note also that M allows internalists to make justificatory use of historical mental states. The people in this example need not be classified as internally alike, since they differ mentally at earlier times.

27 Alvin Platinga, "Respondeo Ad Feldman," in Jon Kvanvig, ed., *Warrant in Contemporary Epistemology: Essays in Honor of Plantinga's Theory of Knowledge* (London: Rowman and Littlefield, 1996), pp. 357–61.

28 Platinga, "Respondeo," p. 259.

29 Platinga, "Respondeo," p. 360.

30 Plantinga's premises establish at most that if a person believes a proposition, then the person has impulsional evidence for that proposition. Plantinga assumes that this evidence justifies the person's belief. However, even if the evidence is strong enough to justify believing the proposition, the person may fail to believe the proposition on the basis of this justifying evidence. In the body of the paper we question the claim that the impulsional evidence is always strong enough to justify believing the proposition and we ignore issues having to do with the basis of the belief.

31 Goldman, "Internalism Exposed," p. 278.

32 Goldman, "Internalism Exposed," p. 278.

33 It may be that if one were to become conscious of the belief, one would also bring to mind some stored justification that one has for it. Thus, if these stored beliefs were occurrent, they would be justified in the fundamental sense. Whether this justification would happen to accompany an occurrent consideration of a belief does not seem crucial. What may be crucial to having a stored epistemic justification for a stored belief is being capable of recalling a conscious justification, or at least being capable of recalling the key confirming evidence in such a justification.

34 Though it is possible for a stored belief to be justified by one's current evidence, in the usual case, one's evidence for a stored belief will also be stored. It also possible for an occurrent belief to have only dispositional justification.

35 Richard Feldman, "Having Evidence," in David Austin, ed. *Philosophical Analysis* (Dordrecht: Kluwer, 1988), pp. 83–104.

36 Goldman, "Internalism Exposed," pp. 278–9.

37 It is, in the typical case, an internal state that is accessible to the believer, so accessibilist versions of internalism can accept this approach as well. We suspect that many internalists will find the second sort of approach to the problem of stored beliefs more appealing. By limiting evidence to current conscious states, the former view limits severely the number of justified beliefs a person has at any time. We do not regard this limitation as clearly unsatisfactory, given the availability of a dispositional notion of justification to account for the favorable epistemic status of many stored beliefs. We shall continue to present both approaches in the remainder of this paper.

38 For example, they can differ with respect to how readily accessible those states must be. It is also possible to hold that the degree of justification provided by a state is partly determined by how readily accessible it is.

39 Goldman, "Internalism Exposed," pp. 279.

40 See, for instance, Sosa, "Skepticism and the Internal/External Divide," pp. 145–57. The relevant example appears on pp. 152f. Goldman cites Gilbert Harman, Thomas Senor, and Robert Audi as having raised similar objections. See Gilbert Harman, *Change in View* (Cambridge: MIT Press, 1986); Thomas Senor, "Internalist Foundationalism and the Justification of Memory Belief," *Synthese* 94 (1993): 453–76; and Robert Audi, "Memorial Justification," *Philosophical Topics* 23 (1995): 31–45.

41 Goldman, "Internalism Exposed," p. 281.

42 Sosa, "Skepticism and the Internal/External Divide," p. 153.

43 Goldman, "Internalism Exposed," pp. 280–1.

44 Goldman, "Internalism Exposed," pp. 281–2.

45 Alston, "Internalism and Externalism in Epistemology," p. 221.

46 See, for example, Laurence Bonjour, "Externalist Theories of Empirical Knowledge," *Midwest Studies in Philosophy*, 5 (1980): 55. In "Epistemology c. 1988–2000" Jams Pryor calls the view *that* endorses the higher order requirement "Inferential Internalism" and identifies several of its proponents.

47 Goldman, "Internalism Exposed," section I.

48 See, for instance, Michael Bergmann, "A Dilemma for Internalism," APA, Central Division, 2000.

49 Internalists who hold that all evidence is conscious can point to evidence such as the expert's feeling of confidence and sense of familiarity while making the judgment.

50 There is a non-evidentialist view that some internalists find attractive. The idea is that a mental fact about people is that they have fundamental inferential abilities. Perhaps this view could also be described in terms of the ability to see con-

nections. But this view denies that this ability is, or leads to, differences in evidence. This is a mental difference, but not an evidential difference.

These two views can also be applied to the original example about the logic student. We said the TA can see that the original sentence has consequences that the student can't see. This is what accounts for the differences in what's justified for them. As we described the case, we interpreted these facts in an evidentialist way, taking the difference in what they can see as an evidential difference. The non-evidentialist internalist alternative agrees that there is a mental difference between the two, but it characterizes that difference in terms of an inferential skill rather than a difference in evidence. It is not essential to a defense of internalism to select between these alternatives.

51 Goldman, "Internalism Exposed," pp. 282–6.
52 For example, distant and complex logical consequences of the basics may not be justified.
53 Goldman, "Internalism Exposed," pp. 282–6.
54 Goldman, "Internalism Exposed," p. 283.
55 Ernest Sosa, "Beyond Scepticism, to the Best of our Knowledge," *Mind* 97 (1988): 153–88. The quotation is from p. 171.
56 The term "recognize" implies that the classification is accurate. There is no need to insist on an infallible capacity here. If there is some such phenomenon as seemingly recognizing a conscious quality while misclassifying it, then it is a seeming recognition which supplies the conscious evidence for the classification.

FURTHER READING

Almeder, Robert, "Dretske's Dreadful Question," *Philosophia*, 24 (1995), 449–57.

Almeder, Robert, "Externalism and Justification," *Philosophia*, 24 (1995), 465–69.

Almeder, Robert, *Harmless Naturalism: The Limits of Science and the Nature of Philosophy*, Open Court, 1998.

Alston, William, "Two Types of Foundationalism," *Journal of Philosophy*, LXXXII (1976), 165–85.

Alston, William, "Level-Confusions in Epistemology," *Midwest Studies in Philosophy*, 5 (1980), 135–50.

Alston, William, "Internalism and Externalism in Epistemology," *Philosophical Topics*, 14 (1986), 179–221.

Alston, William, "The Deontological Conception of Epistemic Justification," *Philosophical Perspectives*, 2 (1988), 257–99.

Alston, William, "An Internalist Externalism," *Synthese*, 74 (1988), 265–83.

Alston, William, *Epistemic Justification: Essays in the Theory of Knowledge*, Cornell University Press, 1989.

Armstrong, David M., *Belief, Truth and Knowledge*, Cambridge University Press, 1973.

Audi, Robert, "Causalist Internalism," *American Philosophical Quarterly*, 26 (1989), 309–20.

Bach, Kent, "A Rationale for Reliabilism," *The Monist*, 68 (1985), 246–63.

Baergen, Ralph, *Contemporary Epistemology*, Harcourt Brace, 1995.

Bender, John, ed., *The Current State of the Coherence Theory: Critical Essays on the Epistemic Theories of Keith Lehrer and Laurence BonJour, with Replies*, Kluwer, 1989.

Bergmann, Michael, "Internalism, Externalism and the No-Defeater Condition," *Synthese*, 110 (1997), 399–417.

Bergmann, Michael, "Deontology and Defeat, "*Philosophy and Phenomenological Research*, 60 (2000), 87–102.

Bergmann, Michael, "Externalism and Skepticism," *Philosophical Review*, 109 (2000), 159–94.

BonJour, Laurence, "Externalist Theories of Knowledge," *Midwest Studies*, 5 (1980), 53–73.

BonJour, Laurence, *The Structure of Empirical Knowledge*, Harvard University Press, 1985.

BonJour, Laurence, "Nozick, Externalism and Skepticism," in Luper-Foy, ed., 1987, 297–313.

BonJour, Laurence, "Externalism/Internalism," in E. Sosa and J. Dancy, eds., *A Companion To Epistemology*, Blackwell, 1992.

BonJour, Laurence, "Against Naturalized Epistemology," *Midwest Studies in Philosophy*, XIX (1994), 283–300.

BonJour, Laurence, *In Defense of Pure Reason*, Cambridge University Press, 1999.

Chisholm, Roderick, *Theory of Knowledge*, 3rd edn., Prentice-Hall, 1989.

Chisholm, Roderick, "The Indispensibility of Internal Justification," *Synthese*, 74 (1988), 285–96.

Cohen, Stewart, "Justification and Truth," *Philosophical Studies*, 46 (1984), 279–96.

Conee, Earl and Feldman, Richard, "Internalism Defended," in this volume.

Crumley, Jack, *An Introduction to Epistemology*, Mayfield, 1999.

Dancy, Jonathan, *An Introduction to Contemporary Epistemology*, Blackwell, 1985.

Davidson, Donald, "Epistemology Externalized," *Dialectica*, 45 (1991), 191–202.

Dretske, Fred, "Dretske's Awful Answer," *Philosophia*, 24 (1995), 459–64.

Dretske, Fred, "Epistemic Entitlement," *Philosophy and Phenomenological Research*, LX (2000), 591–606.

Dretske, Fred, *Perception, Knowledge and Belief: Selected Essays*, Cambridge University Press, 2000.

Feldman, Richard, "Reliability and Justification," *Monist*, 68 (1985), 159–74.

Feldman, Richard, "Epistemic Obligations," *Philosophical Perspectives*, 2 (1988), 235–56.

Feldman, Richard, "Subjective and Objective in Ethics and Epistemology," *Monist*, 71 (1988), 405–19.

Feldman, Richard, "Kvanvig on Externalism and Epistemology Worth Doing," *Southern Journal of Philosophy*, XXXVIII Supplement (1999), 43–50.

Feldman, Richard and Conee, Earl, "Evidentialism," *Philosophical Studies*, 48 (1985), 15–34.

Foley, Richard, "Epistemic Luck and the Purely Epistemic," *American Philosophical Quarterly*, 21 (1984), 113–24.

Foley, Richard, "What's Wrong with Reliabilism?," *Monist*, 68 (1985), 188–202.

Foley, Richard, *The Theory of Epistemic Rationality*, Harvard University Press, 1987.

Foley, Richard, *Working without a Net: A Study of Egocentric Epistemology*, Oxford University Press, 1993.

Foley, Richard, "What Am I to Believe?," in S. Wagner and R. Warner, eds., *Naturalism: A Critical Appraisal*, University of Notre Dame Press, 1993, 147–62.

Foley, Richard, "Quine and Naturalized Epistemology," *Midwest Studies in Philosophy*, XIX (1994), 243–60.

Foley, Richard, "Locke and the Crisis of Postmodern Epistemology," *Midwest Studies in Philosophy*, XXIII (1999), 1–20.

Fumerton, Richard, "The Internalism/Externalism Controversy," *Philosophical Perspectives*, 2 (1988), 443–59.

Fumerton, Richard, "Skepticism and Naturalistic Epistemology," *Midwest Studies in Philosophy*, XIX (1994), 321–40.

Fumerton, Richard, *Metaepistemology and Skepticism*, Rowman and Littlefield, 1995.

Fumerton, Richard, "Externalism and Epistemological Direct Realism," *Monist*, 81 (1998), 393–406.

Fumerton, Richard, "A Priori Philosophy after an A Posteriori Turn," *Midwest Studies in Philosophy*, XXIII (1999), 21–33.

Gallois, Andre, and Hawthorne, John, "Externalism and Scepticism," *Philosophical Studies*, 81 (1996), 1–26.

Ginet, Carl, "Contra Reliabilism," *Monist*, 68 (1985), 175–87.

Goldman, Alvin, "A Causal Theory of Knowing," *Journal of Philosophy*, 64 (1967), 357–72.

Goldman, Alvin, "Discrimination and Perceptual Knowledge," *Journal of Philosophy*, 73 (1976), 771–91.

Goldman, Alvin, "What is Justified Belief?," in G. Pappas, ed., *Justification and Knowledge: New Studies in Epistemology*, Reidel, 1979, 1–23.

Goldman, Alvin, "The Internalist Conception of Justification," *Midwest Studies*, 5 (1980), 27–51.

Goldman, Alvin, *Epistemology and Cognition*, Harvard University Press, 1986.

Goldman, Alvin, "Strong and Weak Justification," *Philosophical Perspectives*, 2 (1988), 51–69.

Goldman, Alvin, *Liaisons: Philosophy Meets the Cognitive and Social Sciences*, MIT Press, 1992.

Goldman, Alvin, "Internalism Exposed," *Journal of Philosophy*, 96 (1999), 271–93.

Greco, John, "Internalism and Epistemically Responsible Belief," *Synthese*, 85 (1990), 245–77.

Greco, John, "Internalism versus Externalism," in D. M. Borchert, ed., *Encyclopedia of Philosophy Supplement*, Macmillan, 265–6.

Haack, Susan, *Evidence and Inquiry: Towards Reconstruction in Epistemology*, Blackwell, 1993.

Harman, Gilbert, *Thought*, Princeton University Press, 1973.

Harper, William, "Papier-Mâché Problems in Epistemic Justification: A Defense of Strong Internalism," *Synthese*, 116 (1998), 27–49.

Hetherington, Stephen, *Knowledge Puzzles: An Introduction to Epistemology*, Westview, 1996.

Hetherington, Stephen, "A Fallibilist and Wholly Internalist Solution to the Gettier Problem," *Journal of Philosophical Research*, forthcoming.

Horgan, Terry and Henderson, David, "Iceburg Epistemology," *Philosophy and Phenomenological Research*, 61 (2000), 497–535.

Jacobson, Stephen, "Internalism in Epistemology and the Infinite Regress," *Australasian Journal of Philosophy*, 70 (1992), 415–24.

Jacobson, Stephen, "Externalism and Action-Guiding Epistemic Norms," *Synthese*, 110 (1997), 381–97.

Kaplan, Mark, "Epistemology on Holiday," *Journal of Philosophy*, 88 (1991), 132–54.

Kaplan, Mark, "Epistemology Denatured," *Midwest Studies in Philosophy*, XIX (1994), 350–65.

Kim, Kihyeon, "Internalism and Externalism in Epistemology," *American Philosophical Quarterly*, 30 (1993), 303–16.

Kitcher, Philip, "The Naturalists Return," *Philosophical Review*, 101 (1992), 53–114.

Kornblith, Hilary, "Beyond Foundationalism and the Coherence Theory," *Journal of Philosophy*, 72 (1980), 597–612.

Kornblith, Hilary, "The Psychological Turn," *Australasian Journal of Philosophy*, 60 (1982), 238–53.

Kornblith, Hilary, "Ever Since Descartes," *Monist*, 68 (1985), 264–76.

Kornblith, Hilary, "How Internal Can You Get?," *Synthese*, 74 (1988), 313–27.

Kornblith, Hilary, "The Unattainability of Coherence," in J. Bender, ed., *The Current State of the Coherence Theory*, Kluwer, 1989, 207–14.

Kornblith, Hilary, "Introspection and Misdirection," *Australasian Journal of Philosophy*, 67 (1989), 410–22.

Kornblith, Hilary, "Epistemic Obligation and the Possibility of Internalism," in L. Zagzebski and A. Fairweather, eds., *Virtue Epistemology: Essays on Epistemic Virtue and Responsibility*, Oxford University Press, forthcoming.

Kornblith, Hilary, "Conditions on Cognitive Sanity and the Death of Internalism," in R. Schantz, ed., *The Externalist Challenge: New Studies on Cognition and Intentionality*, de Gruyter, forthcoming.

Kvanvig, Jonathan, "Externalism and Epistemology Worth Doing," *Southern Journal of Philosophy*, XXXVIII Supplement (1999), 27–42.

Lehrer, Keith, *Theory of Knowledge*, Westview, 1990.

Lehrer, Keith, *Meta-Mind*, Oxford University Press, 1990.

Luper-Foy, Steven, ed., *The Possibility of Knowledge: Nozick and His Critics*, Rowman and Littlefield, 1987.

Luper-Foy, Steven, "The Knower, Inside and Out," *Synthese*, 74 (1988), 349–67.

Lycan, William, *Judgement and Justification*, Cambridge University Press, 1988.

Moser, Paul, "Internalism and Coherentism: A Dilemma," *Analysis*, 48 (1988), 161–3.

Moser, Paul, *Knowledge and Evidence*, Cambridge University Press, 1989.

Nozick, Robert, *Philosophical Explanations*, Harvard University Press, 1981.

Pappas, George, "Internalism and Externalism in Epistemology," *Stanford On-Line Encyclopedia*, 1999.

Plantinga, Alvin, "Chisholmian Internalism," in D. Austin, ed., *Philosophical Analysis: a Defense by Example*, Reidel, 1988.

Plantinga, Alvin, "Justification in the Twentieth Century," *Philosophy and Phenomenological Research*, L (1990), 45–71.

Plantinga, Alvin, *Warrant: The Current Debate*, Oxford University Press, 1993.

Pojman, Louis, *What Can We Know?: An Introduction to the Theory of Knowledge*, Wadsworth, 1995.

Pollock, John, "Reliability and Justified Belief," *Canadian Journal of Philosophy*, 14 (1984), 103–14.

Pollock, John, "Epistemic Norms," *Synthese*, 71 (1987), 61–95.

Pollock, John and Cruz, Joseph, *Contemporary Theories of Knowledge*, 2nd edn., Rowman and Littlefield, 1999.

Pryor, James, "Highlights of Recent Epistemology," *British Journal for the Philosophy of Science*, forthcoming.

Quine, W. V. O., *Ontological Relativity and Other Essays*, Columbia University Press, 1969.

Riggs, Wayne, "The Weakness of Strong Justification," *Australasian Journal of Philosophy*, 75 (1997), 179–89.

Schantz, Richard, ed., *The Externalist Challenge: New Studies on Cognition and Intentionality*, de Gruyter, forthcoming.

Schmitt, Frederick, "Epistemic Perspectivism," in J. Heil, ed., *Rationality, Morality, and Self-Interest: Essays Honoring Mark Carl Overvold*, Rowman and Littlefield, 1993, 3–27.

Schmitt, Frederick, *Knowledge and Belief*, Routledge, 1992.

Sosa, Ernest, "Methodology and Apt Belief," *Synthese*, 74 (1988), 415–26.

Sosa, Ernest, *Knowledge in Perspective: Selected Essays in Epistemology*, Cambridge University Press, 1991.

Sosa, Ernest, "Philosophical Skepticism and Epistemic Circularity," *Aristotelian Society Supplementary Volume*, 68 (1994), 263–90.

Sosa, Ernest, "How to Resolve the Pyrrhonian Problematic: A Lesson from Descartes," *Philosophical Studies*, LXXXV (1997), 229–49.

Sosa, Ernest, "Reflective Knowledge in the Best Circles," *Journal of Philosophy*, 94 (1997), 410–30.

Sosa, Ernest, "Chisholm's Epistemology and Epistemic Internalism," in L. Hahn, ed., *The Philosophy of Roderick Chisholm*, Open Court, 1997, 267–87.

Sosa, Ernest, "Skepticism and the Internal/External Divide," in J. Greco and E. Sosa, eds., *The Blackwell Guide to Epistemology*, Blackwell, 1999, 145–57.

Sosa, Ernest, "Two False Dicotomies: Foundationalism/Coherentism and Internalism/Externalism," in R. Schantz, ed., *The Externalist Challenge: New Studies on Cognition and Intentionality*, de Gruyter, forthcoming.

Steup, Matthias, "The Deontic Conception of Epistemic Justification," *Philosophical Studies*, 53 (1988), 65–84.

Steup, Matthias, *An Introduction to Contemporary Epistemology*, Prentice-Hall, 1996.

Steup, Matthias, "A Defense of Internalism," in L. Pojman, ed., *The Theory of Knowledge: Classical and Contemporary Readings*, 2nd edn, Wadsworth, 1999, 373–84.

Stroud, Barry, *The Significance of Philosophical Skepticism*, Oxford University Press, 1984.

Stroud, Barry, "Understanding Human Knowledge in General," in M. Clay and K. Lehrer, eds., *Knowledge and Skepticism*, Westview, 1989.

Stroud, Barry, "Skepticism, 'Externalism,' and the Goal of Epistemology," *Aristotelian Society Supplementary Volume*, 68 (1994), 291–307.

Stroud, Barry, *Understanding Human Knowledge: Philosophical Essays*, Oxford University Press, 2000.

Swain, Marshall, "Alston's Internalistic Externalism," *Philosophical Perspectives*, 2 (1988), 461–73.

Talbott, William, *The Reliability of the Cognitive Mechanism: A Mechanist Account of Empirical Justification*, Garland Publishing, 1990.

Unger, Peter, "An Analysis of Factual Knowledge," *Journal of Philosophy*, 65 (1968), 157–70.

Vahid, Hamid, "The Internalism/Externalism Controversy: The Epistemization of an Older Debate," *Dialectica*, 52 (1998), 229–46.

van Cleve, James, "Foundationalism, Epistemic Principles and the Cartesian Circle," *Philosophical Review*, 88 (1979), 55–91.

van Cleve, James, "Reliability, Justification and the Problem of Induction," *Midwest Studies in Philosophy*, IX (1984), 555–67.

Wedgewood, Ralph, "The A Priori Rules of Rationality," *Philosophy and Phenomenological Research*, 59 (1999), 113–31.

Williams, Michael, *Groundless Belief*, 2nd edn., Princeton University Press, 1999.

Williams, Michael, "Dretske on Epistemic Entitlement," *Philosophy and Phenomenological Research*, LX (2000), 607–12.

Williams, Michael, *Problems of Knowledge: A Critical Introduction to Philosophical Epistemology*, Oxford University Press, forthcoming.

Wolterstorff, Nicholas, "Obligations of Belief – Two Concepts," in Lewis Hahn, ed., *The Philosophy of Roderick Chisholm*, Open Court, 1997, 218–38.

INDEX

Printed in the United States
129122LV00006B/5/P